Charity in Motions

Charity in Motions

Ten Years of Commentary On Nonprofit Board Service

Renee Kumor

Basics of …
is an imprint of
ABSOLUTELY AMAZING eBOOKS

Published by Whiz Bang LLC, 926 Truman Avenue, Key West, Florida 33040, USA.

Charity in Motions copyright © 2016 by Renee Kumor. Electronic compilation / paperback edition copyright © 2016 by Whiz Bang LLC.

All rights reserved. No part of this book may be reproduced, scanned, or transmitted in any form or by any means, electronic or mechanical, including photocopying, recording, or any information storage and retrieval system, without permission in writing from the publisher. Please do not participate in or encourage piracy of copyrighted materials in violation of the author's rights. Purchase only authorized ebook editions.

This work is based on factual events. While the author has made every effort to provide accurate information at the time of publication, neither the publisher nor the author assumes any responsibility for errors, or for changes that occur after publication. Further, the publisher does not have any control over and does not assume any responsibility for author or third-party websites or their contents. How the ebook displays on a given reader is beyond the publisher's control.

For information contact
Publisher@AbsolutelyAmazingEbooks.com

ISBN-13: 978-0692654507 (Basics of …)
ISBN-10: 069265450X

This is for all the real newspaper people who have supported me over the years: Malcolm Gibson, Bob Whitmire, Joy Franklin, Ruth Birge, Bill Moss and Diane Norman.

Charity in Motions

Ante-Bella Years

In 2003 I proposed writing a newspaper column on issues that faced local nonprofits. I organized this project through the Hendersonville Times-News with two other women. How clever, I thought. I only had to write four columns a year.

Then I learned a sad truth – never collaborate with women younger than you. They get pregnant, or married or go back to school! Soon there I was a post-menopausal, long time married, college graduate with a monthly newspaper column!

During 2006 I would begin developing a cast of characters to enlighten readers, but these early years contained serious and thoughtful essays on nonprofit board service and the challenges and the responsibilities board members faced.

As you read through these essays you will find references to local nonprofit agencies operating in Henderson County, North Carolina. You will also find mention of people, by name, who were active at the time the article was written. I used opportunity to draw attention to their community service and offer praise for the work they performed. Sometimes, you will find the subject matter dated. By that I mean, I may refer to some action, locally or nationally, that was occurring at the time I was meeting my deadline, scrambling for a topic related, no matter how obscurely, to nonprofit work or administrative organization.

Those of you in nonprofit work, whether as a volunteer or an employee or a client, understand the impact charitable work has on a community, especially a small community, you know, much like the places we all come from or work in. Nonprofits are the glue that hold communities together and make our hometowns the best places to be and make us better people by bringing us together.

Board Service

More jobs than people, more work than money, more rewarding than you ever imagined. That's what serving on a nonprofit Board is all about. The nonprofit world is a great place to put your volunteer time. Many of us in the community do it daily – and probably for more than one agency. And these volunteer commitments are designed to fit nicely into our lives – happy volunteers work hard and donate to the cause. But there are some jobs that go begging. Especially Board membership. Every nonprofit is run by a very visible Executive Director, who is hired and advised by a volunteer Board of Directors. It is not the Exec who is responsible for fundraising, it is the Board of Directors. It is not the Exec who sets policy, it is the Board of Directors. It is not the Exec who sets the agency direction, it is the Board of Directors.

Although the nonprofit Boards in our community manage agencies of different sizes and different mission, there is a common thread of responsibility and operation that governors each one. To be asked to serve on a nonprofit Board should be viewed as a serious request from people committed to an agency and mission. One should give equally serious consideration to what acceptance of this appointment means. Those who serve on nonprofit Boards should, must, understand the responsibilities and expectations of such service.

To begin with, a person is asked to consider Board membership because there has been a demonstrated interest in the agency – volunteer support at a committed level or response to fundraising requests. But fair consideration of the Board invitation should encourage some further investigation of the mission and agency goals, including some detailed look into business organization and program operations. Ideally, a request to consider Board membership should be accompanied by an invitation to a pre-orientation that includes a visit with the Exec and Board member to give an overview of the agency and some idea of the role one would play as a new Board member. After a person is accepted as a Board member there should be a more detailed orientation about the agency and its operations.

A Board Nominating Committee is looking for many characteristics for new members. There is the constant need to be developing Board leadership for the future. In fact, in my opinion, stay away from Boards with no term limits in their by-laws. This may be a Board that is really a mini dictatorship and may be stuck in first gear. Agencies shouldn't be surviving on someone's personality. A strong, well-built agency only becomes stronger as new leadership develops.

And what are the expectations of a new Board member? First, attend meetings!! Don't say, "yes," and then be a no-show. And accept committee membership. Each Board member, especially in a small agency, must take responsibility for management activity. Let me explain. Board members, often through committee work, help develop the agency budget, select agency and staff insurance offerings, support the exec with developing personnel policy, develop additional policies, and work on fundraising campaigns. Of course, each of these responsibilities takes time, effort and skill. That's why an invitation for membership is a serious request.

A good Board member also has an appreciation of two important issues, confidentiality and conflict of interest. Operations of the Board and agency should not be cocktail party conversation. Board members should always be willing to answer questions about the agency, but this should be done in a positive manner, no one needs to know about any brewing scandal or petty Board infighting. The other issue, conflict of interest, is often more of perception than fact – but perception is as important as fact and often develops a life of its own. It is up to the Board to define where the line is on conflict of interest. Many Boards have developed guidelines and ask members to read and sign a conflict of interest statement as well as a confidentiality statement at the beginning of the term of Board membership or at the beginning of a new fiscal year.

The biggest responsibility of a Board member, after "being there," is money. Be a donor, be an asker, be a schmoozer at fundraising events. There is no other job, so difficult to many of us than asking for money – but it is the way of the nonprofit world. The mission drives the agency and money makes the agency thrive. Just remember, the board is responsible for the viability of the organization and its programs, the planning and direction of the agency and the funding of all of the above.

Time, Money Crucial to Board Membership

One can quickly become a cynic when working on a nonprofit board. After all, isn't it true that only 5% of the people do all the work? Give all the money? Stay in town? Of course, staying in town means, having time to give. The challenge in building a good nonprofit board is to find that 5% who are available, moneyed and not interested in leaving town.

There are many resources available that outline the types of members that should be on a functioning Board. It is important to look for a variety of talent for your Board. Look for folks who bring certain backgrounds to the table. And look for potential members who bring special skills to the table. It reminds me of looking over a menu in a Chinese restaurant. Pick one from each classification, an accountant, a lawyer – all genders should be represented and all ethnic minorities should be included. Funders are very interested in finding diversity on nonprofit boards. The balance of viewpoints is valuable to an agency. There are always many ways to solve a problem or to address an issue. On a Board with a variety of people, all respecting one another, the discussion usually is helpful and enlightening. The outcomes are always positive for the organization and pave the way for building a stronger Board.

However, there are other criteria that should be considered with the "one from column A" picks. Those criteria include understanding the agency mission, being committed to the mission and vision, and that big four letter word ... TIME. Time commitment needed is often measured by the size of the organization, the age of the organization and the staff support available to the Board. For example, a new or relatively small agency survives on extensive "hands on" time commitments from Board members. As an agency grows and staff is hired, time commitments may not ebb as much as become less day-to-day operations and more policy level service. In a new or small agency Board members may find that time is necessary to answer phones, deal with clients or order supplies. While in an older, larger agency, those roles are filled by staff while Board members deal with hiring auditors, developing policies and supporting the executive director in meeting potential donors or in meetings with potential grantors. Time is the key to good board membership. It takes time to spend in discussion with others on Board issues. It takes time to cultivate donors. It takes time to plan budgets, review programs, support the executive director. Saying yes to Board services means making time.

There are ways to give time on a Board that are as valuable as attending monthly meetings. Each Board member should serve on at least one Board committee. In addition, other Board work includes representing the Board with other groups and in other parts of the community, taking part in fundraising efforts, and recruiting new Board members and volunteers.

Another facet of Board time commitment involves training and orientation. Board members must be kept abreast of the challenges within the organization and the changes in law or mission that demand retraining. It is also the role of Board leadership to design and implement orientations for new members. One of the important tasks that only a Board can do is conduct an annual self-evaluation. Have we stayed on mission; have we reached the goals set down in our planning process; have we recruited and trained new members for the next term? Are we leading this organization in a manner that attracts support and attracts others to join the Board?

There is one more element to evaluate in recruiting a nonprofit Board member. Money. Nonprofit Boards have THE responsibility to keep the organization viable. Not all Board members will be able to give at the same level. All members must understand that membership on the Board comes with an expectation of financial support. The size of the donation is not as important as the fact that a Board member makes a financial contribution. This is also key in Board evaluation. Do all members give to the agency? There should be 100% financial participation by Board members.

Building and maintaining a thoughtful, hardworking Board for a nonprofit is a job for the Board leadership. Finding volunteers with skill, time and interest in making a financial commitment is a full time challenge for nonprofits in our community. Could we be looking for you?

Nonprofits: A Risky Business?

One of the items a Board should review annually is its insurance coverage. As a board sets program goals, fundraising goals and direction for the organization, insurance is a necessary consideration. There should be a review of types of insurance as well as the discussion of balance of costs to the risk to the agency and the impact those costs may have on delivery of service to agency clients. Insurance, you ask? What in the world does a nonprofit need with insurance? Well, let's start with Directors and Officer Liability (D&O). No matter how small the agency is, this type of insurance is necessary. This is the policy that covers board members, officers, volunteers and employees. As the brochure for one company who provides D&O coverage says: "Just because an organization does good works doesn't mean it will never be accused of doing wrong." In fact, as you consider whether you should join a nonprofit Board, ask whether there is D&O insurance for the Board.

I like to break the rest of the insurance needs into building/property and staff. Under building issues there are many things to think about to determine the balance of risk. For example, do you rent or own the agency office? What kind of assets does your agency have? New computers, new phone system? These days some agencies might investigate Equipment Data Processing (EDP) that covers hardware, software, manuals, peripheral equipment. It also may include mechanical breakdown or on-premise electrical disturbances. This is something that nonprofit Boards never

Charity in Motions

had to face decades ago – Now it makes good business sense to review assets and weigh the value of insurance. Another practical insurance may be general auto. Does you agency own and operate vehicles? If staff and volunteers use their own vehicles for agency business, some agencies consider carrying "hired and non-auto" coverage. This protects the agency in excess of the driver's limits should there be an accident.

Then there is an array of insurance options that are driven by staff. First, if there are 3 or more employees in the agency, worker's comp is required – another example of the cost of during business.

There are numerous benefits that an employer can choose to offer employees. In this day and time, many nonprofits find that attracting and keeping good employees demands that they develop a package of employee benefits. The most expensive, health coverage, is probably the biggest challenge to a Board of Directors to fund. It is important for the Board to have a clear and open discussion about agency goals, budgetary impact of the employee benefits and the importance of benefits to the overall issue of employee morale. When a Board begins to investigate this issue, look for a presentation that gives you several choices so that the Board can weigh the benefit to staff against the cost to the agency and balance that with the cost of meeting the agency mission.

Another big discussion should be around retirement benefits for staff. There are 403(b)'s, 401(k)'s, SEP's and straightforward IRA programs. Is the Board ready for this offer? The discussion will include cost to agency, administrative costs, employee investment. Again, finding good outside advisors helps a Board deliberate the question and find affordable solutions.

In addition, there are several other types of insurance

that an agency may consider. One is group life and group disability. In an agency with a number of young employees, no one seems to be thinking about life insurance or disability. This coverage may be a good inexpensive offering that may be paid by the employer as a benefit that may be appreciated when salary increases are not in the budget. Or it may be part of the health package that a Board develops for staff. Finally, many agencies that provide professional services such as counseling or health services will be responsible for the professional liability of their professional staff.

All in all, a board needs to have a strategy for insurance coverage. The insurance issues that deal with property are cut and dry, but the coverage that is defined as employee benefits demands Board discussion and planning.

To prepare for this column I visited with Rob Cranford and Jim Rasmussen of Morrow Insurance. They offered some good advice. The issues of insurance will drive your budget and they caution that your insurance decisions must be made with good business sense. The decisions should reflect Board goals. Jim works with clients developing benefits for employees. He says, if there are benefits that a Board wants to offer staff, start slow, and plan for growth in benefits costs. You don't ever want to take benefits away!

Note: Rob Cranford died several years after this interview. Our community named an award to honor the memory of the Cranfords and their service to our community. In January 2013 I was privileged to receive the Rob and Ginger Cranford Community Service Award for "outstanding contributions to the people of Henderson County."

What You 'Audit' Know About Finances

All of you received your tax forms already. The government is on the ball when it comes to its finances, or at least when it comes to getting its finances from us. And a big part of your reporting is going to depend on how well you have maintained your records. The same goes for nonprofits – their record keeping is important to donor tax returns and to their own reporting.

So at tax time let's look at some of the issues that are important in a functioning nonprofit. First, those donor tax receipts – so important to your donors. That is why financial records management is so important to nonprofits. An agency should have appropriate financial controls in place to receive, record and acknowledge donations. Each donor has the right to expect proper acknowledgment of donations, whether these donations were cash, stock, property or "in-kind" donations. Whether an agency manages this income with computer software or the old fashioned way, the Board has the responsibility to see that a "fail-safe" process is in place.

The nonprofit has tax responsibilities of its own. All nonprofits with receipts over $25,000 are required to file an IRS Form 990. Failure to file or omissions in filing may result in penalties. There are also tax liabilities for any nonprofit that runs a business to help support its mission. If the nonprofit has staff, there is the inevitable need for all the record keeping that comes with paying salaries. A nonprofit is like any other business in that respect. Taxes must be paid, money transferred to IRA type accounts and funds directed to medical benefits.

Another financial question that a nonprofit Board must decide is when to have an audit. The audit is a concrete, professional assessment of the financial health and management of an agency. It is certainly appropriate when an agency reaches certain levels of income and activity. An audit is often necessary for agencies that apply for state and federal funds and is a requirement for many grants. For Henderson County nonprofits interested in certification by the Alliance for Human Services, an audit is required for all nonprofits with annual revenues in excess of $300,000 for a Level 1 accreditation, and an audit is required for all agencies seeking a Level 3 accreditation.

Many donors are also interested in reviewing the financial operations of an agency. There are other less costly options in lieu of an audit. They are a Review, looking at the agency but not in detail and does not come with a CPA opinion, and a Compilation, nothing more than putting information in order, somewhat like a financial statement, again with no CPA "blessing." The decision to engage in an audit is one a board should weigh carefully.

Over the years, nonprofit finance management has gotten more complex. An audit will help a growing agency establish good financial controls. Some of the control issues revolve around who opens the mail, how donations are tracked, how restricted funds are managed and allocated, and how overall reporting is done. After all, a nonprofit is the one place where daily mail often includes checks from donors.

Another issue is check-signing. Although the Board members are volunteers, they have the responsibility for fiscal management. In many organizations, the Executive

Director may have check signing ability only to a certain dollar amount and then Board policy requires a second signature, usually the Board Chair, Vice-Chair or Treasurer. Because Boards are volunteers, an agency usually needs that many authorized signatures to make sure that at least one member is in town when check signing is necessary. For every financial function there should be two people responsible. The Board should also have an audit committee – a group of Board members who sit down with the auditor to review the audit and discuss the issues that the auditor brings forward. The audit contract should also include the preparation of the Form 990.

Completion of the audit is probably a good time for the Board to review financial policies of the agency and to review the financial articles of the Bylaws to make sure that actual operations are reflected in the agency's administrative documents. A nonprofit has to be prepared to demonstrate that financial controls are in place. This is a big responsibility for the Board of Directors and has the potential to be a big liability for the Board.

I would like to thank my friends, Peggy Judkins, retired CPA, and Todd Webb, CPA for helping me walk through these issues. Peggy has a P.S. – check out the IRS website, www.irs.gov and click on "Publications" for a good place to start researching taxes and nonprofits.

Note: IRS now requires all nonprofits regardless of size to file an annual 990.

Hiring an Executive Director

Hiring the Executive Director of a nonprofit agency is one of the most important jobs a Board does. The Executive Director will carry on the agency mission, implement Board policy and be the everyday face of the agency. Whether the Board is looking for the agency's first exec or replacing one, there are many things to consider. The search for a new director needs thoughtful planning. Have you reviewed your mission and goals of the agency? Have you developed a job description that outlines the work – not a job description that can only be handled by Clark Kent?

The exec certainly needs some specific talents and training to get the job done. The search committee may have to determine which talents are most important and which can be learned or which are just icing. For example, is a second language important to your mission or to communicate with your clients? Are you willing to negotiate hours? Must the agency operate at a conventional nine-five schedule, or can hours be flexible? Can the exec work from home?

No matter what talents are important, there is something that can't be measured, nor even described. It is that intangible quality that the exec brings to the agency – as its "face." If the Board is changing execs, the search process may be even more challenging. The agency "face" will be changing. Has the Board reviewed the agency mission and conducted an audit of the agency's strengths and weaknesses? This isn't complex; in fact, it is probably part of the reason that the board is looking for new leadership. An exec may leave, unilaterally, or by mutual agreement, when the mission grows beyond his ability, or the future of the agency requires more of her time, or more emphasis on management than on client service.

When an exec leaves, the Board should work to make an assessment of what are the next talents the agency needs. It is also important to have a clear understanding of what you are losing. Periodically, the Board should work on some sort of succession plan. This is not to frighten the exec but to make sure the Board understands the job she is doing. Much of the measurable parts of the job are probably apparent in the instrument used for an annual review as well as in the job description. But there are a hundred little things that are important to know. For example, how does your exec interact with your donors? Are there some personal relationships that should be protected in a separation? Does your exec have special relationships with other agencies, or leadership roles in collaborations that should be protected for the benefit of the agency even as leadership changes? And then there's the small stuff. Is your exec the only person who knows where the fuse box is; or water shutoff; or who to call when the fax machine acts up? Make sure it is all written down.

Preparing to hire an executive director requires a lot of preliminary work. But, I think that reviewing the applications and selecting some candidates to interview is the most challenging phase of the process. The trick has always seemed to me to find the person who in real life is what they look like on paper. Life being what it is, references are skittish about saying too much one way or another. And there are limits as to where the interview goes. All in all it is a fine dance with choreographed roles.

Here are a few simple suggestions. Let just a few Board members review all the applications and select the top 3-5 candidates. Design an interview process that includes questions and is somewhat scripted. This process should be held closely and be confidential. Be prepared to have current employees apply for the position. Also be prepared for applications from many in the community who are already familiar to your agency through other agencies or personal friendships. Job openings attract a lot of interest – even before the Board has a plan for replacement. In future articles, I will deal with the interview and selection process. Just remember, each Board has a personality and the Board is looking for an exec who fits their needs and their quirks and will carry the agency into a new phase of development and community service. My best piece of advice – never try to replace the retiring exec. No matter how special your previous director was, allow her to be remembered, but not institutionalized. Hiring a new Executive Director means its time to move on.

Surf State Website for Nonprofit Information

So here it was one of those lazy, languid summer days. Nothing to do. The washer was whirring and the dryer was adding to the household humidity. Then Jeannette called. She was in a panic. Her column was due and the family was packing for a vacation. So I agreed to do her column this month. But, I didn't have an idea on paper, or at least on my hard drive. Needing an idea – I did what Gary Trudeau does – I went to the old mailbag!

I decided to pursue a question someone had asked me. "What do you do when you have doubts about a nonprofit?" That's a good question. Where can you go to get information on a nonprofit? What can you do if you feel something is amiss with finances or solicitations? I started at the website of the Secretary of State, the North Carolina Secretary of State that is. Colin Powell has enough on his plate! Besides, most local nonprofits start at the Office of our NC Secretary of State. That is where the paper trail begins as a 501(c)3 initiates work for its incorporation. The site (www.secretary.state.nc.us) has a lot of information pertaining to nonprofits. This is a good site for North Carolina donors to review. There are some helpful hints to use in dealing with phone solicitors. There are reports and listings and a series of frequently asked questions (FAQ's).

Charity in Motions

Our secretary of State also includes a number of links related to nonprofit information.

At the Secretary Elaine Marshall's home page, select the option for "Charitable Solicitations." The web surfer quickly learns that the Secretary is responsible for "Charitable Solicitation Licensing" and shares some enforcement responsibilities with the Attorney General. Clearly, this is the place to research agencies and to report activities that may be questionable. It is possible to download a pdf file on this statute. (And right now, if you aren't on the Internet, I apologize – I apologize that you aren't connected because you are missing allot – but that's another soapbox.) This site offers opportunities to report or ask questions regarding charities and solicitors. The Secretary of State and the State Attorney General have the responsibility for keeping charities and solicitors honest.

Another feature of this site is the "Donor's Telephone Checklist." It is a one-page document that should be kept close to your telephone. It is designed to help a donor query telephone solicitors. The Secretary cautions that one should check a solicitor out before writing a check. In fact, the "Donor's Telephone Checklist" is something to be given to friends, especially those who may fall prey to unscrupulous solicitors.

In addition to these warnings, there is another report that is called "Ten Tips on Giving Wisely. It is another one page document with some thoughtful information. Some of the tips include: Budget for giving ... Ask about matching gifts ... Don't forget you have the right to say no. It is very helpful as a discussion starter for any agency before entering into an Annual solicitation or a capital campaign. This information can serve an agency as well as a donor.

One site I always find helpful is the NC Center for Nonprofits, www.ncnonprofits.org). It is an excellent site for

Board members to find information on topics relevant to all phases of nonprofit operations. The resources and information are restricted to members of the organization. This site is also linked to many other sources.

Of course, on the net one thing always leads to several others. So somewhere in cyberspace I ran into a site (http://nccsdataweb.urban.org) that had more data than anyone could possibly use. But I learned that Henderson County has 239 registered 501(c)3's. And that 104 agencies filed a 990. Remember, all non-profits with receipts over $25,000 are required to file a 990. This is a website for data wonks. There are times when starting a non-profit seems to be the only way to attack a community problem or community need. But do we need 239?

Several things pop into my mind – the confusion of all these related and unrelated services – how does a donor decide? But, this also tells me about our community – we care – we care in large and small sums. We care for every living thing. We care for things that soothe our souls, from our Churches to fine art. We care about the quality of life in our community and our history.

Note: IRS now requires all nonprofits regardless of size to file an annual 990.

Finding an Executive Director Part II

I discussed a process that is always a challenge for a Board – finding a new Executive Director. When Board members start looking for new agency leadership, they should already have completed a lot of preliminary work. They should have a clear, updated job description; have a clear and updated mission and vision for the organization; have a plan for accomplishing the interviewing and hiring process, including identifying members of the interview team. And, finally, have a determined salary range and the factors that will influence the level of salary offer. If you have all this done, you are probably exhausted, but the fun is just beginning.

Before advertising, study the applicable labor laws. Being a nonprofit is no excuse (in the government's eyes) for unfair labor practices. I am only going to mention federal regulations, and I am grouping as applicable by agency size. For all agencies of any size, the following apply:

Equal Pay Act of 1963
Employee Polygraph Protection Act of 1988
Fair Credit Reporting Act
Immigration reform and Control Act
Uniform Services Employment and Reemployment Rights Act (USERRA)
Fair Labor Standards (FLSA)

And then there are some that apply if the agency has 15 or more employees:

Title VII of the Civil Rights Act of 1964
Civil Rights Act of 1991
Americans with Disabilities Act (ADA)

Of course, this is nothing. Type "labor laws" and do a web search. When you regain consciousness from that web experience, just follow some of my simple rules. Make sure the Board knows what they are looking for; knows what job must be done; knows, and defines, any physical limitations. It may be helpful to include the salary range in the employment notice. This will help screen candidates out of your price range. Require that all applicants file the same application forms. An office supply store carries generic employment forms. Then the information is there and easy to compare to determine appropriateness for the position. My summary of all the applicable employment law: Be kind, open, fair and honest with the people you interview. Treat them with respect and have a clear idea of what the agency needs that isn't defined by gender, color, national origin, age or physique.

Design an interview script that will be followed for each applicant. Decide if there will be participation in the interview by the existing staff as well as the identified Board members. In the first meeting, listen. Learn about the candidate. It is important to ask questions that pertain to the job and candidate qualifications. The interview team may also ask scenario questions, such as how would you handle this type of employee situation? Or how would you organize this task? It is good to ask open-ended questions that allow the candidate to talk at length. That type of question may be something like, "Describe the most difficult crisis you had to resolve." Or "Talk about a conflict with a Board that you had to work through." On the second interview, talk about the agency, the job, the facility. Be specific about job expectations and outline performance measures. Stay focused on performance expectations and skills that are necessary to do the job. Enthusiasm, sparkle and blarney are not what get a job done. A good interview team should know the difference between baloney and real beef.

A good team should know what not to ask. Nothing about age or ethnicity. No questions are appropriate if they are related to family situation, such as "Will you need to find day care?" Nor can the panel ask health related questions, like "Do you have HIV?" All the information gained must be related to the job and to the employment situation.

The chair of the interview committee should check the references personally. Look beyond the "handpicked" references supplied. But remember, the same "don't ask " questions also apply to references. Criminal and credit checks are essential at the ED level. Criminal checks usually involve researching public records, but credit checks do not. These checks fall under the "Fair Credit Reporting Act." which states that with the applicant's permission, you can gather this data. This law also requires that, should information gathered cause the applicant to be dropped from consideration, the applicant must be informed upon request.

A Board makes a time investment in searching for a new executive director. Once the position is filled, it is the Board's responsibility to make sure the new ED has the tools to do the job as it was advertised and as outlined by the performance measures. A serious investment of time and thought in the hiring process should yield the Board a long term, capable employee.

Small Business, Nonprofits Have Much in Common

There isn't much difference between running a small business and running a nonprofit, points out my friend Steve Johnson, owner of Southern Alarm and Security in Hendersonville. As Steve says, nonprofits provide a service, have a customer base, both donors and clients, make payroll and work hard to establish a good name in the community. These are the same principles that a small, for profit, business adopts to succeed. The only difference is that nonprofits don't pay taxes on their income.

Steve makes a good point. Once a nonprofit has established itself as such, internally it must operate by the same good businesses practices as the small businesses in our community. For that reason it is always helpful to recruit business people to a nonprofit board. Those board members can help you organize the "business" side of the organization. Business owners and managers add comfort and credibility for your donor base. When a successful business owner sits on your Board and solicits colleagues for donations, it adds a sense of reassurance to the "ask."

Recruiting business people for a Board doesn't happen overnight. All board recruitment is an ongoing process. Look over the businesses in our community. Do they know who you are? Have you worked to establish your presence? Is your mission obvious or must you work on a statement that is clear? Steve has some good ideas here. He suggests that you continue what you already do, newsletters, networking opportunities, donor appreciation. It's what all nonprofits do. But then, he suggests that your organization select a few businesses with whom to build closer relationships. And build those relationships before you need their money!

During our conversation Steve made some good points about donations. First, he suggested that some donors might like to make donations using their credit cards. He says that some folks might respond to a request for large sums if the donation can be financed on their own terms. He also said that some donors may appreciate using a credit card because that adds to their bonus or travel point program on their credit card. That's a good point. This credit card suggestion is even a good idea for us retirees who have used payroll deduction donations in the past.

Businesses can make donations in other ways. For example, some businesses can offer in-kind support. But Steve cautions, an in-kind contribution deserves the same amount of acknowledgment and thanks as a cash contribution. Often helping support a fundraising event by an underwriting sponsorship is an advertising expense for a business but income to the nonprofit. Steve points out that leveraging advertising dollars for event sponsorship has advantages for everyone.

Steve currently serves on three local nonprofit Boards and has served on many others in the past. He has served on boards that have business purposes, cultural purposes and human service purposes. That pretty much covers every type of board service available in this community. He talked about his board service and stated that he goes into service ready to work and knowing he will donate to the organization. Those are the two rules for board service!

Then he went on to say that there are reasons to stay on a

board. And why does he stay on a board? He gets caught up in the passion and energy of the "cause." He finds he is involved with people and/or a "cause" that is very different from his professional commitments and that he enjoys the variety and challenge of different ideas and new people. And he has fun.

Finally, Steve has developed some informal comments on his reasons for giving. Steve's top five reasons why he says he might give to your organization:

– I appreciate the recognition gained, such as advertising or underwriting, from giving
– I know and like the people in your organization
– I'm on your Board or a committee (In Steve's opinion this is a given)
– I really believe in your cause
– Someone went out of their way to thank me last year

And here are some reasons why he might not give to you organization:

– It's late in the year and I'm out, or burned out of "giving" dollars
– I'm not familiar with the cause
– I don't know the people in your organization
– I was never asked
– I was never thanked or acknowledged for last year's contribution

I hope you found this information enlightening. Steve is one of the many small business people in our community who see nonprofit service as an important part of being successful in business. A business owner gives time thoughtfully and nonprofits should go about developing business relationships with just as thoughtful an approach. In that manner both businesses, for profit and nonprofit, and the community will gain.

Year-End Giving; Year-Round Caring

It's November. You are already receiving donation letters from many reputable and worthy causes. It happens every year. Many of you will be generous and many local agencies will spread holiday cheer throughout our community because of you.

Very practically let's look at some pragmatic discussion about year-end giving. Many people start to examine their financial position as the year-end approaches. They realize that some timely donations will have very positive impacts on their 1040. There are advantages to donating appreciated property before December 31. Giving appreciated assets carry multiple tax benefits. They are generally deductible at full fair market value, if owned for longer than one year. This donation also allows the donor/taxpayer to bypass capital gains tax. Then there are advantages to donating depreciated property before December 31. According to one source "The amount of your deductible loss combined with the charitable deduction may actually amount to more than the current value of the investment."

And, of course, the always welcome gift of cash can serve to reduce your tax impact, if you itemize your tax deductions. Through a cash gift it is possible, based on the size of the gift and income, to eliminate income tax on up to 50% of your taxable income. Larger gifts may result in tax savings in as many as six years. Don't you just love the subtleties of the tax code?

Charity in Motions

At United Way, Henry Johnson, the Executive Director, and Amy Williford, Director of Community Engagement, talked about year-end giving. Amy suggested that donors who are giving sums to impact their taxes should be sure to check with their financial planner to help develop a successful giving strategy. Henry has his own year-end giving strategy. He wants to make sure that United Way has helped make donors aware of all giving opportunities in the community. Henry has alerted United Way agencies to provide information on needs and special holiday programs. He has advised his member agencies to list these opportunities at 211, the phone service that works to link those who want to help with those who need help. He has suggested that this strategy should tell donors who is collecting what; who needs toys, or gifts for elderly; and who is looking for holiday volunteers to help distribute the gifts. Amy added that everyone has a big heart this time of year and this is a great opportunity for us all.

In our meeting we also discussed the importance of year-end giving to local agencies. Many agencies are not organized enough, nor large enough for year round development operations, so year-end solicitations are a big part of their fundraising strategy.

Is there any one special place to send your money? I stopped to visit Carol Kitchen at the Department of Social Services. Carol works hard managing the needs of DSS clients against what the various tax-supported programs allow. For example, there really is no line item for, say, Christmas toys for foster children. So Carol has learned where to find the Christmas Spirit. She says that all local agencies work together to make sure community resources get to everyone in need, or alone, or all the things one shouldn't be at Christmas. Of course, the kids have her heart and she makes sure the kids get gifts collected by "Share the

Magic' and by "Toy Run." In addition, she points out that, from Salvation Army to Bounty of Bethlehem, this community is demonstrating that Christmas isn't about tax deductions, it's about the Message.

So check 211, check your Church programs, look into the activities of your favorite agency. And if your donation is worth enough to substantially impact your tax savings, you have been blessed with success in life and we are blessed as a community that you heard the Message, too.

Enron, Martha Stewart And You

If you sit on the Board of a not for profit, or NFP, consider yourself in the questionable company of all the Enron executives and Martha Stewart. That's right, you are suspected of lying to your auditors, suspected of financing offshore terrorists or suspected of money laundering, among other felonies. Things have gotten pretty bad when the sincere folks who serve in the charitable world have no better reputation than a drug trafficker. I started out angry that my good work and community service should be so suspect. But after reading what is possible under the protection of NFP status, my anger gave way to great sadness. I came across a statement by United Way National President Brian Gallagher, as he stated, "... changes in nonprofit accountability have to be made in order to restore trust."

Where and when did we NFP's lose trust? And how can that trust be restored on a community level? One of the first steps seems to be mandated government action. I have only two words for you – Sarbanes-Oxley. This is a piece of federal legislation called "The American Competitiveness and Corporate Accountability Act of 2002. "Since sincerity and piety, honesty and integrity, respect for others and good conscience have been purged from corporate America, something seemed to be needed to revive those ideals. Of course, the solution is federal legislation! What? Does it seem possible that a body that thrives on insincerity, lack of integrity and absence of conscience can address corporate felons? Who knows? But we do know that what's good for the

Charity in Motions

goose is good for the titmouse, or something like that. So for all the corporate felons still at large and for those (Martha, this means you) who have new TV shows scheduled for spring release and for all the NFPs who fund graft, corruption and terror, Sarbanes-Oxley is for you. While the lawyers and CPA's draft new philosophies and yet undeveloped policies to circumvent the legislation, we small businesses and smaller NFPs will do what we always do – follow the laws and comply while we wonder why doing honest "for profit" and "non profit" work seems to be punishable by federal intrusion.

What does the Sarbanes-Oxley Act (SOA) mean to you? More work, more monitoring and more money to comply. As a NFP, your Board should be working on two provisions in this act. The first is "Whistle Blower Protection." An NFP should have appropriate financial policies in place to assure staff, members and donors that funds are monitored, managed and spent appropriately. The whistle blower provision allows some one to challenge, or call into question any financial or management practices. It then allows protection for the whistle blower. An NFP responds to this provision by proactive financial management. Get you books and financial policies in order. If your NFP has an audit every year, the auditor may be suggesting activities or policies that will help your agency design a system of open, understandable management and tracking that will encourage donor and staff trust. Then, develop and adopt a formal "Whistle-Blower Policy." This policy should have a method for dealing with complaints and should prevent retaliation to anyone who "in good faith" calls your NFP practices into question.

The other provision of SOA is "Document Destruction." This provision deals with the destruction of litigation-related documents. Enron sure has added a lot to the meaning of

"Best Management Practices!" An NFP now must have a written, mandatory document retention and periodic destruction policy. The National Council of Nonprofit Associations has developed a list of types of documents with minimum requirements for length of preservation. They caution that their presentation is a sample and suggest that you consult your attorney for issues specific to your NFP. But here are some areas familiar to all NFPs. Documents such as deeds, mortgages, year end financial statements, minute books, charter and retirement and pension records are records that are kept permanently. Keep bank statements and expired insurance policies for three years. Duplicate deposit slips can go after two years, while payroll records, time sheets and withholding tax statements should hang around for seven years.

All in all, this legislation probably demands of NFPs some things that are good business practices. If your NFP house is in order, Sarbanes Oxley will be a blip on your radar, on the other hand, if your NFP is a little disorganized, this legislation sets out some standards to help get you on track. When your organization is distracted by disorganization, it costs money in staff time, donor distrust and board mismanagement.

For further information, go to:
www.independentsector.org/issues/sarbanesoxley.html.

There is a lot of information and some pdf files to download regarding this legislation and impact on your NFP. In addition, Henry Johnson at United Way has a great fact sheet from the above website as well as some sample policies.

Just tell him I told you to call.

Federal Government Scrutinizing Finances of Nonprofits

Overhaul of various financial reporting and financial responsibilities for charities and foundations continues as a topic of interest at the Federal level. The Senate Finance Committee held hearings in April on misconduct attributed to nonprofit organizations. This is a continuation of the adoption of Sarbanes-Oxley a few years ago. The Legislation originally paid attention to financial practices in the business world, but has increasingly turned attention to the nonprofit community. Last month I was sent copies of articles relating to these hearings that occurred during that time. The first was an op-ed piece from The Wall Street Journal, "Death by Bureaucracy," written by, Heather R. Higgins, the co-founder of the Alliance for Charitable Reform (www.ACreform.com). The author called attention to the destructive nature of the potential actions that might come from the Senate Finance Committee hearings. She argued that the responses would be overkill, raising the costs of operation for all nonprofits when only a few are guilty of misconduct. The writer suggests that a more appropriate action would be for the committee to study the real extent of abuse instead of relying on abuses discovered while reviewing a handful of organizations. She challenges whether the appropriate agencies charged with reviewing all the proposed new filings would be staffed appropriately. Part of the federal proposal also includes some method of accrediting charities. If you check out the website of the Alliance for Charitable Reform, you will find their suggestions for legislation and self-policing of nonprofits.

The second article I received was a report on the Senate Finance Committee hearing as reported in the Washington Post. This article refers to nonprofit as "a hotbed of tax evasion and abuse." IRS Commissioner Mark W. Everson "said that the IRS is finding problems in virtually every type of tax-exempt organization." The article continues, "Non profits include not only charities, but colleges and universities, many hospitals, pension plans, trade associations and think tanks ... now totals roughly 3 million entities controlling $8 trillion in assets.

Hmm. My first response as a person who asks for money for local nonprofits – with $8 trillion floating around – I think some one is getting more than their share and it isn't anyone I know! My second response is that there are risks to folks who receive charitable services as well as to donors, if they are ill informed. In fact, Mr. Everson, in the Post article does lament that those who might suffer most would be the people and groups who receive help from foundations and charities. His other concern is defining a mechanism to penalize offenders. He points out that when an entity that pays taxes is found to have acted illegally, that entity can usually expect to pay a penalty, usually double the tax owed. He then points out that inappropriate actions by non-profits need another type of punishment. If you don't pay any tax, doubling the amount owed is meaningless.

Because I am not familiar with the Alliance as quoted above, I went to the website of NC Center for Nonprofits (www.ncnonprofits.org) for a second opinion. The Center's "Public Policy Alert" of April 19, 2005 also reports on the

Senate hearing. The Center website details a national panel of nonprofits' report submitted to help the Senate Finance Committee work toward solutions for nonprofit tax issues. They also support some regulation and some self-policing.

All this is to tell you that giving money or other assets to a charity or foundation, is becoming a lot more complicated for the donor and more challenging to the nonprofit recipients. Charities will have more responsibilities to monitor donors especially gifts other than cash. The IRS suspects donors overvalue donated assets. Charities, even our local agencies, will be required to develop methods to monitor donations. Nonprofits need to be aware of the laws. They should all have appropriate policies in place to ensure correct financial management and board members in place who understand the responsibility of acting as the law requires.

There is a bright side to all this. Although the IRS is telling Congress that tax abuse is rampant in Nonprofits, they are also trying to help. On June 28, 29 or 30 they are offering an 8-hour workshop for small and mid-sized exempt organizations in Charlotte. The cost is $30. In fact, check out www.irs.gov/charities. There is a lot of information there. If you are a treasurer for a local nonprofit, this is a website for you. The workshop has to be a personal decision. Eight hours or so with the IRS could be a challenge. Look what it got Al Capone.

Nonprofits: An Important Sector of Local Economy

Some folks think of nonprofits as organizations of questionable value run by "do-gooder" types with no business sense. Over the last several months I hope I have helped all donors in our community understand that a local nonprofit has to be as well organized and as fiscally responsible as any small or medium business enterprise. Recently, I found a study that measures nonprofits' value in dollars and cents.

According to a report, "Economic Impact Study of WNC Nonprofits," by The Community Foundation of Western North Carolina and the Environmental Leadership Center of Warren Wilson College, 2004-05, our regional nonprofits are an "important economic sector."

In our region nonprofits are not just "do-gooder" human service agencies, but are also hospitals, schools, fire departments, performing acts programs, economic development programs and a variety of other services. In fact, the largest employer in the region, Mission Hospital, is a nonprofit. Most nonprofits manage funds that are similar in amount to many local small businesses. We have talked before about the many accounting challenges that are facing nonprofits and the need to be better organized and transparently accountable to their donors and the IRS. This report makes a point to say that the value of the nonprofit organizations to each community goes beyond the visible community service provided. When we look at local nonprofits, we are also looking at JOBS. We are looking at the capacity of local nonprofits to spend funds within the community. To purchase goods and services is a view of nonprofits that needs to come forward and be recognized.

Here are some points of information listed in the study:

There were 2,105 501(c)(3) public charities registered with the IRS in the 18 counties of western North Carolina in 2001. Religious congregations were not included.

Of the 875 nonprofits meeting the threshold of $25,000 required to file a 990 with the IRS, there is even more breathtaking information: WNC nonprofits receive a total of $1.95 billion in revenue. Revenues are split as follows; 74% from fees and services; 20% from contributions, including 8% from government grants. Those nonprofits support 42,348 jobs – 28,035 jobs are supported directly by nonprofits and an additional 14,313 jobs are generated indirectly from economic activity of the nonprofits.

But let's bring this closer to home. Henderson County, per this report, accounts for 1,736 nonprofit jobs and 685 jobs that are created though indirect support of nonprofits. That represents a payroll of $71,295,855 in 2001. And the study credits local nonprofits with generating $3,208,166 in State and local revenue, or $1,474,610 if nonprofit hospitals and colleges are excluded from the formula.

With the passage of the county's 2005-06 budget, the county commissioners allotted $212,500 to be distributed to a number of human service agencies in the county. In addition, the Partnership for Economic Development received $199,500 to continue work in industrial development and local industrial expansions. There was also an additional sum of $77,500 distributed to local nonprofits with missions serving the environment, the arts and community development groups. I am sure there are some who question the involvement of the county in distribution of funds to any nonprofit.

However, after reading the impact of nonprofits in our community, I would say that the commissioners are wise to be investing in that sector of our economy. That's right, nonprofits are part of our economic landscape – a very successful part by economic development definitions. So when the commissioners invest, not give away, $489,500 to local nonprofits, we get a great return on our investment. We get services that are less costly when provided by the non-government sector of our community. We get measurable economic benefits and we get reliable community programs.

It is important to note that the commissioners are thoughtful and demanding with our tax dollars. They require application and evaluation information. They ask others to help evaluate the program requests. And they expect accountability from the nonprofits.

All in all, when local government gives to local nonprofits and when we make private contributions, we gain. We gain in services, we gain in quality of life improvement and we gain in jobs and positive economic impact.

Board Self-Evaluations

During the recent pleas for donations to help the Katrina victims, we have been warned to beware of scam artists trying to attract donations from sincere donors for victim relief. The reporters always recommend that we give our money to an agency that we know and trust. That's a good rule for all of our giving. Local or national, make sure the agency receiving your money will deliver the service as you believe.

Several weeks ago in this newspaper, there was an Op-Ed piece by Frances Fairey outlining the operation of the Alliance for Human Services. In Henderson County this organization exists to help local funders, namely the Community Foundation, United Way and Henderson County government, by accrediting human service agencies seeking funds. One of the positives of accrediting of local agencies is to assure donors that these agencies are well organized and managed within the good financial practices of non-profits.

The Alliance board has designed a great instrument to use to conduct an organizational self-evaluation. The first form in the packet is very interesting. It is designed to help agencies determine duplicate services. The form helps a Board do a program review to highlight distinctions of its programs from other programs in the community that may appear as duplication. Local donors are very savvy. They are interested in avoiding redundancy. Yet, they are also interested that all in need receive services. Agencies have to be ready to respond to these concerns – working through the questions will be helpful.

Next the packet contains a great checklist of necessary and highly recommended financial policies and procedures. Form C 2005 is designed to help an agency design the appropriate accounting checks and balances to prevent fraud, waste and/or abuse of financial resources. Its a simple checklist, but will have an impact on managing an agency's financial paper trail. Financial evaluation concerns address policies such as: receipts issued for any cash contribution received; expenses coded accurately to the general ledger in a timely manner. For those of you in a very small organization, some of the questions may be a challenge. In a larger organization, there would be staff to address some of the issues, but in the end, large or small agency, the Board members need to be involved in financial issues and policy development. After all – this is the primary Board responsibility.

The next section of the packet is the "Self-Evaluation Matrix." The matrix lists accepted standards and practices of good organizations, then asks the agency to rate its performance in these areas. The standards measured in the matrix cover several categories. They are: Mission and Program; Legal; Governance; Financial; Charitable Fund Development; Public Accountability and Ethics; Public Policy and Advocacy; Collaboration and Partnerships; Human Resources and Compensation; and Constituency Development and Services. It looks at agency mission and its relationship with agency organization. It looks at Board organization, offering a great checklist to assess the Board functioning level. There are some categories that speak to client services and community need.

The process for accreditation that has been developed by the Alliance is a great instrument for any agency to use as a preorganization guide or a self-evaluation tool. Whether your agency serves anything from the arts to zoos, the Accreditation Packet is something to use to check your organizational health.

The point is, local nonprofits have tools and mandates to make sure they are who they say they are and do what they say they will do. This is not an idea that exists just for Henderson County agencies. All national agencies with local offices go through a rigorous assessment on a routine basis from the national office. So the local group of the Boy Scouts, Girl Scouts or the local Consumer Credit Counseling offices are already meeting standards necessary for a well-run, creditable, established fundraiser and service provider. The Alliance helps local human service agencies move their organization to those standards.

In recent years accountability of an agency has become very important. Donors want the same kind of information regarding a nonprofit as they want for any type of financial investment. Those concerns and the rise of donor sophistication have made nonprofits work to a higher level of accountability and measurable outcomes. If you sit on a local nonprofit board, or are thinking of seeking nonprofit status to serve a community need, email the Alliance for Human Services at ahschair@hendersoncountync.org. Ask for the Accreditation packet.

Note: The Alliance for Human Services was dissolved in 2010 and no longer advises county funders.

Christmas (Thrift Store) Shopping

The merchandizing frenzy is in full swing. Buy this – buy that. Everyone on your Christmas list needs a rhinestone potato peeler, or some other assault on good taste. So what do you do? You have this list, you want to serve the Christmas spirit, yet, you want to give gifts that reflect your warmth – not scream "last minute, desperate selection!!"

I just happen to have a friend, no names, please, who always has some good suggestions, matching those on my list with just the right gift. So I have asked Mr. X to help us put Christmas shopping in perspective this year.

"Mr. X, thank you for meeting with me today," I started.

He looked at me and toyed with his white beard. "You know, I haven't got all day. I have people to supervise and livestock to feed." I think I even heard his boots stomping in impatience, like the anxious prancing sounds of his "livestock,"

"Its well known, Mr. X, that you work very hard establishing lists of folks and gifts and are pretty good at making it all come together. How about some shopping clues for me and my friends?" I smiled.

The smile got me nowhere. He kept me at his door. I was going to have to be happy with doing this interview in the snow. "Listen, here," he started, "I don't have too much time. And this year, I don't have the funds I used to have. What with tsunamis, hurricanes and earthquakes, me and my staff have been spending early and often using funds we don't have." (No, I'm not talking to the President!)

"But, Mr. X, many of us are struggling with those same challenges. We have been helping as best we could afford, to relieve some of the suffering related to these tragedies."

"You have? And your friends, too?"

I nodded.

"Hmmm," he mused. "Maybe there is more to you than meets the eye." His eyes twinkled. "Maybe I can help you and your friends."

I got my notebook and reminded myself that this wasn't the time to worry about subpoenas and identifying news sources.

"As I said," he began, "its been a tough year. So many folks have needed so much. This isn't a year to give random, tacky gifts. This is a year to give warmth, food and shelter." His belly shook with some secret laughter. "I like to do my share of unexpected, but useful gifts. Remember that year you got the C-clamps?"

"That was you? No wonder I could never get the kids to admit to that gift!"

Now his belly shook like a bowl full of jelly. "I thought it was great! And it didn't cost much, and fess up – you use them all the time, right?"

"Yes! How did you know?" I asked suspiciously. Then another question occurred to me – did I get them because I was naughty – or nice?

His grin broadened and his rosy cheeks bounced above his beard, squeezing his eyes between cheek and bushy white brow. "That's my point!

If it were, I was lost. And I told him that.

"Exactly!" he said as he laid his finger aside his nose. "There is more to giving gifts than the receiver's goodness. It's based on the giver's goodness. That's why I give gifts from the heart. Even in times when money is tight. Look around, there are plenty of ways to give with fun and joy and warmth, without breaking the bank.

And I like making my money go really far. So I ....

My pen was ready, here comes the stuff Special Prosecutors dream about – sugarplums, indictments, candy canes, grand juries ... but I'm forgetting my assignment.

"... shop at nonprofit thrift stores."

Ugh? Did I miss something? What a let down! I opened my mouth, but he spoke first.

"I bet you think you heard wrong? Did I disappoint you?" Wow. No wonder this guy knew when I was sleeping and when I wasn't paying attention.

"Let me explain. Often we can't help everyone that needs us. Giving money to charity is one way of getting support to those in need. But another way is to support charitable enterprises. And at Christmas time what better way than shopping at their thrift stores? They are the best places to find gifts that are one of a kind, personal and within your budget. You can always find old records, an old piano or two; books, furniture, T-shirts that say the darndest things and so much more. But the best thing is that you are supporting a good community service and you are saying 'I love you' to some one too important to ignore at this time of year. You give twice and that makes up for a whole lot of naughty."

Was he serious? I had better things to do than talk to some bearded guy in a red, sooty suit. But I gave it a try. You know what I learned? Local charity thrift stores rock – and shopping there gives each nonprofit the ability to spread their warmth in the community while I can give gifts that have special meaning.

Happy Holiday shopping!

Finding Nemo

A nonprofit Board should always be on the look out for fresh talent – new Board members. This is usually the time of year the nominating committee starts to look for those new members for midsummer elections. Everyone is talking about the Pro Draft – that's what the nominating committee is – the committee looking for some one that has that special "something" to help the Board succeed. This candidate must have staying power, stomach for the hard stuff, heart for the long haul, and courage under fire.

The first rule – no stereotyping. For example, we have a Congress that thought a guy lobbying for clients and throwing around money had staying power. What did they get? A thug who is singing like a frightened canary. However, look what the gang got when they bet on Nemo, a little clown fish with heart, courage and staying power. The trick is to find the true measure of a candidate. Don't be afraid to look at some unlikely folks, and match the Board's needs with the talent around town.

Second rule – follow the money. If there are consistent donors to your agency, give them a good study. Their financial commitment is an indication of their belief in the mission and may translate into volunteer Board service. Many donors prefer to have their money do their service. But ask. Sometimes, it's the right offer at the right time. Even if the offer is declined, your donor has again learned how much your agency values him or her.

The third rule – never date your sister (or brother.) I'll bet you wonder where I'm going with this. Stay with me – it'll make sense. Often, an agency is tempted to invite a retired employee to join the Board. WRONG. There are two types of folks who should not be asked to join the Board. A former employee and a former client. That doesn't mean that they aren't good folks who would work hard and give their all. They may give more than anyone wants. Look at these potential candidates and just remember the inverse proportions of math. The further away in time a person is from employment or from assistance from the agency, the better the chance that such a person will became a great Board member. So let some time elapse before the invitation is made. And give the invitation serious thought.

The fourth rule – good vibrations. The yin and yang keep the good vibes going. Look for a pessimist and match that person with an optimist. Just don't let them sit near one another at meetings. By pessimist, I mean more than some one who is negative. It should be some one who nitpicks, finishes thoughts and always tries to wrap up the current discussion before the Board leaps to a new, unrelated topic. This person says things like, "I thought we decided at the last meeting to...." or "I may have missed something but exactly who is going to ...?" Be grateful those folks are paying attention. Because, remember that optimist. That's the person who grabs a loose thought and has the whole Board voting to try some venture unrelated to mission, but spectacular in concept and crippling if it fails. When they both agree, the Board is onto something big.

Fifth rule – save the last dance. As I look for Board recruits, I like to hold a position open. That flexibility is probably in your bylaws. Something like, "the Board shall be not less than, nor more than..." I like to never reach the more than, so that there is always an opportunity to invite a midyear participant. Sort of bringing some one in from the bench. Of course, make sure the nominee is some one the Board members know. That's the value of the nominating committee working year round and keeping a "draft" list that the Board discusses periodically. But why would you need a mid year entry? Well, Boards and agencies are like any good soap opera – vice, virtue, sex, embezzlement. The crisis can be anything from the death of the Board Chair (sorry all you chairs!) to a financial brouhaha. As the drama unfolds a new person with a calm demeanor, familiar with crisis management, and respected in the community for solid thinking can strengthen a board to act appropriately.

There you have it – some one old, some one new, some one – oops, wrong column. Building a Board is like recruiting a good team. The Nominating Committee should always be scouting the community for candidates who have qualities the Board needs – commitment, caution, daring, experience and especially heart. Make sure the list of potential Board members includes some one who can make the next touchdown or hold the line. Don't ignore some one going against type, like the clown fish with the gimpy fin – He's got what it takes.

The Bella Years
2006–2011

After writing this column for several years, I developed a new format to get my point(s) across. I created a world, the Land of Lost Board Members and introduced readers to a number of characters who discussed nonprofit board membership in their community. The most famous character, Bella Pelorizado, was a nonprofit ED who had naturally curly hair. In the early articles her hair provided its own commentary. Bella soon evolved into a nonprofit consultant who worked with a group of community activists: Joshua Biggly Huge, community philanthropist; Coach Amos Alonso Upright, long serving board member on many boards; Cash Now, CPA to nonprofits; Al Truistini, community do-gooder.

These characters had their fans. But they also had many readers who told me they never understood what I was trying to say! But they were my friends and read the column anyway.

Cosmic Questions

Sometimes we need to evaluate life with and without nonprofit Board participation. With that in mind, I visited the Land of Lost Board Members. It's a sad place, neither here nor there, misty and gray, random meeting minutes floating through the air and a bylaws quagmire at the edge of Main Street. There I found a forlorn soul. He was a sad looking gentleman with a great emptiness about him.

"Excuse me," I ventured, "Can I help?"

"Its 'may' not 'can.'" He looked at me. "I was the newsletter editor for thirteen and three quarters years. Did that matter? Nooooo. They started putting the letter online – who knows all that software? Not some useless oldie like me. Folks enjoyed my newsletters. They liked the insider jokes, the cogent pleas for funds, the popular volunteer corner. Folks stood in line to be the volunteer of the month." Sigh. "But now, nothing. Do I matter anymore?"

Wow, I struck it rich on my first encounter. "What do you mean, do you matter? Of course you do. There is always more work to be done!" I was on a roll. "You haven't been abandoned – you should just consider that you have been reassigned. Agencies have to grow and change, but that shouldn't mean you aren't useful."

"Do you think so?" Was that hope I saw in his eyes? "Do you think they still want me? What could I possibly do for them now? Its probably time for new thinking." A tear spattered on his shoe.

"You're right. Each year, it is time for new thinking. But that doesn't mean the old thinking was wrong or useless. And on close examination, you may find that new thinking is only as good as the old thinking that laid the groundwork

Charity in Motions

for ...."

"Are you suggesting that my service and work continues to have value?"

"Exactly. And if you helped build a strong agency, future board members will be grateful for your work and vision."

"Just a minute here, girlie." I turned to find myself facing a disheveled woman with a pitted and scratched identity badge. Her name and agency affiliation were obscured, but her title, Executive Director, stood out.

"Are you addressing me?"

"You bet, girlie. Are you one of those folks that keeps telling old board members they are still wanted and useful?" She demanded.

"I ..."

"Just as I thought. Why do you keep encouraging them to stay in touch? Good-bye to old thinking is what I say! I want my agency to move and I don't need deadwood or tired blood getting in my way." She was militant.

"So, what are you doing here?" I asked.

She looked around. "I was sent here to look for contributions."

"No you weren't," interrupted a hovering Spirit of Members Past. "You were sent here for CONTRITION."

"Contrition? What? I'm in hell?"

"Well, it's not Kansas," breathed the Spirit.

"Or Oz," piped up my sad friend.

The old Exec looked at us. "Where am I?"

The Spirit of Members Past sort of harrumphed and was wadding up some old finance committee reports to fling.

"I think," I ventured, "that you are in the Land of Lost Board Members to atone for the way you may have treated old board members. My guess is that you didn't respect them for past service, nor value the continued contributions that they could make to your agency."

"Well, what do old timers know?" she stomped.

"They know your history, they are loyal. They usually have given countless hours and steady financial support to a cause they believe in."

"And what happens to us?" the little man cried. "Abandonment, neglect. All I know is I need to continue to belong. I can see that times change and new ideas should come forward. But my past work and commitment should count for something." He was glowing as he spoke.

"Well, I can see that we're on the road to learning a good lesson here today," I was smug in my self-satisfaction. I was ignored.

"What's that you say?" the Executive Director's voice quivered as she turned to the gentleman. "Abandonment you say? Ha! What about me and the agency? One day you're there, the 'go to guy' for every problem, and the next day you've dropped us for a sexier issue, a younger ED." She swallowed a sob.

I thought there was a moral here somewhere, but I was busy dodging bound copies of Strategic Plans, besides my new friends were lost in their reconciliation under the protection of the Spirit of Members Past.

Know When to Fold

There is a little known spot in the Land of Lost Board Members that I visited recently – The Cemetery of Dissolution. I was to meet a young woman who was asking for some advice. She said I would recognize her by her lovely naturally curly hair. I spotted her under the fundraising viburnum with its aroma of fresh cash and tinkling sounds of its coin like leaves.

"Hi," I ventured.

Her head of Shirley Temple curls swirled to reveal a charming, energetic countenance. "Are you Renee?" she asked as one long curl flopped across her nose.

"Yes, I am, and you are Ms. Pelorizado?"

"Just call me Bella."

"OK, Bella, why did you ask to meet with me?"

"I want to close down our agency. And I need some guidance." Curls bounced as she spoke.

"May I ask a few questions? That will help me direct you to an appropriate course of action."

She nodded as several curls covered her left cheek. The curls seemed to have thickened and grown in the last few minutes.

"As you may know, Bella, North Carolina General Statutes Chapter 55A, Nonprofit Corporation Act, Article 14, outlines dissolution. Are you being forced to dissolve because of some corporate or administrative issues? Or judicial dissolution because of fraud? Or...." Above her head curls spelled out "NOPE, NO, NADA."

"No, this is completely voluntary." She tried to push some of the curls behind her ears.

"We just found the cure and we don't need to work hard

anymore."

"Wow, found the cure!" I was impressed. "What an accomplishment to be able to speak to such a greater good. What have you cured?"

"We didn't really cure anything, it was genetic research to find a cause and alter DNA to help humanity rise to a new level of perfection." She twirled a ringlet around her pencil and stared off across the polished dissolution markers.

"And?"

"Oh, we are the Barely Hairy Alliance. We have been funding genetic research for years to find the gene that gives you naturally curly hair." She pushed armfuls of hair from her face and looked triumphant.

"Who would pay for genetic research for curly hair?" I've been doing fundraising a long time and funders do have standards!

"Bald foundation directors, bald legislators, bald CEO's. I must say it was very easy. But success has been a challenge." She was now sitting under a mound of curls.

"So you want to stop what – fundraising, research …?"

"The agency. I am tired of those researchers," she hmmphed. "Money, money, money to do more research, and they keep getting side tracked, mapping and marking other diseases, finding solutions to genetic engineering ethical issues. You know stuff outside my, I mean, our mission." I watched as a few healthy ringlets inched toward a small oak at the cemetery edge. She didn't notice this growth as she continued, "So that's why I contacted you."

"Me? I don't know anything about genetic research."

"You know something about nonprofits – and I want to shut this one down – no more Barely Hairy Alliance, no more wild-eyed genetic researchers stalking me. I found my answer …." she croaked as her hair pulled her from the bench and was tangling itself into tree branches.

"Well, as I told you," I shouted as I trotted after her, "follow the guidelines of NC General Statutes Chapter 55A Article 14. It will tell you to prepare a plan of dissolution; make arrangements for the disposal of assets, transfer title of property. Your board must also make sure that all bills are paid and that no debts exist. In addition, it is helpful to work with staff to make sure they are paid before the corporation is dissolved." She indicated she was listening while she tried to get control of the curls. I continued. "Your incorporation papers may also have some directions that you are obliged to heed, such as naming an agency who will receive your assets. After all North Carolina regulations require that nonprofit assets be given to another nonprofit. The incorporation papers may have anticipated dissolution and designated an agency." I arrived breathless at her side.

"What do you mean give away our assets?" She was indignant. She continued speaking as she expertly scissored her tangled curls. "I raised that money. I did all the work. I deserve something for my time and commitment to this project." She stood and brushed herself off. Fresh curls began to inch down her back.

"You are raising ethical issues here, Bella. Conflict of interest." I gasped! "Are those curls a result of Barely Hairy research grants? Did you intimidate researchers into stepping outside appropriate practices to accommodate you? Enrich you? Curl you??" (I know you saw this coming, but I was a little slow.)

"I need those assets to pay for hair maintenance, and ..."

"Not according to North Carolina law." This place was getting scary. "Look, Bella, I've answered your questions. I have to go now."

She was outraged. She held the scissors in a threatening manner and glared at me. I swear some of the curls glared too.

"I'm sure I'm late for a meeting somewhere," I shouted over my shoulder and, like the song, I was "Gone."

Donor Database Management

Drinking coffee at a sidewalk cafe in the Land of Lost Board members is what you would expect. The land is neither in day nor night, hot nor cold, so the coffee is tepid and old. But I needed something after my surreal meeting with Bella Pelorizado. She is working to shutdown her nonprofit while she tries to handle a head of out-of-control Shirley Temple, regenerating curls. This might be a three-cup afternoon. This job certainly had ... wait a minute. Across the sidewalk there were some of Bella's curls scampering along a park bench. They seemed to notice me, now they are moving around like a cheerleading squad. They're spelling ... HELP! Yes, several disconnected ringlets lined up along the bench back spelling Help, and they were "looking" at me. I walked over to the bench, and in what felt like a Lassie moment, I asked, "Is something wrong?" They quickly disassembled their word and stood at attention, they all nodded. What appeared to be the spokes ringlet, tossed a curl toward a side street. They all jumped down and scampered toward the street. So I followed.

We came to an alley filled with the detritus of nonprofits. They halted and spelled SHHHHH on the rim of a dumpster. I could hear voices. Peering around the dumpster, I saw Bella tied to a pole, her curls had been shorn and they were cowering in the alley dust and debris. Bella's head had been wrapped with duct tape so it looked as though she were wearing a turban. Two people were arguing. One was a man holding a razor. He was arguing with a woman while he tried to keep the ringlets at bay by waving the razor.

"What are you doing to Bella?" I demanded. "Who are you people?"

"I'm Karen Terrier, rhymes with Perrier," she answered nervously. "I need to learn from Bella before she retires from fundraising. Bella is the master, the..."

"Yeah, yeah, yeah." The man silenced her. "I'm Mac Velly," he looked at Karen, and added, "rhymes with Jelly. Bella's my catch. She can't leave the industry without passing on her skill to me."

"So you've tied her up and shaved her head?"

"I guess things got out of hand," Mac tried to explain as he turned to face me. "That hair," he gestured over his shoulder, "kind of puts you on the defensive." The ringlets began inching through the dust toward Mac's feet while his back was turned.

"We just wanted some information on donor data base management." Karen sort of shrugged, "you know, should we buy some software, or sign a contract for an online service? Things like that"

The ringlets were closing in, so I said, "Managing and growing your database is an important part of running a successful agency. There are several methods, purchased software or online services, that allow an agency to stay current, file and maintain donor information, and even manage volunteer and client data. A growing agency needs to investigate donor management options."

The ringlets were in place. Mac was curl tackled. Karen was pushed against the dumpster. Bella's eyes were wide, and her duct tape turban was expanding like a pan of Jiffy Pop! I was too late. I had never seen duct tape explode! Curls tumbled, scurried, spelled unprintable words!

I finally reached Bella and released her. She removed the last bit of duct tape ... from her mouth. She was furious.

She turned to the curlnappers. "What do you mean treating me like this. I was willing to share my donor management knowledge with both of you, but now you can go to ...," as the curls spelled you know what in the alley dust.

"Renee is right. Successful agencies need to think about what information concerning donors is important to have on hand and easily accessible. You have to consider cost. For example, which has advantages to your fundraising strategy, an up front investment in software or a continuing monthly fee for online services. In addition you should consider privacy and confidentiality. If you go online, what are the encryption protocols? Also look at training and tech support. How easy is it to ask a question, change your information fields? Those are things good agencies would explore." She stopped in mid pique, "but as for you two, I don't give a ...." And the ringlets completed the thought.

She stomped out of the alley. Her shaved head already had a new curl crop while the rescue ringlets formed up in military parade formation and followed her out in curl cadence. Hut, hut, hut.

Was It Worth It?

One of the forlorn community notice boards in the Land of Lost Board Members was covered with overlapping, over hyped, blurred fundraising announcements for unreadable agencies. They all ran together – "come to our breakfastlunchdinner during winterspringsummerfall for the event of a lifetime! Help our cause. Join our team. Spread the word." Right in the center of all the fundraising flotsam was a fresh appeal. "Fundraising Event Evaluation" one night only presented by the CPA to NFP's, Cash Now, Biker CPA.

I checked my calendar. I didn't want to miss this session. Cash doesn't waste time or money. He gives his advice and dares a client not to listen. The ad said the presentation would be at the abandoned drive-in. I walked out of town to the meeting location – an old movie screen tilted to one side with weeds growing around the speaker poles. But the snack shop was abustle. One of the rules of fundraising – good food rivals a good story. There was Cash handling cheesy fries and a 40-oz. soft drink. He spotted me and shouted, "Hey Renee, will you be at the workshop this evening? I've got some great info to share with my clients."

"Cash, its good to see you. I thought you had given up the not for profit crowd for, well, more cash."

"I did, but it just wasn't as much fun. I like working with people who raise money for ideas and turn it into community service. The for-profit world sometimes seems to work by sleight of hand and guile. This is more rewarding." He managed to say all that and finish his drink and fries without getting anything on his leather jacket.

"Come on over to my office. Let me give you a rundown

Charity in Motions

on the show tonight." He pointed in the direction of a motorcycle.

We walked over to his Harley with a sidecar. "Still using the same office, I see."

"Yes. this is the most efficient desk on three wheels. Technology allows me to keep the overhead under, if you know what I mean." He reached into the sidecar and brought out his laptop and projector. "Look at this stuff." He focused his PowerPoint projector on the sagging drive-in screen.

"I did a study of how my clients raise money and tried to develop criteria for evaluating the events." Slides flashed on the screen. He kept up a commentary as they blinked by.

"See there? I want my clients to start thinking about several things before planning an event. They should know their market audience. Design an event that suits the audience and makes sense for their cause. Then they need to build a budget of potential income and expenses. Does it make sense?" He kept talking as he compulsively twirled his Blackberry on his biker chain.

"Cash? Those slides went by mighty fast. May I have a copy of the presentation?"

"Sure, how do you want it? I can e-mail it now." He snapped the Blackberry into his palm. I must have looked puzzled because he said, "This land is Wi-Fi. But maybe I can just burn you a CD." I must have still looked lost because he then sighed, "Well I guess I can Xerox a copy."

"You have a copier in the sidecar?" I didn't hear his answer because he was pulling some fresh copy out of his "office." I rifled through some of the notes he handed me and found I had more questions.

"Cash, why do you think this is an important topic?"

"Well, Renee, agencies put a lot of time and energy into fundraising. They need some guidelines to help evaluate the results. You know, was it effective? Did we reach our audience? Did we have a realistic budget? Did everyone help or did we overburden our director?" He flexed his CPA muscles under his jacket, then continued, "An agency works hard, but if there isn't an evaluation component, that agency may be spending energy on something that has no return. Its all a dance." He swiveled his hips, "They may be doing a gala's worth of work and end up with sock hop receipts."

Just then his sidecar rang. He turned to me, "I love technology." He took the call and concluded it with a directive, "Yeah, yeah, just stand by your fax, it will be there in a second."

"You have a fax in that thing?"

"Hey, this is my office ... my clients expect all the same services that a for-profit expects." His Blackberry dangled on a chain from his belt, the projector lightbeam created a halo around his buzz cut as he turned to add, "I got to get this workshop done. My clients expect good advice. And I am committed to keeping them fiscally sound. You know my theory, if Congress has caught a megamillions multinational corporation doing funny books, you can bet they want to make sure some $100,000/year not for-profit isn't getting away with something the least suspect."

"That's sounds so cynical, Cash."

"Not in this business. NFP's do so much good. I'm privileged to work with them." His eyes twinkled. "Besides, who else would accept me in a business meeting in these duds?"

Plan Your Donation Year

This is the time of year that we start collecting those random receipts to prove we – paid alimony, had no capital gains, practiced some level of stewardship at our Church. You know – tax time. You have a file where you have stuffed all those letters that nonprofits are required to send you – $25 here, $75 less the cost of the meal there and various, spur of the moment responses to asks. Well, look it's over. Is this where you want your money to go? Or in our case, is this where we want our money to go. Or, the question in our house, "I don't remember this donation, did you give some money to …?"

Last year, 2006, was an especially, "did you give money to…?" year. I don't know how we got so out of sync. There I was looking at sending a check to Artist Who Paint with Yogurt while Stan, believing that teaching a man to fish, yada, yada, yada, was preparing to send money to Bait for Belgium, when we met at the computer waiting for Quicken to open.

"You've got to quit giving away all this money," he pontificated as his finger jabbed the computer screen.

"But, my causes are better than your causes," I whined.

A synopsis of the donations for the year was offered by Quicken. There it was. We had been generous this year, and it was close to Christmas, we still needed money for presents for the grandkids. It was too late to call back funds, but it certainly showed us that we should consult each other more on our donations. Especially when we discovered that we were supporting competing ideologies – ESPN Anonymous vs. ESPN Embrace Me.

You review you portfolio and the status of assets and review your overall financial position each year. Why not look at your giving history? For example, is your money going to a cause that has your heart and your interest? Are you supporting a cause because its good work benefits a family member or friend, whether it's the arts, scouting or shelter and safety? Are you familiar with the upcoming needs of your favorite agencies – will there by a capital campaign in 2007? Is there a new program that will expand service opportunities? What about location? Do you want your money to stay in local agencies, travel to your former hometown or go across time zones? And what about emergencies – Katrina, Tsunami, famine – the global array of need?

Then there is your Church. Most folks consider Church giving as separate from other donations. However, consider what your pastor will ask of you this year. It may mean altering your overall giving budget. Is there a new mission, a new outreach? Will that money be easily found in your current resources or must another aspect your giving be reduced?

So here are some guidelines to review your giving. Look back over your checkbook. Try three years. Is the amount of money more or less constant? Who are you giving to? Are the agencies receiving your money those with whom you have a familiarity. Or are you just giving out of habit? You might find a visit to a website or, if local, an actual site visit may help you renew your commitment to giving.

Now review all those requests you got for end of year giving. Apply the same scrutiny there. Visit websites and actual locations. Maybe you will find something more compatible with your interests at this time. You might even find a new volunteer opportunity for the new year.

Next examine who you are. Are you supporting what you believe in? Your review may find that your money has been going to a program that doesn't quite feel comfortable with your personal outlook on life. That doesn't mean that the agency is wrong, or bad. It only means that you have different opinions on a solution. Its also people. Consider who is asking you for funding. There are dynamic fundraisers who make you actually feel your money working, help you enjoy the outcome of your donation, make sure you experience the joy of those who receive your gift. This may be another factor to include in your evaluation.

The final question – when you give as two – Who's on the official family list? Negotiate a reasonable list of his and her donations. I know this is 2007, but we still have genders and we still have many charitable needs.

Remember, when you look back in 2008, you should reflect on these decisions and find that you have added a new, more fulfilling dimension to you family giving.

Board Member Self-Evaluation

There are many ways to look at a Board of a non-profit agency to determine if the leadership is functioning and productive. A Board may look back at last year's progress or look forward to projects, goals and objectives for the coming year. This all sounds suspiciously like Strategic planning or the dreaded annual Board retreat. But, face it – these activities are Board evaluations. Another type of evaluation is the type that asks each board member to look at his/her performance and contribution on the Board. This type of self-evaluation may also include peer input from other board members. Other board members are encouraged to add their two cents to your personal view of your own board participation. My advice, don't bring your ego with you into this discussion.

That's how I found myself sitting with my friends, Cash Now and Bella Pelorizado. We met at the coffee bar on Main Street of the Land of Lost Board Members. It was a semi-gray day, with the weather being neither hot nor cold, the sky neither light nor dark.

"I've asked you here to help me fill out my member self-evaluation for my service as a member on the Board of Drifting Do-gooders." There was a copy of the form and my responses for each of them.

Before I could say anything more, I lost control of the session, as Bella roared, "What do you mean that you express appreciation for what others do? You've never mentioned my hair." At that her uncontrollable curls stuck out on all sides of her head and scowled at me.

"Active listener?" challenged Cash. "I talk numbers and you run. But if you disagree with me, you criticize my tattoos, my hair cut, my hog office........."

"And keeping the Chairman informed?" interrupted Bella, "remember when I chaired our Annual Spring Flutter and you reorganized it behind my back?"

"But, Bella, that was the time your hair......," the curls went on alert, "got caught up in a fight with that wig salesman. Remember, I only had time to get the room decorated, make nametags, find you, bandage your head. There was no time to consult until you regained consciousness. See right here where it says I am willing to initiate action to further the mission of the agency?"

"That's no excuse," she hrumphed as her hair spelled "LOSER" at me.

Cash was not as threatening as Bella's hair, but he did have more to say. "I wonder if you really understand your job description?" He pointed to another evaluation item. " Get your reports out in time? I can remember a meeting where we never saw you." He looked more closely at the evaluation form. "Wait, is there a line here for attendance?"

"I wasn't there Cash because I was tracking down Bella when she had been kidnapped ...."

"Blaming me again!" Bella was outraged. "I do everything for you, promote your skills to my friends." Above her head, her curls kibitzed, as they wrote "WHAT SKILLS?" She continued, "and you never invite me to your kitchen for ad hoc discussions."

"Bella, you're always welcome in my kitchen" I responded, as Cash's chair scraped on the floor. "You too, Cash."

"Maybe, you're not as much or a slacker as I first thought," Cash proposed. "Maybe I just don't understand people that don't catch on to my numbers."

"But, Cash, that's why Boards are teams. There should be experts in many areas. and they should respect and value the talents of all members. Good members listen, ask good questions and help the agency serve its vision and mission." I paused and thought a moment. "When did I ever criticize your tattoos, hair cut, or office?"

"I think that was me," confessed Bella. We looked at her for a further explanation. "Don't you remember? I wanted to use some of my program funds to buy a new dress for our volunteer appreciation dinner and you wouldn't let me."

"That's because it would have been illegal," he barked back at her.

They were lost in a rehash of an old argument. I picked up the tab, saying "It's on me today folks," and left them while Cash's curbside office hog was ringing and Bella's hair was joining the discussion with unprintable remarks.

When Your Number Comes Up

Those lost on the treadmill life in the Land of Lost Board Members hear stories of salvation and resurrection. It's not often that we witness such an event. Salvation, resurrection, you ask, is this place a monastery? Let me explain nonprofit salvation and resurrection. We struggle for years raising funds, selling the cause, managing mission drift and goal gouging always trying to stay true while watching other issues grab their sexy moments in the sun. But nonprofit life evolves by ordained design. Your time comes and your time goes.....but salvation, resurrection!! Sometimes – your time comes again.

As you all have read we can no longer make ethnic slurs, spread social class insults, dis global warming scientists, nor believe everything you hear. The dormant concern for global rights and individual responsibility is front page. Humanity has been put back in the human race.

Who would have thought the impetus for change and for raising us to a higher level of human awareness would have come from China. Yes, you heard me, China. America has rallied, our pets will no longer find themselves risking fur and paw by eating tainted Chinese food.

"Yeah," grumbled my friend Bella Pelorizado, "that risk goes back where it belongs – people who eat carry-out." Bella is a little behind in reclaiming her humanity. I ignored her and continued typing.

This was the beginning of renewed interest in the world

Charity in Motions

around us. People are listening to the news, people are concerned that there are risks and threats to face in life. Folks are going to be ready. No one would threaten Fluffy and get away with it again. With America on alert, the perfect storm has happened. With ear to the ground and eye on the prize, people are listening and evaluating information. Then, the unimaginable happened. The Supreme Court said the environment counts, that the EPA should do their job. What could this mean for The Alert?

"It means," spoke a man behind me, "that it is all right to come out of the environmental closet. It means that recycling is not a four-letter world. It means water should be positively drinkable and air should be breathed and not seen. Now we all understand what the court wants to conserve!" Cash Now, nonprofit CPA biker flexed his muscles.

"You're a closet environmentalist, Cash? " I asked.

"Yes, and that closet was getting plenty crowded." He looked like he was ready to carry on about owls and smog, but I had a deadline. No time to talk. I kept typing.

The world turned inside out as The Alert, keeping their ears to the ground heard disgusting discourse, incivility and crude invective sprinkled with racial and sexual harassment. The Alert were shocked, appalled...

" ...and sore." said Bella. "Keeping your ear to the ground can make you a little stiff. So The Alert are angry, and sore, not a good mix."

And there they were. The Alert stood up and shouted. "We have almost had enough. We don't want floating values – we want rules of human engagement. We want respect for all of us and for the world around us." As they spoke, small buds of dormant issues appeared in the Land of Lost Board Members. Blossoms danced along the horizon, critical concerns awoke from years of hibernation. It was a new time, another season had finally come. Former nonprofit leaders were seen dusting off their mission statements.

"When your hot, you're hot." chanted The Alert.

The old ideas didn't need much tweaking, they had been valid all along. The Alert had just been hypnotized in the high beams of an SUV, they had been dulled by transfats and been confused by the shock jocks.

What does this mean for the future of the Land of Lost Board Members? Well, it means that issues and agencies we haven't heard from in awhile will be back in touch. There will be new life breathed into old staples like concern for your neighbors and respect for the world around us. We will be encouraged to discard stereotypes, and we will be reminded to nurture our children from cradle through college.

So Bella, Cash and I gathered at the edge of the Land of Lost Board Members and watched as all the resurrected and the recycled left us Lost behind and walked toward the sun.

Will You Remember Me?

In a land where it is never really day nor night, never really happy nor sad, we inhabitants sometimes forget that there are people and events that deserve to stand out in life. That is why I was wandering through the gray and withered landscape of the Land of Lost Board Members' cemetery. It was time to reflect on ….

"Hey, little lady," sighed a voice from the far side of a tombstone. "Out here thinking, eh? I come here often to do the same thing. But thinking doesn't make the sun shine." He looked up at the gray sky.

It was my friend and community benefactor, Al Truistini. "I didn't see you there. How are you feeling?" He shrugged. "You know," I continued, "this is a small place and word gets around when one of our heroes is not well." I smiled at him as I found a perch on a nearby stone.

"Yes, I know word does get around." He drew his coat more tightly around him. "My illness has caused me to reflect on my life in this community and the work that will be my legacy, maybe sooner than I would like, eh?"

I tried to say all those things one should say when faced with honesty and courage of the dying. I didn't succeed in saying anything. He looked at me with eyes that were tired. He gave me a soft smile and patted my hand. We sat silently for awhile as he traced patterns on the ground with his walking stick. It was so peaceful, and he so quiet, that I almost didn't hear as he asked, "Will you remember me?"

"What do you mean 'Will I remember you?' How could I forget you? My mentor, my inspiration. The person who taught me how to take my heart and turn it to commitment, the person who............"

He chuckled. "You can really get going, can't you?" He struggled to catch his breath.

"I mean," I sputtered, "that your work is all around us. You have served this community at many levels, buildings stand because you designed great capital campaigns. The homeless are sheltered, the local artists have venues to display their work and perform, local children are safer."

"Will you remember me?"

"I know I'll remember you, Big Al. Everyone will remember you. We will build monuments, or name streets, or set holidays as our homage to you and your example."

"Of all that I taught you, your only response to my question, is you want to give me a plaque?" He continued to trace a pattern on the ground with his walking stick.

I struggled to understand this conversation. This community had gained so much through Al's generosity. Services for the needy quietly worked day and night because of his organizational skill and his ability to get folks to work together. There were many folks in this community who had grown, had expanded their capacity to give because Al had taught by example. Giving had become second nature to so many. This was a community that found their heart in their wallets. "That's what you mean!" I was so excited I slid from my perch. "You want us to remember you in a way that will help your work to continue."

He smiled softly as he glanced down on me all tangled in his walking stick and some memorial nasturtiums. "Sometimes it is really a challenge to get you from A to B." He coughed again and continued. "I don't want my friends to be distracted by my passing. I want them to use it as an opportunity to recommit to this community in all the ways that I value. If that happens, in this little patch of gray humanity, I will have lived for something!" At that he thrust his walking stick into the sky.

The conversation had taken its toll. Al slumped in his seat. An alert groundskeeper came to us and helped Al into his equipment cart. Things happened quickly after that, rescue, resuscitation, an ambulance. But before he was wheeled into the ambulance he looked up at me and asked, "Will you remember me?"

Al Truistini had offered at lot to think about. Many of his friends would do exactly as he wanted. They would be generous to Al's memory, offering funds to the projects that Al inspired. In years to come, we would continue to remember his kindness and charity. This was Al's final lesson. And we all would have the answer the next time any of our other committed and generous friends might ask,

"Will you remember me?"

How Full Is the Glass?

Capacity is one of the big buzzwords in Henderson County. Do we have water capacity to handle our growth? Do we have sewer capacity to all flush at once? Do we have road capacity to handle all those folks moving in, but not staying home? So I wasn't surprised when I eavesdropped on a discussion about charitable giving capacity.

In the Land of Lost Board Members I was enjoying a tepid glass of fat free, sugar free, extra strength latte while I listened to the conversation at a nearby table. Two people were discussing how much is too much. One of those was my old friend Bella Pelorizado. She had recently closed down her successful nonprofit organization and had gone into the consulting business. Sitting with her was a gentleman looking worn and tired. He was another old friend, Buff Now, the older brother of Cash Now, CPA to the nonprofits. Buff had organized a community support service that relied on local community professionals to supply free service as volunteers. They were talking about the gifts of time and talent that so many nonprofits receive from loyal volunteers.

Buff asked, "How long can I keep going back to my volunteers and ask for more – free service, free supplies, free advice? I worry that soon my volunteers, willing to take a few free clients, will find that their paying clients are less than the free ones. So I wonder is there a number, or maybe a percentage of free to pay?

Buff had organized a community nonprofit call Fitfree, designed to address fat, ugly people and change them into something more appealing. In fact their vision statement is 'From appalling to appealing – the e is the difference – exercise, energy, eat less.'

Charity in Motions

Buff had a cadre of fitness professionals offering free service and training to his clients. So that was the dilemma – when did a fitness coach feel the pinch? But that is the question many nonprofits face, when have we asked for the final straw?

Bella nodded in agreement as her amazing curls jiggled behind her ears. "I know what you mean, we must be respectful of our volunteers."

"Bella, how do I balance the requests for free service with available volunteers?" Buff could not sit still for long and stood beside his chair doing an impromptu workout. "Bella, *two, three, four,* "give me a standard," *five, six, seven, eight*, "how about some criteria for service management?"

"OK, Buff," *puff, puff,* (Bella gets winded just watching exercise!) "I'll take a stab at it. I think you should try several approaches and be flexible." Buff stretched and bent. "Ah, I see you are flexible." She fluffed her hair. "I recommend a two phased approach." Her hair scribed, 'Phase One!' She began, "Set limits on your free asks of your volunteers. No coach should have more free clients than any other coach. I do think," she said, "there is a limit to the number of ugly people one can face during a day." She thought some more, "How many fat and ugly people are you working with?"

"Lots."

Her hair bounced and spelled UGGGLY above her head.

She fluffed again and her hair spelled 'Phase Two!' She was coming to the BIG IDEA, as she said, "Now you have to develop a plan to build capacity." She sat back and looked at Buff. He stopped in mid flex. "Let me explain," she hurried on. "You have plenty of clients, you have donors anxious to keep the ugly at bay. What you need is more volunteer capacity. More volunteer coaches! This town is growing, Buff." Her hair was electric, she was on a roll. "There will be plenty of fat, ugly people moving in, but there will also be plenty of healthy, fitness types, too. You just have to find them. Look into every gated tennis court, on every private golf course. Some of the folks you find will be healthy. They will also be interested in becoming good community members. Some will choose to volunteer to deliver meals, some will want to help in a literacy program, or help at a shelter, or thrift shop. But some will be offended by ugly and want to work with you. You just have to get your plan of recruitment ready. Expand your capacity to offer volunteer opportunities to those who value health and exercise. There you have it – planned growth to serve all those needing exercise!"

Bella had done it again. Capacity is the issue and building it is the challenge.

The Smoke Filled Room Part 1

Board member recruitment is an everlasting job for a board. It's important to always look for fresh faces and ideas. Board members are looking high and low for people interested in service, skilled in team work, able to understand a balance sheet, or just some one who is breathing. It is a sophisticated process that should be operating year-round. A board never knows when a tragedy or life change will strike membership. Some groups are more skilled than others in successful recruitment. This has led to the myth that there is a Mr. Big or some such persona pulling the strings in some smoke filled back room and the popular, donor favs, get the best board members. In the Land of Lost Board Members, where it is never really light and never really dark, a smoke filled room could operate under your nose and not be noticed.

Then one day I walked passed the Recycle Shop and thought I would stop. And the myth became fact. The Recycle Shop is the place to buy and sell, recycle if you will, old audits, strategic plans, old letterhead, old computers, various consultant directories, but you get the picture. Behind an old shower curtain at the back of the store, I heard this discussion as the cigar smoke stung my eyes.

"I'll give you one lawyer for two retirees," growled a gravel voice.

"I got a lawyer, what I need is some one to help with our marketing plan." twittered a singsong voice.

"Well we need a lawyer, but it has to be a woman, and does anyone have a CPA?" countered a courtly drawl.

"That's all well and good but I need folks who can spend time as volunteer office help." The gravel voice was impatient.

Behind the curtain several board chairmen and membership recruiters were bidding on potential board nominees. There were bits of paper around the floor, charts on the wall and an old flypaper strip hanging from the 25-watt bulb in the low ceiling.

As I continued to listen, the gravel voice said, "I want to trade you for Cash Now." He looked at the woman next to him. "I served with Cash in the past and want him with me on this board. And I don't want to take a chance on some unknown CPA."

"But that's incestuous," I blurted

"Don't you come in here and talk dirty, girlie," he growled.

"You should be raising new leadership, not relying on the good few who are always there. Why it's like everyone sharing the same shoes."

"I told you to watch that kind of talk. We don't go along with folks who are sharing clothes – what next your underwear?"

A woman gasped and fainted.

"See what you've done. I told you we don't go along with you transvesti sorts," the growler said. "Look here, girlie, we don't want new folks that we got to get used to coming into our clubs."

"These are boards not clubs!! You need new people to bring in fresh ideas and new energy," I argued.

"If we wanted fresh, we'd open the window, ya hear?"

"But you won't do your agency any good if you just recycle your old friends. No matter how hard working and dedicated, they will give out under the challenge of running from one meeting to the next without time for rest and reflection. You can't fundraise year round for several different groups before all the messages blur and your friends aren't sure what you believe in."

The fainting woman revived and said, "Oh, dearie, I know what you mean – sometimes I'm not sure if am asking for money for kids or cats."

"Why, I remember one time, I went to a fundraiser for one of my boards and discovered that the money would go to develop a competing program for another one of my boards," grinned gravel voice.

"See!"

"Well I solved my problem," he continued, "I started another agency and blew them both out of the water."

"Somehow, I never think of warfare as nonprofit." I looked around at the people in the room. "All I'm saying is that there are better ways to develop board membership."

The man with the gravel voice rolled the cigar around his lips, looked at those gathered in the back room, then nodded at me. "Well, we ain't got all day."

I coughed, "First, lets open a window."

The Smoke Filled Room Part II

In the Land of Lost Board Members, I recently joined a group of nominating committee chairs as they bartered, traded and stole board members from one another. I was appalled at the situation and firmly told them that there was a better way to build board membership. Of course, in a land where it is neither dark nor light, nor hot nor cold, my reception matched the environment.

"Listen, girlie, we have been doing our nominations this way for years. Its comfortable, and no surprises." The man chomped on his cigar. I stood close to the open window.

"He's right, dearie," chirped a woman on a wobbly stool, "we trust our friends, and in spite of the confusion --"

"What confusion?" I asked sensing and opportunity to enlighten them

"Well, you know, sometimes forgetting which board we're serving, confusion with mission and confusion at fundraisers, but," she giggled, "it usually works out."

"Ah, ha. That's why you have to rethink this method. Board recruitment is a constant process. You nominating people should be trolling the community looking for new recruits. You should have an idea of the talents your board could use. You should be looking for members who bring to your board a diverse membership representing the entire community. You shouldn't just be looking for retreads." I was eloquent and polished in my delivery.

"Yeah, right," snarled a man in the corner. "We have

looked, we have asked varieties of groups. We have tried churches, civic clubs, local barber shops, but everyone is too busy, too committed to something else or too tired."

"In this country studies indicate that over 50% of people volunteer in some capacity in their community. And in midsize and small communities the percentage increases. It is also important to understand that volunteering cuts across economic groups and include the young and the mature." I tried to be encouraging, "so recruiting good people is challenging."

"We have the classic conundrum," pontificated a gentleman lounging against the wall, "Is our community half full or half empty?"

"Professor, button it up. You know we work better when your vocabulary takes a rest.," growled the cigar smoker.

"What I mean," the Professor continued," is that we can think of this as an opportunity. Half of our community is still out there waiting to be tapped."

"But how do we find them?" moaned the fellow in the corner.

"Maybe those folks not volunteering, don't really know they're needed," I speculated.

"We have looked," protested a lady with knitting needles, "we've had teas, we've had booths at the festivals and fairs. We advertise. No recruiting event has been successful." They all nodded in agreement.

"Maybe they don't know we are talking to them. Maybe they haven't realized that volunteer opportunities are what they need in their lives," the chirping lady replied.

"Great, I feel like we're out looking for lost hikers and they don't know they're lost." An unlit cigar stabbed at the ceiling. "So how do we convince the unlost to figure out that we are trying to find them?"

"The unlost? I like that term. We want people who will

self identify and self select for volunteer opportunities. They just don't know what an impact it will have on their hearts and souls."

"There you go again Professor, we are looking for the unlost who don't know they have a need to be found and don't know they could volunteer and don't hear, read or see volunteer opportunities for themselves and don't know where to start. And they will self select without information." He took the cigar out of his mouth and challenged the listeners.

"That's it," we all cried, "you have a great idea!"

"What did I say?" The cigar danced around his teeth.

"You just laid out a strategy for growing the recruiting pool for potential board members," I explained. He looked skeptical, but I continued. "You suggested that people don't realize their talents are needed nor do they know where they are needed. We need to help people find opportunities. Teas and socials aren't the answer. Inviting people to sample the work or help develop solutions may be the answer I think we just start by suggesting that folks think about joining a United Way panel to review agency requests. Panel work for United Way allows a volunteer to study some great agencies and evaluate their programs. Steve, Pam or Sandy at the United Way office would love to hear from everyone.

"Does this mean the community is half full or half empty?" someone asked.

"It means," concluded the professor, "we're optimistic that the best of the people not volunteering, the unlost, will self select into community service."

Tax Deductible No-No

"You know Dasha and Pasha and Sasha and Lenin...."

"Wait, its my turn, Grab your coat and get your hat, leave your millions on my campaign steps...."

"Just direct your feet," chimed in a third voice, "to the Socialist side of the street."

"For Liberals I have known before who have traveled in and out my door," There was a burst of laughter. The singing quartet giggled and squealed as they enjoyed the late October heat wave in the Land of Lost Board Members.

"What are you folks doing, preparing for some sort of a fundraiser, dinner theater, talent show?" I was confident that this was another committee meeting for a local nonprofit fundraiser.

They all looked at me. "We're trying to raise funds to support our candidate. We've got people to elect. Policies to influence. That's why we have organized our new nonprofit, 'Onewhorules.'"

Sometimes a wet behind the ears twenty something is too easy a target, but I resolved to be charitable. "Are you telling me that you're planning to mix politics and nonprofits? Because that's so illegal. Politics has no place in the world of charity and good works. Wait, I didn't mean it that way. Politics should be kept behind... no, no wait. Charity is not political." I thought about that and decided that it was the best of a bad statement.

They looked at me. I continued, "According to the IRS, a tax deductible nonprofit must have a public purpose. That can be a religious, charitable, educational, scientific or literary. Political activity and lobbying are definitely not any of those."

"But yes they are. Our candidate has a moral purpose, supports education and reads."

"I think your missing the point. You can present information about an issue. You can't lobby for an outcome and be deductible. You can present facts about an election topic, organize a forum where all candidates have free access to the audience, but you can't campaign for a specific candidate. A Church or a non profit can get into big trouble lobbying or campaigning."

"But," one of them sputtered, "world peace, tax issues, our candidate has solutions, integrity."

I looked into those star spangled eyes and nodded. "Look, I'm not saying that politics isn't important and that people your age shouldn't be in there fighting for your political future. I'm just saying that the political campaign of a deserving candidate stands alone. That activity is governed by a different set of IRS rules and guidelines. Get involved. Get out the vote. Just decide whether you are getting out the vote as a good American activity or if you're getting out the vote for your candidate. The time and money you invest will have different restrictions under IRS code."

"Isn't it horrible that there are so many restrictions on personal freedom and the political choices we make."

"Amen."

"I told you, churches and political candidates don't mix either." These young people were having a difficult time catching on.

"Why are we even bothering if we're stopped in our tracks with every good idea?"

"You haven't been stopped, I'm just telling you that yes, there are rules, yes, there are guidelines, and, yes, you should be involved at all levels in your community. There is a time to campaign for a person. There is a time to campaign for a new building. If you are honest, and if your story is a good one, people will listen to you and give their support, emotional and financial, under any banner. The case has to be made and the rules obeyed. Aren't you paying attention, people give money to charity and to politics. People chose what is important to them and sometimes the issues transcend deductibility."

"If you're a Church or a community agency providing service or advocating for issues, you have to be aware of the restraints on political activism. There is a line to walk and a line to cross and there are serious consequences to your group and to your candidate, when those lines blur." I hoped I was making progress.

"Wait you guys, we have another song, M-I-T," two of them sang out. "A-R-Y," came the reply. They all looked at one another. Their eyes told me they had learned the lesson. Charity and politics don't mix.

Clique-ity Clack

It is a year round job to recruit volunteers for all sorts of jobs. Often it is from that volunteer pool that many non-profits, or even civic clubs find future Board leadership. The biggest mistake many groups make is to put a tepid welcome forward to the new faces. If some one new walks through the door, that's your first and 10. But there's a lot of ground game before you make a touchdown. And I mean ground game. Any passing game, no matter how skillfully executed doesn't allow for that face to face, shoulder to shoulder, side by side, get acquainted and get to work atmosphere. In a passing game its possible to overlook the diligent for the flashy only to find that the flashy have no hands to receive nor the ability to find the end zone.

This sounds a little footbally, but I just happened to meet up with Coach Amos Alonzo Upright, you know him, the guy Notre Dame should have hired. Coach was sitting at the coffee shop in the Land of Lost Board Members chatting with some forlorn looking citizens. By the look of them, I thought they were Monday morning quarterbacking the local NFL team. Coach called me over.

"Hey, Coach, good to see you this morning. Have you replayed last weeks' games this morning?" I asked.

"Honey, some of those games would have been better off not even being played the first time." The group at the table nodded in agreement. "But that's not what I want to talk to you about." I sat down.

"These folks," he gestured to those at the table, "need some help. They just tried to volunteer at the Land of the Lost Athletic Boosters and were ignored. Just listen to their story."

The meekest of the group began in a quivering voice. "We all are financial supporters of the Lost Bawlers, and we decided that there was time in our lives to give some hands on help. After all the quarterly newsletter always invites folks to help, to show our spirit." He cleared his throat. "So the three of us went to a meeting as instructed in the newsletter. And no one talked with us. Well, that's not true, some one handed us name tags and asked us to fill them out. And that was the last thing anyone said to us." The other two nodded. He continued, "We waited, we stood, we sampled some food. We looked around the office, looked at all the volunteer opportunities. But every time we approached someone they ran off to talk with someone else." He concluded, "They talked with the Senator, they fawned over that glitzy radio personality, and they trotted after that lady with the curly hair. But no one had time for us."

"Let me get this straight, you walked in to volunteer and were ignored?" I was puzzled.

"In spades," said the Coach. "I sit on that Board and I noticed them in the background. Let me tell you, Honey, I am trained to spot talent. I could tell after two minutes that I was looking at some great team players."

"Well, Coach," I teased, "are you going to take them back in for a more personal recruitment opportunity?"

"That's what I want to do, but they are disenchanted with the organization now. And I can't tell you how hard I've tried. I was hoping that you could convince them to try again."

"Coach, I don't belong to that group. All I can say to them is keep looking – when you find the group that welcomes you, join that team. Agencies and organizations don't understand that first impressions work on both sides. Your friends may not have a look of potential to many of your Bawling membership, but there is a group out there that will see in them the promise that you see, Coach."

"But we need them – well, if the Board met them, they would know that we need them."

"The board never took the time, Coach. They chatted with celebrities, chased glitter and ignored a true volunteer gift. It's a lesson many groups learn too late. They run to the flash and miss the game close at hand. When a new face comes through your door, take time to get their measure. Welcome them as much as you welcome a long time worker. And long time volunteers should do the same. Don't stand at a gathering and just talk among yourselves – draw in the newcomer, make all welcome, not just your friends. Remember, an agency is only as strong as the recruitment for new membership is successful."

"Well, shoot, that isn't helping me. I wanted these folks on our team. They are solid. They would play their hearts out for us," he protested.

"I guess that's a lesson to take back for your Board to add to their play book."

"One more football reference," he growled, "and you can pay for your own coffee."

Investing Advice

As usual, Main Street of the Land of Lost Board Members is a great place to strike up meaningful, challenging conversations. At the recently redesigned crosswalk intersection, I found Joshua Biggly-Huge, a local philanthropist, financier and political curmudgeon. He was searching through the pockets of his expensive overcoat. "Mr. Biggly-Huge, may I help you? You look quite distressed."

"Dear me, I am. I have misplaced a stock tip that I received from my CPA, Cash Now. That boy has a great investment sense." He turned out several pockets.

"Can't you just call him for a reminder?"

"No, no, he's out of town for the holidays. But you are on to something maybe some one else in town would have that information. Let me think, stocks and investments, hmmm."

"Maybe one of Cash's friends. He does a lot of work with Bella Pelorizado, the nonprofit consultant."

"But what would nonprofits know about investing and managing money?"

"Nonprofits have to be great managers. In fact a donation to a well run nonprofit should be measured in much the same way you study your personal investments. The pay back may not be in increased wealth for you, but in the expansion of quality service for the community. You should investigate management of a nonprofit in a manner similar to the scrutiny of a business investment." I was irate.

"Humph." He was indignant. "I do believe I give a lot of thought to my donations."

"You're right," I softened, "we all respect you for your generosity and even your vision in directing and helping support a variety of nonprofit agencies."

"That's better." He continued to hunt for his stock tip.

"Maybe some of Cash's clients would know the information. He does some consulting for local government."

"We know **they** can't manage money." It was a declaration that he expected to go unchallenged.

"We do? How do we know that?" I challenged.

"Look at what they do. They take our tax money and spend it on falling down buildings, slipshod service – always just missing the mark. That's why I joined the 'Hell No Taxes PAC.'" He struck a Jeffersonian pose as a Hummer struck a City of the Lost utilities truck.

"I would argue that taxes are another form of investment and I would challenge you to measure need and result and management ability as part of your tax position."

"What do you mean?" he waved his arms and distracted a bicyclist. "They can't manage. They always need more, they never do anything for me and my friends." He recited his usual litany against government.

"I think you're blaming local government for all the taxes you pay, just because they're the closest government." I was trying to make sense of his philosophy.

"They don't do anything for me and my friends." If he were a lesser man he would have stomped his foot, instead he pounded on the hood of a Prius inching its way through the intersection.

"This conversation is getting awfully political, Mr. Biggly-Huge, but maybe instead of crying 'too much tax,' you should look at local government and measure the service being provided to you and the community, then measure the result in the quality of community life, for us and for our children.

"Quality, service," he dodged a car spinning in the crosswalk, "are two words that cost money!"

"Think about it this way, as a tax payer, you own our

buildings and are the Board of directors who sets a standard for elected officials. This is much like the model for a corporation and for a nonprofit. You have certain expectations and you understand that there are costs. It's the results that you look for. Why not have that same standard for local taxes as you use for stock investment and nonprofit donations – be willing to pay for good management, for well thought out proposals or to maintain services and projects that serve the community. Communities that strive to serve the past by following your tax philosophy, are communities limping to the future – and certainly not welcoming investment, economic growth or -"

"That's all well and good" he interrupted,"but I don't like taxes and nothing you say will ... ah, wait, here is that note." He unwrinkled it and read, "Invest in municipal bonds." Six vehicles came to a screeching halt at the four-way intersection.

Expect the Unexpected Every Day

What to do on a snow day? Did you ever notice how so many of us find reasons beyond reason to venture out on those risky days? It's the same everywhere, including the Land of Lost Board Members. In a land that is never day or night, nor light or dark, the snow comes in the same quality – already gray. Walking through the not quite frozen, not quite thawed grey-gray slush, I slid into the office of the local newspaper, the Timely Donations News. I was planning a trip to anyplace warmer and sunnier and wanted to stop delivery until my return. The lobby was quiet, but I could hear a familiar voice in the reporter's pool. It was my friend, Bella Pelorizado. Bella is a former nonprofit executive director who has moved onto a lucrative consulting business.

"Bella," I waved across the anti-press terrorist barricade, or is it the antiterrorist press barricade, or is it the terrorist press... never mind. "Bella, what are you doing here?"

Bella released the barrier lock, lowered the bulletproof shield, raised the steel impelling spikes, and welcomed me into her office. "What do you think?" she asked as she gestured around her cubicle. It was cluttered with tech equipment, old newspapers and letters. "How do you like it?" She glowed in the mess. "I have a new job. Its only part time – but it just suits me!"

"You've become a reporter?"

"No, no. I'm the new agency help lady – you know the Dear Abby of nonprofits."

"Bella, I can't think of anyone better suited for the job!" I looked around at the clutter. "What questions do your readers have?"

She held out a derelict piece of paper with coffee stains and chocolate smears. "Listen to this – Dear Bella, My agency is having trouble getting Board members to take their service seriously. What can I do to revive their commitment and increase their service hours?" She put the letter aside and began to type, "Dear Slob,..."

"Bella, that's cruel."

She ignored me and continued. "Dear Slob, if the rest of your work is like the letter I received, you have to clean up your act and probably your desk before anyone takes you seriously. I bet your agency needs cleaning, organizing and decluttering. It's a new year, act like it."

"Whoa, I think that's a little harsh."

She ignored me and read a second letter aloud. "Dear Bellicose," she paused and turned to me, "I think they're getting sensitive don't you?" She continued – "Dear Bellicose, I never thought I would be writing to you, especially after the advice you published in your last column,.."

"Your last column?" I asked.

She waved a disinterested hand, and continued, "But I'm in trouble. My finance officer just sent a card from Bora Bora. And now, if I could figure out how to access the books on his computer, I'm sure I would find no bank balance. What can I do?"

"Dear Loser, And I say that because you have probably lost your capital campaign fund, your reserves and any restricted funds that you manage for special programs. You are at fault and so is your Board. There should always be a lot of double-checking going on when one manages donated funds. Or, as you have learned, there will be a lot of double-dealing going on. Where were you and the board? What was the treasurer doing, how about the finance committee and where was the audit committee? Fortunately for you, the Board is as much at fault as you are – losers and slackers all of you." She pounded away on her keyboard as she reworded her response. She giggled and smiled, her interesting hair did its usual ringlet dance as it spelled out LOSERS.

"Must you be so harsh? Won't people respond better with kindness and understanding?"

"By the time they get to this desk," she glanced around the office, "they are too far gone for kindness." She picked another letter from her pile. It was wet and the ink had smeared. She sniffed in disgust, but as she read her countenance became more sympathetic. "Listen to this," she said, " Dear Bella,

"Please excuse the condition of my stationery, but I am writing this as rain pours down through the office ceiling. You can tell by our letterhead that I work for a respected agency that provides good, cost effective service to this community. The rain is my problem. How do I get my board to understand that maintaining our place of business, you know, keeping up the building we paid for with a valiant and successful capital campaign, is imperative? Won't donors become suspicious or at least think we are foolhardy for not doing practical, though not sexy, maintenance?"

Bella's hair was afire with indignation as it spelled, POOR GIRL and MORE PAILS, while Bella pounded out her reply. "Dear Drip, You are correct. No donor keeps giving to a place that can't manage all facets of a nonprofit. I don't care what the edifice is, if you used some one else's money to build it, you should take care of it. Your Board is missing the boat and mismanaging donation dollars. Hope you dry up soon."

"You know, Bella, even when you are being supportive, you sound mean."

"You know," she looked right at me and so did her ringlets, "You get on my nerves."

More Advice from Bella

It's been a month now and I thought I would check in with my friend, Bella Pelorizado to see how her new job was going. She had taken a job at the Lost Timely Donations News as an advice columnist for nonprofits. Since I'm a regular visitor to the pressroom now, I only needed an eyeball scan and a walk through the airlock to gain admittance. Things were quiet in the pressroom when I arrived. All one heard was the clackity of keyboards.

"Bella, how's it going?"

She stopped the clackity and looked up. Her hair was tangled in the mouse and there were stained papers and envelopes around the floor. "I'm overwhelmed. Everyone has problems and they think I can solve them."

"That's what happens when you claim to know a lot." I wasn't sympathetic. With Bella friendship is a combat sport.

She ignored me as usual, and pulled a letter from under her desk. "Just listen to this. Dear Bella, My friends and I have a great idea. In fact we have a plan in place that will be exciting for the whole community. We call it the "Frugal Design Showcase." She stopped and glared at me. "Do you know what this group is planning?" She waved the letter in my face. "A model home will be decorated using furnishings from local resale shops operated by nonprofits. The event will take place the weekend of June 20th. Tickets will go on sale prior to that date. Please help us spread the word."

"Of course," I nodded, "that's from Terry."

"Don't you mean Terri?" she sniffed.

"What?"

"You know, Terri with an "i" not a "y."

"You could see the words I spoke and know I used the

wrong spelling?"

"I'm in the print media, we see all words."

"You can't tell if I misspell when I speak!"

"You misspelled misspell." She glared at me as her active ringlets made a series of "sass's" in the air.

"OK, OK, it's Terri," I conceded. "I think she has a great idea. She has organized a number of nonprofit thrift shops and has had a builder volunteer a vacant house to display rooms decorated with items from the shops. Pretty clever." I was happy to contemplate a new and vigorous idea. Sometimes folks in the Land of Lost Board Members get too gray and dull. We need people with energy and talent to revive us and try new ideas.

"I think it's a terrible idea." Bella was angry. "How could she?"

"How could she what?"

"I used to be the thinker around here. I'm the expert in collaboration. I know a thing or two about solving problems. Originality is my middle name." She started to pace around her office. Her hair spelled out insults.

"Bella how can you be angry?" I asked. "You were hired here to help nonprofits. I think that means you should be a cheerleader for an event like this. I have heard you challenge other nonprofits to work together and to forget turf issues while staying focused on service." Bella continued to pace and ignore me. I tried again. "Bella, you have always been a voice that supported ideas and helped organizations deliver quality. Where's the old Bella?" I waited as her hair spelled "power" and "revenge."

She stopped pacing and returned to her keyboard. "I know," she said as she began to type, "I'll put the idea on my blog and claim it was mine. Then a few days from now, I'll do a press release and imply that Terri just did what I told her to do."

"Bella," I was horrified. "You have a blog? I mean, you can't be that dishonest! I thought journalists lived by a code of ethics."

"Who do you think I am, David Brooks?"

"Your bosses here at the paper might get upset," I offered. "I'm sure they have an expectation of honesty." That seemed to reach her.

"You're right." She was reluctant to admit defeat. She turned and asked. "Do you think if I tell everyone how great Terri is and remind all of my readers to attend the event that Terri will invite me to do a preview tour?" She looked sweet. Her hair was calm. "And if she isn't nice to me," she stamped her foot, "then I'll blog her!"

Her hair rejoiced and spelled, "She's back!"

Voting for Nonprofits

Nonprofit organizations stay away from politics, but that does not mean that nonprofit volunteers and staff should stay away from the political process. So on the day after the North Carolina Primary election I wandered down Main Street in the Land of Lost Board Members. As usual, the early morning crowd had gathered at the coffee shop to dissect the election outcomes. Some folks had backed candidates who had lost their races and some had backed those who had won. There were discussions about various issues that had been placed on the ballot. All in all, it was much the same conversation that had taken place throughout the country after each state primary.

Some of my nonprofit friends were talking about their role in the recent election. It was enough to hear that they had been involved in the election to make my head spin. Didn't they know better? Haven't they learned anything about their roles? And that's just what I said to them as they huddled around a table in the back of the shop. I was in great form. I was righteous. I found I didn't have a leg to stand on.

"Calm down," said my friend, Cash Now, CPA of the nonprofits. "We know what we can and can't do. We all wanted to be involved so we found a great way." They all nodded.

My friend, Al Truistini, our local philosophically liberal donor patted my arm and explained, "We worked at the polls. Isn't that a great way to be involved? It was a heartwarming day."

Cash continued, "I helped a young woman who had just become a citizen vote for the first time. She came in with her husband. He had finished voting quickly at his machine and stood across the room and watched as she worked through the ballot consulting her notes. The new voters are so thrilled when they work through the ballot and hear the machine printer record their votes. Its times like that I think those machines should play a tune and shoot off sparklers."

Al interrupted. "I worked with a very feeble woman who had to be helped to the voting machines. We even had to bring a chair for her to sit as she scrolled through the ballots. Technology doesn't deter a serious voter. They catch on quick and always seem eager to have us poll workers leave so they can get on with the process."

"And all those folks who carried sample ballots and notes to make sure they got their candidates right. Do you know what that means?" Cash looked at us. "It means they prepared for the election. They may have searched websites, consulted with friends or attended forums to listen to candidates answer questions about the issues."

"What about the Moms and Dads who brought their children along? I was touched. What a great way to teach that voting is important." Said Mr. Joshua Biggly Huge, philanthropist and antigovernment conservative voter.

"And I was helping at the "Kids Voting" Table," chimed in Bella Pelorizado, nonprofit consultant and news columnist. "Those kids all had opinions. You could tell they had studied about the election in school and heard their parents talk about it."

"It was very uplifting, agreed Joshua Biggly Huge. "I had the privilege of helping a blind woman vote a curbside ballot. It made me think about how important voting was to so many people. I watched handicapped and elderly people come to the polls in spite of infirmities. They were so committed to our democratic process. Many bragged that they never missed an opportunity to vote. It was an inspiration."

"And those kids," said Al Truistini, "the ones who were voting just for the first or second time – so young and so serious."

"I know what you mean," said Cash, "I am a One Stop Warrior. I've worked at one of the early voting sites for several weeks. I saw my share of people with health restrictions make their way to vote. I saw Moms bring baby carriages. I saw young men and women of every color in our community come in to cast ballots."

The gang seemed very pleased with themselves and were enjoying the camaraderie that grows from a job well done. Then Bella shouted, "And we got paid!"

"I'm giving my check to No Nukes is Good Nukes," said some one.

"Well, I'm turning my check over to Nukes Are Nice." Came a reply. The discussion deteriorated to slogans and name-calling.

Cash led me from the table and whispered, "It's the morning after and we're right back where we were yesterday." He patted my arm and added, "but we all voted."

Bella's Big Blowout

We all came rushing into the ER at Lost Land Memorial Hospital after receiving an urgent call from Dr. Stat Convalesky, local physician in the Land of Lost Board Members. It was the usual setting, gurneys, needles, eccentric staff, but that's another column. Cash Now, local accountant, and I arrived together joining other friends already pacing the waiting room.

"Is Bella okay?" gasped Cash. We had all received a call from Dr. Convalesky telling us that Bella Pelorizado, well-known local nonprofit advocate, had been brought to the ER.

Dr. Convalesky walked into the waiting room and we all rushed forward to get answers to our concerns. He began by saying, "She is in no danger." We relaxed. "She will have to stay overnight. But I think you can all come back for a quick chat." We followed him into the spotless and shining ER examining room. There was Bella lying on her stomach on an examining table, a white sheet flecked with blood draped across her.

"This is an outrage," roared Joshua Biggly-Huge, "Is no one safe in this community? Where were the police, Homeland Security? What's that Congressman's name?"

"Please remain calm," cautioned Dr. Convalesky. "My patient needs to lie still and not be excited."

"How did this happen, Bella dear?" asked Al Truistini. He had a way of soothing our concerns and also working to calm Bella's fears.

Bella turned her head to look at us. "I just went to speak as a community advocate at the annual public budget hearings." Her active head of curls spelled, "Pain."

"We saw you on TV," I said. "You did a great job. You

Charity in Motions

talked about need, spoke in support with statistical evidence and testimony from other community members and service providers."

"And," marveled Cash, "you did it all with respect and decorum, never losing your temper or calling people names." We all nodded. Some of us had seen the dark side of Bella's temper.

"Your arguments were lucid," said Joshua, "encouraging local leaders to balance funding solutions and build partnerships to develop new ways of solving problems."

"Thanks," spelled her hair.

"I was impressed with the way you challenged local leaders to face issues, not put them off to an unknown future. I particularly like your metaphor," Al thought a moment, "oh, yes, a decaying tooth doesn't heal itself, only encourages more to rot with it." We were all glad we had brushed and flossed that morning.

"So what happened? Did they shoot the messenger?" laughed Cash.

"No, I got a little carried away."

"You mean you were escorted from the meeting? I didn't see that on TV."

"No, I was so eager to make my points about issues I thought needed attention, especially since I would be speaking in the new meeting room," she spoke softly, "I planned to have a little demonstration, sort of a stationary parade float."

"In the new government meeting room? But I didn't see that on TV."

"I thought, with that high ceiling and those beautiful windows, I could create something that would speak to community need such as elder issues, concerns for children, the responsibility of leaders to find solutions within the community, collaborations, synchronizing assets."

"Synchronizing assets? But I didn't see that on TV."

"You would know what I'm talking about, if the float had worked."

"But we all saw you on the broadcast of the meeting. After you spoke, the meeting ended."

"No, not quite," she put her head down and spoke into her pillow, "It blew up." Her hair responded, "Kaboom!"

"Blew up?"

"Everything." Her voice was still muffled, and we strained to hear. "I hadn't considered the amps and the length of my extension cord and the challenge of water and electricity together, and a few other technical things."

"You blew up the new meeting room?"

"Not exactly." She moved uncomfortably on the hospital table. "The display blew up, shorted out the building, and showered me with shards of glass as I ducked under a podium."

"Was anyone else hurt?"

"No, just the part of me that couldn't fit under the podium." She laid her head back on the pillow.

Dr. Convalesky said, "She'll be fine in a month or two just as long as she sleeps on her stomach and doesn't sit on anything too hard." He signaled that it was time to leave.

As we tiptoed out of the room, we turned back for one last look as her hair spelled.... Well, we weren't sure what it was spelling. Dr. C looked at the confused hair and said to us, "Lets go, the sedative must be working."

Eavesdropping on Life

People in the Land of Lost Board Members are the same as everyone else. Cell phone courtesy is a nonexistent art. We become hostage eavesdroppers wherever some very personal conversations take place – in the Mall, on a bus, in a restaurant. That is why I was shocked when I heard my friend, Bella Pelorizado talking on her cell in the grocery store check out line as she spoke about her IUD. Everyone in the line heard her. I knew her well enough that I felt an intervention was necessary.

"Bella," I tapped her on her shoulder. She looked at me and quietly said, "Gotta go," to her phone partner.

"Bella, I have to say that I am embarrassed to be listening to this very public conversation about your IUD."

"But it's such a great idea and a marvelous method to accomplish our goals," she said proudly.

"Bella! It's a very personal method," I countered. I was pained by her behavior. "We are not interested in your method."

"But of all people I thought you would be interested in how it operates," she pouted.

"I think I know how it operates." I was really gruff.

"How could you? We just organized this effort yesterday." She placed her phone in her purse and brought out a report. "Don't tell me you already know about Interdisciplinary United Donations?" She waved the report at me. "Or as we like to call it the Lost IUD."

This conversation was attracting more attention than her phone call had. But I pushed forward. "I'm sorry Bella, I thought you were talking about something else." Recovering, I asked, "What is this new method?'

"It's a new community concept that encourages synchronizing assets with verified community need across agencies and supporting public private partnerships."

"That sounds like something United Way would do," I stated.

"Yes! United Way, or as we like to say UWLOL, is the originator of the process under their 'Think United' campaign."

"LOL?"

"Land of Lost."

"I get it. I'm with you now. So tell me how this will be working?"

Her magnificent hair, spelled "Now hear this!," as she began to explain, "IUD is broken into two parts, one is STD."

More ears strained to hear our conversation. Even the checkout clerk held a bag of chips in midair waiting for our discussion to continue. "Bella," I whispered, "You can't say STD"

"Strategic Thinking Dynamic." She was snippy now and her hair spelled "Don't you know anything?"

"Bella, you seem to be using terms, acronyms, in different and, I might say, challenging ways."

"Well, get used to it. These are different and challenging times that call for WTF."

I heard a gasp, a little old lady in the next check out line, fainted on her papaya. Bella looked around unconcerned.

"That's my point. People can't keep thinking they know everything, because what you know changes daily, what's bad is good, what's black is white." She was on a roll. Her hair spelled out initials that left no question in anyone's mind about what it meant. Bella continued, "A community has to look at the needs it has, respect the current method of addressing need, but continuously evaluate service success, access and progress. If the old method doesn't do any more than keep people static, instead of moving them forward, then it is time to rethink delivery, maybe even rethink the need. In addition, there are new concerns facing a community everyday." Many shoppers were nodding their heads in agreement.

"You're correct," I said, "changing economic times, changing political alignments influence the non profit picture. Donations fluctuate with real and perceived solutions and even with cash on hand. Solutions ebb and flow with the leadership available to direct solutions and with a community willing to work for the common good." I was getting her message.

Folks were cheering in the grocery store. They understood changing times, nonlinear economic conditions. They were aching for new solutions. They wanted to be a part of making a difference and creating life-changing opportunities

The mood was electric as Bella summed up, "That's why those of us on the UWLOL, IUD committee, STD subcommittee use WTF as our motto."

I wiped my brow as I cautiously asked, "And that motto in real words is?"

"Welcome the Future."

Note: I was inspired to write this piece while standing behind a lady in the grocery store checkout line. She was talking into her phone and the line of shoppers heard her side of her IUD conversation! I wondered who she was having sex with, 'cause she wasn't real sexy!

Puzzling Over Life

Here I was sitting on Main Street in a normal gray summer day in the Land of Lost Board Members. What a day to just sit and do the crossword puzzles in the Lost Timely Donations News. Hmm, a four letter word for 'Singin' in the -.' '*Rain!*' An eight-letter word for 'Pouring cats and dogs.' '*Storming*.' A three letter word for ...

"It's a puzzle, my boy," said Mr. Joshua Biggly Huge, local anti-big government philanthropist. I peeked around the thirsty landscapery on Main Street and saw my friend, Cash Now, local CPA and nonprofit financial management guru, in deep conversation with his richest for profit client. They were probably having a client-privileged conversation so I returned to my puzzle, a three-letter word for 'Not dry,' '*Wet!*' I was filling in those little boxes.

"But, sir," I could hear Cash pleading, "times are tough for local charities. I think you might consider some interim commitment to UWLOL as a way to help folks through some tough times."

Ignore them, I told myself, this is a private conversation. I had more relaxing things to do. "I find that whole thing so annoying," said Mr. Biggly Huge, "LOL, what is that, some kind of palindrome?"

"Sir, that means Land of Lost." Cash continued his argument. "As I was saying, we might look at restructuring your annual donations," here Cash's voice became enticing, "You know, for tax purposes, and help out now when the money is needed."

Hmm, a seven letter word for 'Cure-all.'

"My checkbook isn't a panacea for this communities' ills,"

Charity in Motions

growled Joshua.

Thank you, Joshua, I thought, *'Panacea.'* Thirty six across, a nine letter word for 'Draw off in a vapor?'

"Right now I'm as strapped as everyone else. My investments are not performing. My real estate is not moving. I'm having to wait longer for rents and loan payments." Joshua sounded troubled. "My boy, I know what problems are out there. I sit on a couple of Boards. Agencies are seeing donations ebb, demand increase and even reliable government support for certain activities withdraw or evaporate."

That's it, *'Evaporate.'* This was a puzzle I could work in ink.

Their voices were quiet for a few minutes, then Cash interrupted my thoughts, "Maybe we need to share these problems with the entire community? Your friends and my friends might be able to help with a solution"

"What do you have in mind?" asked Joshua.

"I'm not sure," said Cash. "We could challenge our friends to give what they can, or maybe attend a fundraising function for some agency. Or we could just encourage them to keep the pledges they made, even if it means stretching payments out an extra year or smaller amounts over shorter intervals." Cash was frustrated. "I know what my clients are going through, both those that are for profit and those nonprofit. It's a tough year."

I was trying to think of a seven-letter word for 'Panting or puffing.'

"I know what you mean," said Al Tristini, a community benefactor. It was said that Al never met a nonprofit he didn't like. "My checkbook is gasping." Cash and Joshua welcomed him to their sidewalk table.

It just came to me, *'Gasping.'* This puzzle was doing itself.

Behind the thirsty shrubs the angst continued. Al was

relating his concerns for some of his favorite agencies. "There are so many demands for service, medications, school supplies, food pantry items." He stopped to survey his audience. "Men, we need to draw attention to the need. This is not the time for subtle feel good campaigns. This is time for the gloves to come off."

A six-letter word meaning understated, with that "t" in '*Evaporate*' as the fourth letter. Wait what did Al just say? '*Subtle.*' Whoa, could I get any better than this? Fifty-two down, 'Balance,' eleven letters with the first 'e' in '*Evaporate*'.'

The men kept talking. Their voices carried concern. "I think we know what to do," said Joshua. "We have to alert our friends and associates in the community. We all have a responsibility to keep a community equilibrium.

'*Equilibrium.*' Does that have eleven letters? I was getting to my last clue, 'Give away to; bestow; contribute to; aid.' It's a six letter word that fits the 'o' in 'storming' and the 'a' in 'gasping.' Do you get it?

Guess Who?

Some holidays have more of an impact on a community than others. And sometimes, certain holidays come just when they are needed to help people play with reality without alarming too many observers. As we prepared for Halloween many citizens looked for ways to help stressed nonprofit agencies. One popular method was to host a festive gathering and sell tickets to attend. Joshua Biggly-Huge, local Lost philanthropist was hosting a Halloween candy tasting costume drop-in gala for a few of his favorite organizations. We were excited about the event and looked forward to the disguises.

"Boo," said a Richard Nixon lookalike, while her hair spelled out 'Guess who?' Of course it was my friend, Bella Pelorizado.

"Hey, Bella," I said while clutching my bag of candy.

"How did you know it was me?"

"Richard Nixon is dead."

"So are a lot of people," she sighed as she slipped off her mask. "It's just no fun this year." She looked longingly at my bag of candy. "Everyone is holding on to what they have. No one wants to spread the sugar around." I held my candy behind my back.

"I can relate to that," said Amos Alonzo Upright trying to look tough in his pumpkin costume. Coach Upright has been one of Land of Lost's athletic boosters for years. "I can't get anyone to fund my new program, RULES, Referee and Umpire Lasik Surgery. They seem to think everyone has health insurance."

"Alonzo, you're getting political," cautioned Cash Now, CPA to nonprofits and the financial conscience of Lost board members and nonprofit staffers. "You can't talk about health care. You can't talk about the sugar subsidy either," He looked at Bella.

"What sugar subsidy?"

"I told you not to talk about it." Cash was at his wits' end as he cautioned against political activity by nonprofits. No one was listening to him. It didn't help that he was wearing a Bambi costume. I was grateful he hadn't seen Bella's costume.

"I see you got my invitation to Buck$ for Treats," welcomed Joshua Biggly-Huge, our host. Even Joshua was disguised. But I wasn't sure what he was disguised as, so I asked.

"I am my favorite thing," he said, "a tax deduction." He was in a large trash bag with a dollar sign painted on the side.

"No politics," moaned Cash.

It is always important that nonprofits be reminded about refraining from political endorsements or opposition to candidates, especially during an election year. It was time for a gentle reminder. But we were interrupted by Birdie Inkstain, ace investigative reporter for the Timely Donations News. "How do you guys think this election is going to fall out?"

Talk about a deer in the headlights look! Cash Now couldn't believe the question. He opened his mouth to caution all of his friends and clients to not say a word. Birdie never gave him a chance. She plunged right on, "Aren't you cute in that outfit," patting him on the nose, "I think I ran over your twin last week." Birdie turned to everyone and asked again, "So how's this gonna end?"

"We don't talk politics because we work for nonprofit agencies," explained Cash. "The IRS would be unhappy."

"Look, I'm standing here talking to Bambi, a pumpkin and a dead politician," she challenged as she threw the remains of her coffee into a nearby trash bag. Unfortunately, it was Joshua's bag. The way that bag went hoping down Main Street suggested that he was surprised by the wet, cold beverage. His antics distracted Birdie for a minute, but she refocused as she cajoled, "Come on, I want opinions."

"Birdie, we can't give opinions on candidates," explained Coach Upright. "We have to protect our nonprofit status"

"But you must have opinions on issues? Don't you do advocacy for you causes?"

"Yes, we do," admitted Bella. "We know that much of the work we do in the community is enhanced or hindered by public policy decisions. For example, those who are child advocates want to raise awareness about issues of child health, safety and education."

I chimed in, "Those of us who have been around a long time like to point out that aging isn't fun when public policy decisions act counter to the needs of the elderly."

"What about those of us who like to stay active and appreciate parks and playing fields? We have to get our message out, too."

"Great," smiled Birdie, smelling a story, "so tell me, which candidates are listening to you?"

"All of them, we hope."

Losing a Friend

In the Land of Lost Board Members, no loss is so great as the death of a community advocate, a community visionary. When it happens the community needs time to mourn As time passes a community must then regroup and find the next generation of advocates and leaders. When money gets tight, good organizations survive. When talent and leadership pass on, good organizations survive. Surviving doesn't just happen. Those who led us, built their vision for the future of our community every day that they were with us. They strengthened us to carry on after them.

On this sad day, even the usual grayness of LOL seemed darker. I found several of my friends sitting quietly at the local LOL coffee shop, sharing reflections of members who were gone.

"I remember him saying to me," sniffed Bella Pelorizado, local nonprofit scribe and consultant, "That by continuing his work I would keep his memory alive."

Cash Now, CPA to nonprofits wiped a tear from his eye, "She always told me to remember the children. They will carry on after us."

Amos Alonzo Upright, retired coach and athletic booster, ran his hand through his hair as he reflected, "Damn, I thought he would always be around."

On the table was the local newspaper open to the obituary page. It was a grim reminder that our community had lost several doers and dreamers in the last weeks.

"We lost their vision," mourned Bella.

"We lost their energy," whispered Cash.

"We lost their heart," sighed the coach.

"Wait a minute," intruded our local nonprofit news

reporter, Birdie Inkstain, "you guys are sounding like real losers." Birdie can be ruthless with her energetic zeal. We sat up straight. She had our attention. I hadn't seen anyone with her kind of energy since the Music Man came to River City. She jumped onto one of the Main Street planters and sang out, "We didn't lose anything. They left us with ideas. They left us with well-run agencies. They left us with plenty of work still to be done."

"Remember the laughter?" We nodded

"Remember the generosity?" We nodded.

"Remember the passion?" We nodded.

In her own way, Birdie was telling us that a worthy life is a life worth remembering.

Birdie's words were an inspiration. I could see the energy and commitment coming back to the table. Our little circle of sadness was rethinking itself.

"You're right," nodded Cash Now, "We haven't lost what they taught us. They didn't take the vision with them. They taught each one of us something about ourselves and about serving our community."

"Now you're getting it," encouraged Birdie.

Bella slammed her fist on the table, "I know better than to let misery win. It's time to recommit to success. Every community leader we lost mentored each one of us in ways that would take advantage of our talents. We won't be clones of those we lost, nor simple echoes of their work. We have trained with the best. We will move forward defining our community future in new ways." Her fantastic curls spelled, "Amen."

"We'll never forget the principles and the ideals," sang out Coach Upright. "We'll never forget the time given in service of our community. We'll never forget their lesson, their example."

"That's more like it," cheered Birdie, "think about how

grateful we are for what we learned. Think about the power of their legacy. Be thankful that we were here to learn." Then she looked at each one of us as she raised her arms high and said, "Be forever challenged by their example, their courage and their love for our community." She stepped down from the planter, put her hands on the table, looked each one of us in the eye and said, "We never lose anyone when we keep faith in what they taught us."

We sat at our table and watched the breeze scatter the leaves. Then, the newspaper that carried the notices of our mourning fluttered and drifted on the wind. As we sat and watched, the paper floated above and blended into the gray sky of the Land of the Lost.

Obtuse You Say?

Vague is the underlying spirit in the Land of Lost Board Members. Nothing is black or white, everything is gray, or is it grey. Whatever. Being a land of no opposites or extremes, someone of my sensibilities is often maligned and vilified for my stand on practically everything here in my hometown. I sighed and whispered to the wind for understanding.

"What are you talking about?" asked my friend, Bella Pelorizado. "No body maligns you. No body understands what you're saying." She invited me to sit with the usual gang. They were spending the afternoon enjoying themselves at the LOL coffee shop

"I don't think it's that bad," offered Mr. Joshua Biggly-Huge. "We just wonder why you talk in words of four or more syllables when you only need to say yes or no."

"That's not fair," defended Al Truistini. "We know what she means, we just would have gotten to the point sooner."

"And with less pompousness, pomposity, and not so pompously," offered Cash Now CPA to nonprofits.

"Maybe you're right," I sighed, "My husband says...."

"You have a husband?"

I ignored Bella and continued, "He says that he...."

"You have a husband?" came an echo.

I ignored that, too, as I said, "that he can't understand..."

"A real husband?" asked Bella, " one that you..."

"Fight with?" finished Coach Amos Alonzo Upright.

"Spark with?" winked Al Truistini.

"Yuck, aren't you guys too old?" gagged Cash Now.

"Yes, I have a husband. Yes, he is real. Yes, we fight. And, how old is too old?" I looked at all of them with my best witchy stare. "Now, will you listen to me? I need help. Many people tell me that I make my points the hard way."

"Or not at all," offered Coach Upright.

"Now, now Alonzo," counseled Joshua, "let's listen. She might get up on one of her soapboxes and we'll be entertained for the next month." They all laughed.

"But I have an important message this month. I have to be clear. I have to make my points unequivocally."

"And pompously," muttered Cash under his breath.

"You go ahead, honey," Bella cooed. "I do enjoy your ditzy thinking. It makes my life seem almost normal. Her hair flashed, "Soapbox!"

"Now you're putting me on, not taking me seriously, waiting for me to tumble and stumble into the neo-reality of this gray-grey LOL mindset." I was hurt.

"I told you, Alonzo, keep quiet. She's her own worst enemy."

"Neo-reality?" questioned Cash. "I thought you just hung around here for the gossip."

"She doesn't gossip," said Al Truistini, "she's too busy fighting neo-reality with neo-delusional abstract irrationality."

"That's a good one, Al," crowed Cash.

Suddenly they all stopped their teasing and harassment. I had been sinking lower and lower in my chair at the Main Street Coffee shop.

"I think we got through," said Cash cautiously.

"What?"

"This had been an intervention, honey," apologized Bella.

"We had to talk you down from the strange places you take us."

"But I have a message," I pleaded.

"Just say it plainly," urged Joshua.

"We need help," I said. "It's Christmas time, and our

community is seeing over an 11% increase in requests for clothing; a 27% increase in individuals seeking food; 48% increase in people seeking help for rent relief; a 31% increase in families seeking funds for household heat."

"In other words," I took a deep breath.

"In all our words," the gang sang out, "This season, give to someone who hurts."

Coming Home

Everyone knows about the economy and it's impact on local charities. Some of the unintended casualties of a down cycle are surfacing in the Land of the Lost. Stumbling down Main Street in a daze of paper and maps was our local real estate maven, Lottie Softsell.

"Lottie, are you OK?" I asked.

"Sweetie, you just don't know what I've been through," she answered.

"I think I do," I said sympathetically. "Times are tough for everyone."

The secret speaker boxes on the street were playing, "Nobody knows the trouble..." Lottie was in such a state that she took off her spiky heels and beat a little speaker until it was silent. The tune continued from the other speakers along the street. She ran to the next. Cash Now, CPA to nonprofits, was able to intervene and get her under control. She burst into tears.

"Lottie, this isn't like you. Why, we've seen you laugh in the face of the Planning Board, turn your back on the Board of Adjustments, go toe to toe with the Freddie, Fannie, EPA, TVA, DOT. What has put you so out of kilter?" Cash asked with real interest.

"HOA's," she sniffled.

"Is that one of the new re-re-mortgaging tools coming down from the feds?" asked Coach Upright, community activist.

"Maybe it's a new loan bundling instrument developed by AIG or Lehman, or the Russian Stock Exchange?" offered Joshua Biggly-Huge, community philanthropist and

Charity in Motions

businessman.

"Do you think it could be a new level of certification for property managers?" guessed Bella Pelorizado, well known nonprofit consultant.

Through all this speculation by the usual suspects on the street, Lottie continued to sob. There was no other solution but to ask at the coffee shop for the secret elixir – two day old Colombian blend. If that didn't focus Lottie she would be out of focus, er, out of, er, well, this stuff would do whatever was needed.

"So tell us, what's HOA?" begged Cash Now.

"Home Owners Association," she wailed.

"And that's a problem?" speculated Joshua Biggly-Huge.

"You know," I interjected, "HOA's account for a large number of nonprofits in a community." She raised her shoe at me.

"But what do they do?" asked Coach Upright, "raise money?"

"Not really, they have dues," answered Lottie.

"Cure disease?" wondered Al Truistini, local benefactor.

"Not really, they may have architecture committees to stamp out ugly."

"Save the environment?" asked Cash Now.

"No, but they may hold ownership of common property in a neighborhood."

"They certainly sound harmless," soothed Bella.

Lottie wailed again. When she calmed down, she said, "They should be harmless, but a neighborhood dispute can be onerous, destabilizing, spiteful, egregious, petty, vindictive...."

"Are you talking about local neighborhood disputes or international military actions?"

"What's the difference?" Lottie looked at us, "Sometimes these neighborhood disagreements end up in our local courts."

"Lottie, do you know anything about local mediation services?" I asked. "Our community has mediation and dispute resolution options that may be more effective than court and provide long term solutions to neighborhood arguments."

"Just as long as it's a process that ends up with a clear winner and a clear loser," she said.

"How about if it just ends up with good neighbors?"

Lean and Mean, I Mean

"Bella, I've never seen you work up a sweat." My friend Bella Pelorizado, sought after nonprofit consultant, was doing a streetwise workout along Main Street in the Land of Lost Board Members.

"Listen, honey, these are lean and mean times." She huffed and puffed as she pressed orange traffic cones over her head for a count of thirty-five.

"Lean and mean?" I was puzzled. "Are you referring to the tight economic situation? The demands on local services by folks who have never had to ask for help before? That supplies and funds are running low? So supplies are lean and that means not everyone gets all they need?

"No, I mean I'm working out so I can lean on my donors for more money." She flexed her muscles and then did fifty push-ups at a fireplug.

"Do you think there may be other interpretations of lean?" I asked, "Like reviewing the budget and cutting out some items. Cut spending, cut the heat, cut the electricity."

"Yeah, right." she sneered, "Cut the c--." I couldn't hear the rest of her remark as she run up and down the Gazebo steps for two minutes. She stopped while she took her pulse and then pondered, "If I turn down the heat, my staff gets meaner and I get the budget leaner?"

"Maybe you're right," I conceded. "But I'm sure lean includes looking at cost cutting measures, that you, your staff and clients can live with." I thought a little more and then offered, "How about leaning on one another?"

Charity in Motions

"I can relate to that" huffed Bella as she completed 37 reps of some complex ab to pecs to ab to gluts to ab to collapse in front of the coffee shop. She leaned on Cash Now, nonprofit CPA, as he sat sipping a black coffee. Cash was showing how to get lean. He pushed her to the ground. I guess he's also working on the mean part.

I helped her up as I continued, "I mean agencies work together, lean on one another for support, share resources, manage services with no one absorbing all the costs."

"I see what you mean," Coach Upright said as he helped Bella grab the chin up lamppost. A crowd had gathered to watch Bella complete her street fitness program. I soon lost their attention as they counted out her chin-ups. She worked through some other cardio set of some mysterious stretching pirouette. She came to rest leaning against a parked car. "Bella," I cheered, "What a great demonstration of lean!" I waved my arm toward her and the car that was supporting her.

"You're saying that lean might not mean cut the fat, but look for someone stronger to work with?."

"I think I'm saying both. Be cost conscious, but also build alliances and friendships. No one is in this alone."

"Yeah, but what about mean? You're saying mean doesn't mean mean. I mean we should think of mean as," here she paused as others tried to help.

"As ugly? As average? As intend? As a verb? An adjective?" Came the street chorus of definitions.

"As a headache," surrendered Bella. "You're not listening to what I mean to say, and you're acting mean, mean, mean."

"Which translates to pesky, wicked and vulgar." I proposed. "So I guess you have to decide which mean you mean – an adjective, a noun, or a verb. Do you mean that you intend to be shameless or dangerous? Or do you mean to say you will determine your future, or that you will aim for your survival.

"What did you do, have a Thesaurus for lunch?" Cash asked.

"No, I'm on a diet. I'm not eating carbs, or fats, or sugar, or spice, or taste."

"That explains everything," Bella sniffed. "Diets make everyone lean and mean.

Opportunity from the Bottom Up

"We are being lost in the shuffle. No one hears us. No one knows our pain," shouted a strange looking man on Main Street.

I poked my friend Bella Pelorizado and asked, "Who is that guy?"

She shrugged. "Maybe we should tell him that standing on a planter on Main Street in Land of Lost Board Members could get him arrested. Then he would really understand pain." She watched him a moment, then said, "Or maybe we just sit here and enjoy a latte while we watch him get arrested." Bella is always practical.

"Don't you want to know what his pain is?" I asked, getting curious.

She stared at the wild-eye, middle-aged, disheveled man. "His pain may be as entertaining as his antics," she mused. Bella was becoming jaded in these tough fundraising times.

"Hey, you," she called to the stranger. "So what's your pain?"

He stopped and looked as a grateful tear came to his eye. "You're the first person to ask me. The first person willing to listen." He grabbed a bough on one of the dwarf, leafless trees in the planter and hung his body out over our curbside table.

"Whatever." These days Bella had no patience with whiners. "Come on my latte's getting cold."

"I'm forming a new nonprofit. Do you know anything

about non-profits?"

I interceded before she slugged him. "Sir, we know a little. Do you mean you're organizing a nonprofit to find a new cure for your pain? What cure, or pain or service is it?"

"WHAM," he said and we ducked. "No I mean, its name is WHAM."

"Which means?" we prompted.

"White, Heterosexual, Adult Males." He then started speaking in a preacher like cadence, "We need help. We're losing jobs, losing portfolio value, losing hair. Where will it end? We whammies have to stick together."

"Have you lost your job?"

"Yes, and my faith and my wife and my dog. There is no salvation for me. Life has let me down. Even my government has failed me."

"You mean you worked for a government?"

"Wasn't I a taxpayer? Of course I worked for a government."

"So now you're an unemployed Republican?"

"No."

"An unemployed Democrat?"

"No, an unemployed whammy." He was bordering on hysteria. His eyes spun around and his hair stood on end. The bough he had been clutching broke and he tumbled to the curb. Bella threw the remains of her latte in his face. He broke into sobs,

Bella pulled him up from the curb and looked him in the eye. "The world is tough for all of us these days. It's time to dig in and help out, fella. We're beyond crying over spilt milk. Sop it up and use it."

I am always impressed with Bella's take no prisoners attitude.

"Is that all I'm worth – spilt milk?"

"Only if you wanna be," replied Bella as she flipped him

into a chair at our table. The recent funding challenges and her lean and mean approach to life made her formidable.

"I want to be what I was, employed, useful, involved," he moaned.

"Then volunteer," she offered. He opened his mouth to protest.

"Is there something wrong with volunteering?" she challenged "I don't think you see volunteering as an opportunity." Her posture reminded me of the browbeating interrogator of old movies.

"Opportunity?" he squeaked.

"Yes, take that talent you have that no one in the private sector needs right now. Keep it honed. Take your skill to a small nonprofit, help them in financial planning, IT solutions, marketing and PR chores. Any local agency would appreciate you. You would keep your skills current. Or add to your resume by learning something new: become a mentor for a youngster, do home repairs for the elderly and disabled, deliver a meal, try court mediation, environmental advocacy, even fundraising. You will meet other volunteers and community leaders who will appreciate your talent and think of you when they have an opening for a paying job. It's win-win."

"Wham," he whispered as he understood.

Mean as the Devil

"One, two, three," Bella Pelorizado panted as she dragged a cart down Main Street in the Land of Lost Board Members. Her count echoed off the low gray clouds, the usual April weather, which actually is no different that any other weather. Her hair was working as hard, spelling out 'lift,' 'pull,' 'breathe' in rhythm with Bella's count.

"Bella," I asked, "Where are you going with all that equipment?" She had Pilates gear, floor mats, body balls, weights and ropes in her cart.

"I'm going to exercise a board."

"Exercise? Do you mean you'll do some long range planning or teach them some practice drills in developing a mission statement?"

"No, they said they needed to be exercised."

"So are you working on abs, or weight training or cardio?" This was not the usual type of consulting work for Bella.

"I really don't know." She pondered a moment, "They just said they wanted to get the devil out."

"You mean you're going to exorcise a devil out of a Board?" That sounded so Stephen King.

"What the devil are you talking about?" she demanded.

"The devil," I said.

"The devil what?"

"Not what, who?"

"Who?"

"The devil." She looked at me confused. "Bella, I think someone has called you in to conduct an exorcism."

"The devil you say." She dismissed my answer.

"Yes, the devil." I was firm, and curious. "Who wants your help?"

"FATE, the Fallen Angel Temporal Endowment. Their mission statement is – Nothing is IMP-possible."

"Bella, I'm worried that you're going into something paranormal and scary. Are you sure you'll be safe?" (Notice I didn't volunteer to go along to help.)

"Hey, I've been working out – I'm lean and mean." She flexed a muscle. "And I'm a nonprofit professional. I go through hell for my clients."

"But are you up to the devil?"

"I'm always up to no good'" she shrugged, "Does that count?" With one more flex, Bella continued on her way.

Soon the skies over the Land of the Lost got darker. In a land that is never day or night, it seemed as though night might win the day. There was far off thunder, while lightning and a strange acrid smell filled the air. Then the skies cleared and returned to gray, day had won. The air cleared. A lost bird sang. Local citizens came back out on the street to stroll and meet for coffee.

Bella came by pulling her cart with equipment. "It was the devil of a meeting." she exclaimed. "These people were all possessed."

"So it was an exorcism," I cried.

"It wasn't an exorcism," she replied. "It was an exercise – ism. They just needed to get the devil out of themselves and listen to each other."

"What did you do?"

"I did the first thing every personal coach does. I worked their sorry arms and legs until sweat poured. Then I ran them through some stretching movements and didn't let them quit until they all could touch parts of their bodies they hadn't touched, or even seen, in years."

"Bella, how did you get them to do all this?" I'm always amazed by Bella's improbable successes.

"I got meaner than the devil. I wasn't going to waste my

time on a board that was failing because they wouldn't listen to one another."

"I don't understand."

"This group does good work in the community. They raise money to feed and shelter many of our neighbors who are going through tough times. So, if they didn't stop fighting and attacking one another, their mission would fail."

I snapped my fingers, "If the mission failed, many clients would not have services."

"That's it." She dropped and did twenty push ups, then continued, "I faced the devil, made them face their biases, their hostility toward one another and convinced them that working together is a far more appealing goal than self destruction is." Bella fluffed her amazing hair. "It's astounding how easy it is to get someone's attention when they haven't the breath left in their bodies to argue." She turned to leave, "I give the devil his due. When he doesn't want a good thing to succeed, he stirs up problems. And I'm here to tell you that no agency that I value is going to the devil."

Amen.

Showcase Shopping Day

In the Land of Lost Board members there are dull days and duller days. But each year there are events that, almost suggest, well, maybe almost, or sort of almost, suggest a brighter livelier time ahead. The conundrum – when all around you is duller than dull, can you recognize success, or hear a tree fall in the forest? Or both?

It's spring in the Land of the Lost and the smell of success is in the gray air. "They're doing it again!" shouted Bella Pelorizado as she steered her stolen grocery cart down Main Street.

"Doing what?" asked Cash Now, CPA to the nonprofits.

"The Frugal Design Showcase!!!" Bella stopped at my sidewalk table at the Lost Cafe. "If you remember, last year the non-profit thrift shops sent items of quality, and whimsy, to the frugal designers for placement in a lovely, newly constructed home. Attendees were invited to purchase the items." Bella looked closely at me, "What did you purchase last year? Come on, tell. I know you were there."

"I'd tell you all that I bought," I whispered, "but I told my husband I only spend ten dollars."

"Last year was a great event," said Coach Alonzo Upright as he shook out his reusable shopping bags. "I found a chess set and a recliner for my den."

"It was a success," agreed Joshua Biggly-Huge, local philanthropist, signaling his limo to the curb. "The event created a paradigm shift in merchandizing perception by highlighting the great buys at the nonprofit thrift stores of slightly used items." We all would have to think about that statement later.

"You shopped at the Frugal Design Showcase last year, Joshua?" I was shocked.

"One never knows where one will find an antique of value and worth." he sniffed.

"You found a valuable antique?" asked Cash, who was surprised that Joshua even knew the word, 'frugal.'

"No, but I certainly enjoyed the challenge." Joshua stood beside his car.

"What challenge?" asked Al Truistini.

"Looking for my donations, my antiques. I found Mother's old table in a bedroom and the mirror from the guest room in the marvelous wall display in the great room." Joshua opened the trunk of the limo and showed us what he was taking to his favorite thrift store. "The thrift stores are collecting items now for the event." Joshua held up a crystal decanter. We all oohed. Then he showed us a small desk lamp. We aahed.

Folks along Main Street stopped to look into Joshua's trunk. They pushed, they shoved. Joshua teetered and fell in upon his furnishings. The trunk lid closed. People pounded on the limo trying to get at Joshua's great stuff.

Coach Upright attempted to calm the crowd. "The Frugal Design Showcase will be June 19 and 20," he shouted. People cheered.

"Get your tickets at your favorite thrift shop," added Cash. The throng lunged at him. "This year, according to the flyer, many items sold on Friday of the showcase will be replaced with new items for the Saturday showcase." Applause, whooping.

"Don't be discouraged," sang out Bella, as a crowd swelled, "you can purchase a $25 two day ticket to shop 'til you drop." The mob cheered.

"Tickets are already on sell at participating thrift stores." More cheers. "Of course, there is a lot of prep work for an event like this. That means, clean out the house, get your treasures to your favorite thrift store." Whistles and shouts.

The gang watched Joshua's car pull away and we all thought we heard him shouting from the trunk but it was difficult to hear with the horde chanting, "Showcase, showcase, showcase."

Recruit Board Members Year Round

In most of the world there are four seasons, In the land of Lost Board Members they are Audit, Strategic Planning, Nominations, and Fundraising. This is nomination season. Local Boards of non-profits usually spend May and June asking old members to reenlist, seeking new board additions and selecting new board leadership for the coming fiscal year. This leads to some very strange gatherings.

I was walking along Main Street in the Land of the Lost looking for a quiet, cool, dry place to rest after a long day of doing nothing, when I heard a loud discussion.

Bella Pelorizado, local non-profit consultant was trying to facilitate an energetic meeting among several local community minded citizens. "You need to think about new board members before now." She was really exasperated. "Haven't I told you, board recruitment is year round?" She pushed her unruly, uncontrolled hair out of her face. Her curls were sending messages to the small group, such as, 'Loser,' 'Are you Deaf?' and, 'Who cares?' The group was so used to the curls stepping into their conversations that Coach Alonzo Upright turned to argue with a belligerent curl.

"I've heard Bella," he snarled at the curls, "but life overwhelms us. We seem to put Board maintenance issues on the back burner when other issues face our agencies." He hung his head, repentant.

'Poor baby' spelled the sympathetic curl.

Joshua Biggly-Huge, local philanthropist, patted Coach

on the arm and said, "I know what you mean, Alonzo. We try every year and some how lose our way."

"Let's get down to business," ordered Bella, "we've got to get this done, the clock is ticking." Bella pulled out her expandable easel and white board. Dry markers materialized at her fingertips. "Let's review again." The little group watched as she magically whisked a board recruitment action plan on the white board. "First, analyze what you've got. There are several matrix available to help you categorize your board." They all looked at her puzzled.

"You need men and women." They nodded. "You need certain skills." They nodded. "You should pay attention to age and ethnicity. You should reflect the makeup of the community. You might even want to have board members who are or have been clients, and you especially want people who support your mission." They nodded, but to Bella they looked like dashboard bobble heads.

"But, how," begged Al Truistini.

Bella handed out papers with a grid for doing quick analysis of board members. The little group studied the information and then started to fill in the blanks. "See?" encouraged Bella. "Now that you know who is on your board and what talents they bring, let's look at who isn't."

"Isn't what?" asked Cash Now, CPA to local nonprofits.

"Who isn't there," explained Bella. "A strong board is a diverse board, peopled with different talents, careers and life experiences. That includes real basics, like age and gender, but should also reflect the ethnic diversity of the community."

"When I do this," offered the coach, waving his chart, "I see what you mean." He passed his chart to the others. As each person completed the form, they shared with one another.

"By golly," whistled Al, "I see what you mean. My board seems to be older folks."

Birdie Inkstain, local news reporter, had been listening and studying the information passed among the group. She glared at Joshua. "I don't see any women on your board." Joshua moved his chair closer to Cash.

"Based on all of this information," offered Cash, "My board could use a twenty something,"

"Age!" sang the gang.

"Asian." Cash ticked off another trait.

"Ethnicity!" roared the group.

"Attorney." Cash waited for a response.

"Career!" The gang was proud of itself.

"From Etowah," concluded Cash. Silently the group compiled the information of the perfect board member. They moaned.

"The Holy Grail of board members," sighed Joshua, wondering if such a person existed.

"That's why I'm telling you that board member recruitment is a year round job. Young Asian attorneys from Etowah don't grow on trees. Nor do any other board members, they have to be cultivated."

"Year round!" concluded the coach.

The Many Phases of IT

As economic times have gotten tough, the Land of Lost Board Members has become an escape destination for many oblivious and heedless types. So I wasn't too surprised when I met a hapless stranger coming out of the Main Street coffee shop the other day. At least, I thought he was coming out of the coffee shop.

"May I help you, hapless stranger?" I asked moving my gym bag to my other shoulder, so I could wave my hand in front of his dazed eyes.

"Are you talking to me?" he asked, looking around the street as though he had never seen this place before.

"Why, yes, I am. You look lost, forlorn, spacey, abandoned, desolate."

He held up his hand. "Are you the one they talk about, you know, the one who gets carried away with IT in her word processor, you know, Inappropriate Thesaurusing?"

"They talk about me?" I was flattered. I take attention anyway I can get it.

"Sort of in passing," he said. "I was on an IT call to one of my clients."

"I love technology," I swooned.

"Not that kind of IT," he said, "I mean Improbable Tabulations."

"What's that?"

"You know," he said, "making ends try to meet in these tough economic times."

"Who are you? A finance officer, a board treasurer, someone from Fannie or Freddie or AIG?"

"Can't you keep quiet," he cautioned, "I'm here on a mission." He looked up and down the street and then over his shoulder. "I'm not supposed to be here."

"Then where are you?"

"Anywhere else. But if I were here, I would test my system to help you local fundraisers. Times are really tough. If my plan works, most nonprofit agencies will have more money than they need."

"Why? Are you going to start printing it? Because there is no money for quick fix investment scams – besides that's already been tried." It had been a tough financial season. I was becoming a little jaded.

"No, we're going to hack, I mean, tap into community resources that we have ignored in the past," he whispered.

"You mean steal money?"

"Shhhhhhhh." He pushed me behind a planter. "Not exactly steal. I mean steal is such a concrete word, and I was thinking something more virtual, more IT, you know, Illusionary Transfer."

"Hmm," I said, "That sure beats asking anyone for money."

"You've got it." He looked up over the planter to make sure we were alone. "Governments tax. We'll sort of do the same, but better than taxing – no notices, no bills, no receipts, you know, IT, Invisible Turnover."

"That sounds much easier to me than a capital campaign or an annual appeal." I was thinking this guy could really be helpful, as long as we avoided a 150-year prison term.

Just then the usual gang came tumbling out of the coffee shop. They came up to me as Coach Upright said, "We were waiting for you inside."

"Do you mean me or him?" I asked.

"Him who?" asked Joshua Biggly-Huge.

"Can't you see the hapless stranger?" I asked.

"You're scaring me," said Cash Now CPA to the nonprofits.

"I told you that you shouldn't visit that gym as often as you do," cautioned Bella Pelorizado, nonprofit consultant. "You're not tough enough."

"I am, too," I argued. "And I'm talking to this IT guy who's come here to tap local resources to help fundraising efforts."

They all looked around, but no one seemed to notice my friend. I looked around, and I couldn't see him either. "Maybe you're right," I sighed, "Too much exercise can make me see things." Coach Upright patted me on the shoulder, and my friends all walked down the street to their afternoon appointments.

As they walked away the hapless stranger spoke, "This is going to be easy."

"Where did you go?" I was confused

"I was always here. This is the information age, nothing is secret and nothing is real." Then he dissolved into some nano ion dust cloud.

I shifted my gym bag to my other shoulder as I thought that Bella was correct, too much exercise makes me IT, you know, Insane Thinker.

New Year of Board Planning

In the Land of Lost Board members, summer is wrapping up, but who can tell when it's never light nor dark nor day nor night. Non-profits have a somewhat obscure seasonal cycle, too. For many agency boards, the beginning of the organizational fiscal year had just begun. New Budgets have been adopted to support program, fundraising plans have been debated and new board members are, ah, er...

"Exactly!" punctuated Bella

"What?" I looked at her.

"You're thinking about the new board year."

"I am, Bella. I let it sneak up on me this year," I confessed. "I'm so unprepared." I wondered if I should cry or be angry. I wasn't sure which would get her to do my work for me. I decided to cry in anger. "How do I raise these new members to excellence?"

Bella looked at me as she sat on a curbside bench. "What are you doing with them?"

"Well, oh, they come to meetings, ah, and, ah....."

"Exactly." She snapped her fingers in my face.

"What?" It's August. It's hot. How can I think?

"Do you have a plan to welcome new members? Does the plan include an orientation? How about a mentor, you know, an old member welcoming and working with the newbie?"

"What?" I yawned. The dog days are here.

"Exactly. How many new members are on your board this year?" She tapped her foot waiting for an answer.

"Three." I leaned.

"How did you get them?" Did Bella have to talk so loud?

"Well, our treasurer was standing in line at the grocery store and he met a woman. They chatted about a pomegranate recipe. He got her number." I threw out my arms. "The rest is history."

"Did the woman know about your agency before the invitation to join the board?" asked Bella.

"No, I think she just wanted more pomegranate recipes, or something else that our treasurer had to offer."

"Exactly. You have a new member with no background. What are your expectations?"

"I just hope she shows up to help us reach a quorum. I don't know what the treasurer expects."

"How about participation?"

"Well. They're adults. I don't think I have to know about their participation."

"On the board." Bella's voice was nuanced in a manner I had never heard before.

"Oh, what do I expect her to do for our agency during her service on the board?" I have to start getting to bed earlier.

Bella looked at me. "I don't even want to know about the other two new members."

"They're very fine people. One is a retired corporate executive. He's been a long time donor and asked to expand his level of activity in our agency. He brings some skills we can use. And I think he's allergic to pomegranate."

"There's one more member." She wiggled a finger at me.

"The other member we got for that diversity thing. She, or he, well, we're not sure which, but the person seems interested and we needed someone different."

Bella took a Mason jar from her bag and chugged the clear liquid. She wiped her mouth with her ShamWow. "You've done everything wrong."

"I know but I was desperate."

"Desperation doesn't build viable leadership strength for the future."

I hung my head and hoped she would disappear.

"Look, let's try to salvage something of this current board and then get you organized for your next round of board recruiting." Bella patted me on the back, then tipped the liquid from her jar into my coffee cup. "Here's where we start." She pulled a white board and easel from her bag. "Each new board member gets an orientation that includes discussion of your agency and programs and a clear statement of board member expectations. Have some work and committee assignment options ready for the new members to accept. Next assign a mentor to the newbies." She tapped my head. "I'd let the treasurer mentor on his own time." I understood.

"Using your board development committee as the leaders, analyze your members by age, talent, and other criteria meaningful to your board. Are there holes in your talent pool? Or are you gender biased? Age? Develop a list of people that meet your board needs, NOW!" I emptied her jar into my cup. "Include all current board members' suggestions in that list. Ask their help in meeting and recruiting potential members. Conduct informal orientations about your agency. By March your board development committee should have a clear idea of who in the talent pool is interested in board service and who has what you need at that time.

Bella took her empty jar from me as she concluded, "Board development isn't a last minute exercise. It's a year round sport."

Health Care for Clunkers

In the Land of Lost Board members, national issues sometimes sneak into local discussions. So the gang was settled at an outdoor cafe, sipping coffee and discussing proposed, pending and played out public policy decisions. It was a heated discussion. Bella Pelorizado, consultant to nonprofits, had lost control of her curly hair. They were on opposite sides in the health care debate. The curls wanted single payer. They wanted to be able to salon shop.

"Bella, does your hair know that salon treatment is not included in health insurance?" I asked.

Her curls went wild accusing me of all sorts of things, you know, like wanting to shave grandma's head. "You shouldn't talk like that in front of them," warned Bella, "One person's disease is another's cure."

"What does that mean?"

"My curls think salon treatment is necessary for their good health," sniffed Bella.

"But it's hair!" Amos Alonzo Upright, famous coach and community volunteer, stated the obvious.

The curls scampered across the table and spelled horrid words at Coach Upright.

"I think we have to calm down the animosity in this debate," intoned Joshua Biggly-Huge, our community anti-government philanthropist. "We should all be able to listen to one another's views." Then he turned to Bella, "How could you think single payer would work?"

Charity in Motions

"It's not me, it's my hair." Then Bella beckoned us all closer and whispered, "Don't say anything about dye panels?

"You mean death panels?" asked Cash Now, CPA to nonprofits.

Bella's hair spelled out, "We will pick our own time to dye."

"But don't they understand what these health proposals mean for the future of the country's deficit?" asked Joshua. "Our children will pay for our excesses. Clunkers, aliens, insurance as the evil menace in a public option plan to buy your old car. Where will it end?"

Did I miss something, I wondered. I wasn't following this debate. So I foolishly asked, "Are we confusing policy issues?"

"Non-citizens need cars, as much as we do." Al Truistini, a community benefactor, pounded the table.

"Aliens get no cars," argued a bystander, "And no health insurance either. Who even knows what blood type ET is?"

"I think you misunderstand the term alien," I suggested to the stranger.

"No I don't. When they beamed me up, they helped me understand it all." He looked at all of us around the table, "And they want single payer, too."

What's their position on death panels?" Cash asked.

"They were pained to see all those cars snuffed in their prime. It was like looking in a mirror and seeing their own civilization on the engine block." The man disappeared with a sniffle.

"We don't need to listen to a fool like that," said Joshua, waving his hand to dismiss the piddling stranger. "We can solve all these problems right here, with common sense and open minds. How about portability?" He threw the question out with gusto.

"I think you should be able to carry all the insurance you can lift anywhere you can afford to go," replied Cash.

"Preexisting conditions?" asked Coach Upright.

"That's a little tougher, isn't everything pre-existing? You know living, eating, growing old?" asked Al.

"I guess what it means, if you're not getting old, overeating, smoking, drinking or diseased, you can ask to be considered for extended, free enterprise, health care coverage," offered Bella. "With as many payers as you want and as big a discount for your clunker as you can manage."

"I think you're letting the opposition brainwash the citizens and confuse the issues." Joshua was tastefully disdainful.

"What would you like to say?" I asked.

"We haven't listened to all sides," Joshua said. "We need to think about this more. We need to watch our cost containment and save Wall Street first."

"SIGH."

They all looked at me. "I thought I could get away from the debate here." I threw my arm out to encompass all of the gray of the Land of the Lost, "to the place where nothing is ever resolved and nothing is ever completed and no answers are ever expected."

"Sounds to me like you shouldn't want to get away from public policy debate," groused Bella, working at curl containment, "It's a responsibility."

If Kermit's American, Prove it

No matter how hard you try, changing the focus of public debate takes on a life of its own. Citizens become embroiled, enmeshed, entranced, entangled in ideas that morph into forces beyond what is sane and realistic, factual and viable to the discussion. For example, many LOL citizens have become fixated on the issue of alien healthcare. Or to be specific, their new war cry is: No ID; No ER. I know it's an extreme position, after all who's carrying their proof of citizenship with them as their mangled body is rushed to the hospital for repair. And if a baby is coming – does it wait for its mother to be approved for, well, you can see prenatal care become post-partum before the documents arrive.

So I was not surprised to hear a story on the LOL Main Street Coffee bar and Tanning salon. "Aliens should get no service," stated Joshua. "They can go back where they came from to get a leg sewed back on."

"I can't believe I'm hearing this," cried Bella Pelorizado, "after all I've been through this week. My friend, Kermit, was visiting. While he wandered along the walking trail through the miasma of late autumn, he was attacked." She wiped a tear from her eye.

"Attacked in our town?" We were appalled.

"Yes, right here." Bella blew her nose. "We rushed him to LOLIPOP (LOL Intensive Patient Operations.) They wouldn't take him. He looked different. They said he wasn't one of us." Her hair spelled out, 'It's not easy being Green.'

"I knew he wasn't an alien. He was as documented as the rest of us. I rushed home to find his papers."

"I say if he looks different, he's an alien," a stranger screamed who had been listening to Bella's story.

"I looked and looked through his luggage," Bella continued. "But who carries documentation when visiting a friend, in your own country? I faxed his family and they sent photos of the lily pad of his birth, but LOLIPOP wouldn't accept that, and Kermit went into rapid decline as we tried to think of another angle."

"Did you consider using his tax returns as proof?" asked Cash Now, CPA to nonprofits.

"We tried that but the tax people said they couldn't give out private information except to the person who it belonged to, but if I wanted to know anything about anyone's private life, try Googling him." Bella sighed. "I tried but only found a reference to that sad affair with his co-star. And we all know it ended badly, well for her, it did." Bella's hair spelled 'Bar-B-Q gone wild.'

"Didn't that prove to LOLIPOP that Kermit was not an alien?" Coach Upright asked the obvious.

"Not at all. The ER director said who else, but an alien, would date such a pig?" Bella couldn't speak any more, she just put her head on the table and sobbed. We all tried to comfort her. We made suggestions about ways to establish authenticity, viability and citizenship. We despaired at the thought of a person being denied care because he looked different, and that care would be withheld until the LOL post arrived with proof of legitimacy.

"Is this where public discourse has taken us?" sighed Alonzo Upright.

"Can we not find the charity in our hearts to care for those in need without creating barriers to services?" Al Truistini asked the cosmos.

As we sat wondering what had become of our better selves, a currier biked down the street, paging Bella. We waved and he came over to hand her a note. He waited impatiently until someone thought to hand him a coin for his service.

Bella opened the loligram. We watched as she read, then sobbed. Her hair spelled out, 'He croaked!'

Cash picked up the loligram and read: *Dear friend or family member,*

Your friend expired at our doorstep waiting to be validated. Too bad. Next time he'll know better. Come get his carcass.

The caring folks at LOLIPOP

As we sat stunned by Bella's sadness and loss, the manager of the cafe brought his board out with luncheon specials, first on the menu was frog leg soufflé.

Never Bored by Boards

When the Land of the Lost local nonprofit boards are recruiting new board members they usually invite a prospective member to attend a board meeting. This lets the board members get a measure of the prospect and allows the prospect to see how the board functions.

I had been invited to be looked over and to look over the board of the Hole Ball of Wax, an agency committed to solving all of the world's problems each month. Their mission statement: 'If thermal nuclear war hasn't occurred yet, we're a success.' I thought the mission statement was a little too broad, but you can't argue with success.

I arrived at the meeting a few minutes early and was handed a packet of information by the chair. Twenty seven pages that included: minutes of the last meeting, (6 pages); financial report, (twelve pages); agenda, (half page); minutes of the finance committee, (half page); minutes of the marketing committee, (half page); minutes of the personnel committee, (five pages); minutes of the fundraising committee, (half a page); executive committee minutes, (one page); flyer for a fundraising event for another nonprofit.

"I'm sorry," I apologized, "I should have given you my email address so that you could have sent this to me before hand.

"Honey," replied the chair, "we don't do advance. It's all we could do to get this information together this morning, before the meeting."

Charity in Motions

"Wouldn't board participation be more focused if this information went out ahead of time? I asked.

"I don't want focus, I want attendance. If you tell them what's on the agenda, they won't come." She waved the agenda at me and I scanned the half page of type. It looked normal. Approve minutes of last meeting, accept treasurer's report, reports from committees (minutes attached to this agenda), adjourn.

Hmm, I thought, maybe the discussion and decisions will stem from the committee reports. I quickly scanned the minutes attached. Nothing. Each one reported the date of the meeting; those in attendance and a statement that said: *Discussion followed on the agenda items. No decisions. Meeting adjourned.* Except the fundraising committee whose closing statement read: *Another fight between the bingo group and the black-tie gala. No decision. Fight continued after adjournment.* I was getting a bad feeling about this board.

People were straggling in accepting their packet of information at the door, then flopping into chairs and ignoring the information they had received. About ten minutes after the designated meeting time, the chair did a quick nose count and stated, "We have a quorum." Someone growled. A chair scraped against the wall. The meeting was called to order. Holding the agenda, the chair asked, "Anycommentontheinformationreceived?" She spoke so fast I thought I saw her words appear as a flash of energy from her mouth. No one moved. No one even looked at her. Another flash of energy, "Minutesapprovedandfinancesaccepted." Then she smiled sweetly and asked in a very condescending tone. "Any committee chairs have anything to report?"

There was a general rumble and grumble. As the chair scanned the room, a latecomer walked in, laden with books and papers and accompanied by a large dog. Once the new comer found a seat, the dog crawled under the table at his feet.

"We're glad you could make this meeting, Horace." The chair was not happy and I wasn't sure whether she was talking to the man or the dog. They both snarled. I looked for a way out of the room, wondering if that window would open and if I would survive a two-story landing.

"If there is nothing else to come before this board, I think we can..." Horace, the man, shifted in his chair and cleared his throat. Everyone sat up, even the dog. "Yes, Horace?" The chair said it in a voice that dripped challenge. We all held our breath.

"I think we have to talk about revising our financial policies, today." Someone screamed, someone threatened Horace with bodily harm. The dog barked.

"Why didn't you say that before we did the agenda at executive committee?" the Chair asked authoritatively

"Because I wanted everyone to hear me," said Horace. Well, he was honest. He had the stage. "We don't ever discuss anything here." Horace was frustrated. "We don't make decisions."

As I went out the window, I thought, Horace sandbagged the meeting to get his idea on the agenda. The chair was keeping her authority too close and not sharing leadership and responsibility with the board members so she was paying the price. And I was hanging by the seat of my pants on the flagpole of a building thinking I was better off than all those left in the meeting.

Charity Begins at Home

"Hack, hack." What a sound, I thought. It sounded worse than H1N1. Is there a newer version out, H1N1.2? I followed the sound. It was my friend Bella Pelorizado, sitting behind a coffee display in the Land of Lost Board members.

"Bella?"

"I've been hack, hack."

"I can't understand you with that horrible cough."

"I'm not coughing. I'm saying I've been hacked."

"Hacked?"

"As in someone got into my email account at graymail.lol.

"But that's my email service."

"Then be careful. Some crazy hacker working from a renegade server sent everyone in my address book email saying that I was supporting the Abyssinian Cave Dwellers' capital campaign as my holiday cause. Then," she was almost vibrating in her anger, "the email suggests to all my friends that they support this project with lots of cash, too!"

"How did you find this out?"

"My mother called and asked why I refused to send money to her Christmas Santa Soiree? She was upset." Bella's hair spelled, "Momma's mad."

"So I called my attorney to check my risk, or liability, or...stuff. He wouldn't take my call because he's irate that I'm not sending my usual donation to Attorney's Against Grinches." She blew her nose. "Then I called LOL my ISP and they said I wasn't real because my account is now controlled by an offshore cave dweller, so they couldn't give me any information."

"This is terrible. What's happening to your annual donations?" I was interested because Bella always gives my favorite charity a little something every year.

"This is a troubling year for charities." Bella was concerned about local LOL charities. "Everyone is maxed out – food pantries, services for elderly, services for children, to say nothing of the arts and groups who love animals and who work for environmental issues." We sat thinking about the doom of donations.

Always willing to turn negative events into life lessons, I asked Bella, "So what does this tell us?"

"Tell who?" asked Coach Upright, as he glanced behind the coffee display. "Bella, I didn't see you sitting there. Why aren't you sponsoring my Christmas 5K, Jingle Jog?" The coach was clearly miffed. "It's bad enough that you aren't supporting me, but you want me to send money to a cave dweller?"

"I think you should sit and listen to Bella's problem," I suggested.

"Bella has a problem?" snapped Joshua Biggly-Huge, sarcastically. "Her problem is reneging on her promise to support my annual Holiday Bounty meal. She's been there every year, raising funds, giving her own donation, cooking, serving........" Joshua wiped his brow in despair or disgust, I wasn't sure.

Cash Now, CPA to nonprofits came running down the street. "Where is she?" By this time we all knew who 'she' was. "She can't do this. I can't file her taxes if she's claiming donations to offshore cave dwellers with no approved non-profit status." Cash made me proud. He always had his hand on the pulse of non-profit action. But I had to move quickly because he was trying to get his hand on Bella's throat. This life lesson might deteriorate into combat.

"Help!" her hair pleaded, as Bella tried to explain. "I was hacked. You've been duped." Now she was sobbing. "I thought you were all my friends."

Time for a life lesson, I thought. I opened my mouth to teach.....

"Now, now," Coach Upright was consoling Bella.

"There, there, young lady," Joshua offered.

Cash was contrite. "Bella, you're a generous donor and outspoken advocate for our community. In these trying times, we should have known that you would stick with us to make certain all people have what they need this holiday season."

The men consoled Bella as she calmed down. They each promised to help clear her name, work as hard as she does for our community, and never believe an email that sounds too crazy to be true. But most of all they all promised to follow Bella's holiday rule, give locally because charity begins at home.

A life lesson for all of us, as we celebrate the joyous season.

Another Kind of Nonprofit

"It's another year, Bella. Have you any plans to make it memorable?" one of the Land of the Lost gang asked.

"Not really. I was thinking about retiring this year." Bella toyed with her coffee cup.

"Where's that woman that knows everything?" We all looked at Bella. No one had ever accused the rest of us of knowing everything.

"Are you talking about me?" Bella glared at him.

"I got a problem with my homeowners association."

Bella clutched her heart. She turned pale then her eyes rolled back in her head. I thought that was an extreme reaction even for Bella. Coach Upright threw a glass of Gatorade in her face. She sputtered back to coherency. "Please not an HOA. There's no worse organization in the world."

"I'll say," advised the stranger. "I painted my home this color." He threw a paint chip on the table.

"Pink?' gasped Cash Now, the CPA to nonprofits. "That's such a girlie color."

"In some cultures," the man informed us, "It's considered good luck." He put the chip back in his pocket. "Besides, it's called rustic rose, not," he shuddered, "pink."

"A rose is a rose," spelled Bella's hair. Everyone nodded agreement.

"Well, they, the Home Owners' Association, say I have to repaint it."

"Never challenge your Home Owners' Association," whispered Jonathan Biggly-Huge. "I tried once. They claimed to have had design review responsibility on my house and directed my architect to make changes."

"You have a lovely colonial manor," I said. "We all enjoyed your Christmas reception there."

"I didn't plan on a colonial manor." Joshua looked at us as the information sank in. "I wanted an alpine chalet."

"We have a guy in our neighborhood," confided Al Truistini, "Who put black plastic on his windows."

"So you couldn't see in?" asked Cash.

"Or vice verse," nodded Al sagely.

"What do they do in there?" asked curious Cash.

"Who knows? They put black plastic on the windows, remember?" Al was puzzled by the action.

"I always thought that you had big windows so your neighbors could see how much more you have than they do," observed Jonathan.

"Or vice versa." Al Truistini always faced truth.

"Here's what happened to me," said Coach Upright. "I wanted to add English Ivy to my fence post and the HOA said it would take over the neighborhood in fifteen years. I said we'd all be dead by then. After I protested all my grass died, overnight." We all shivered.

"They claim to be protecting property values, but old neighborhoods are valued for their eclectic charm, not military rankness." Coach was on a roll so we didn't ask if 'rankness' was the word he wanted. "My HOA lets people do some strange things and they aren't fair or evenhanded in their decisions. I think it depends on who gets elected and who's overthrown."

"Overthrown?" we chorused.

"Yeah, it takes a coup to get some of these folks to retire." The others seemed to agree.

"We can't find anyone to serve on our HOA board anymore," sighed Jonathan and Al together.

"These are all the reasons HOA's are pains in the...," Bella didn't say it but her hair spelled it. "They are non-profits and should be transparent and non-despotic. But some of them seem to get carried away.

"What do you mean transparent? Are you talking about windows again?" I asked.

"No. All the members should have reasonable access to financial information. Minutes of the meetings should be available to all members. Often HOA's own common property through out the development and that property must be maintained. Sometimes they even own the roads which must be maintained. It's sad to see an HOA board ignore the real purpose for their existence." Bella looked at us and summed up the discussion. "The members of an HOA should always be treated as neighbors first."

There Are No Easy Answers

When times are tough the tough hold a fundraiser. So one Saturday morning in the Land of Lost Board members there was the thirty mile skip for jaundice, the kissing booth for canine dental health (can any one say dog lips?), a dress-up ball for nearsightedness and a dress-down ball for the perpetuation of edible art.

"Where will it all end?" asked Bella Pelorizado, local consultant to nonprofits.

"I have to agree," moaned Joshua Biggly-Huge. "My checkbook can't take another plea."

"Don't say that Joshua, I was just going to ask you for a matching grant for my Guts Away Sauna day to support a scholarship fund for sous chefs," said Coach Upright.

"There has to be a better way." Bella was pale and disheartened. "We can't go on like this. Someone must have an answer." We all looked at her.

Finally Cash Now, CPA to nonprofits had the nerve to say it aloud. "We all thought you had the answer." We stared at Bella.

"There's only one thing to do." There was a glimmer of the old fire in her eyes. "We have to go see LOLA.

"Not LOLA" shivered Coach Alonzo Upright.

"It's not the end of the world yet," argued Al Truistini, community benefactor. "Can't we wait until things get really bad?"

"Who's Lola?" I asked.

They all looked at me. I shrugged, "I'm new here. I mean

Charity in Motions

I've been around a while, but not when things have been this bad for raising funds for local nonprofits." Al patted my arm.

"LOLA is our own oracle, affectionately (I heard someone snicker) called the Land of Lost Avatar," explained Joshua.

"Like that new movie?"

"I think more like the Wizard of Oz movie." Cash rolled his eyes.

"But the Wizard was fake and only told everyone what they already knew or had or something." I looked around for Munchkins to begin singing and dancing.

"We're going to see LOLA and that's that." Bella stood, pushing her protesting hair out of her face.

We marched on for what seemed like a half mile, tripping over failed skippers and avoiding the kissing booth where a slobbering German shepherd was waiting for customers. We walked passed barrels of useless strategic plans and crumbling mission statements. Up we climbed, through the mist until we arrived at the pinnacle, the apex, the little anteroom of LOLA. A creaking door opened and we tiptoed in. At the back of the large room was a curtained wall, but you've probably seen both movies, I don't need to say more.

LOLA's voice rumbled from the curtain and bounced around the walls. "Why have you come?"

"Oh great LOLA," chanted Bella, "We need to be guided by your knowledge."

"What is it? The soaps come on in a few minutes," rasped an irritated voice.

"Oh great LOLA," intoned Cash Now, "Please bestow your wisdom. How can we survive in these times of diminished donations?"

"Eat less," roared LOLA.

"Oh great LOLA," sang Coach Upright, "help us carry on

our good work."

"Jellyfish like to sing and dance. Hurry up, I only have time for one more."

"LOLA the powerful," wept Joshua, "When will the bad times end?"

"Iodine sublimes. Gotta go – close the door on your way out." The room became silent and we could hear "All My Children" theme music.

"I feel better," said Bella as she smoothed her objecting hair.

"Feel better? I didn't understand a word he said." I was befuddled.

"But that's why I feel better. No matter how bad we think it is, LOLA has it worse. Can you imagine being up here in the fog, trying to make sense of what's happening in the nonprofit world?"

"There must be a lesson here someplace," I commented.

"That's the lesson." Bella was disgusted with my lack of savvy when it comes to dealing with an out-of-the-way oracle. "There are no easy answers. We had to trek up here to be reminded that we'll survive by doing what we always do – work together to effectively manage community resources and community need."

Agencies Need Good Volunteers

Balloons floated along Main Street in the Land of Lost Board members. They weren't advertising anything, like a fundraiser or a webinar on fundraising, or a book on fundraising. They just floated, some fat, some thin, all a dull Mylar gray.

"Bella?" I asked the Land of Lost nonprofit consultant, "what are those balloons?"

"Not what, who?" She stared after them as they drifted from lamppost to building cornice along the street. "They're lost volunteers." One balloon got too close to our table at the coffee shop patio and she kicked it back into the air. Returning to my question, she continued, "They're loose volunteers, floating around after being ignored, or dismissed. Nature protects them with a polyester bubble until another agency comes to rescue one of them."

"How did they get there?" I found if I stared hard I could see their little faces pressed against the Mylar, woeful sad eyes begging to be rescued, you know, that pound puppy gaze.

"It's the same old stuff," she explained.

"I don't know any same old stuff," I moaned. After all these months I still had no sense of how this place worked.

"See that one over there." She pointed to a balloon with a sag in the lower hemisphere. That one got canned for having an idea better that the hired fundraiser." The she cocked her hair toward another. "And that one got PV'ed because she questioned the displays at the thrift store. And that one self

PV'ed because he never got thanked or praised for his efforts."

"PV'ed?" There we go again, another LOL acronym.

"Polyester-volunteered." She saw the question in my eyes. "Sometimes agencies use the method to dismiss volunteers and sometimes volunteers self-PV. They leave an agency and put themselves out there for better opportunities." Then her hair made little curly arrows in the direction of another balloon as Bella explained, "He was a board member who said the word accountability one more time than the Bylaws allowed." Tisk, spelled her hair.

We watched as three balloons came together and merged into one.

"That's trouble," Cash Now, CPA to nonprofits, predicted as he joined us for tepid coffee. "Those three are probably old friends who like to work together. It's all or none for some agency."

"Isn't it a good thing when friends recruit friends to work for a good nonprofit?" I wondered if the coffee was making me dumb.

Joshua Biggly-Huge joined us as I finished my question. He stared at the balloons then stared at me and sighed. "When good friends work together, they sometimes present a force strong enough to challenge a weak agency board or executive director. They challenge the status quo, run amok with energy and ideas." He shook his head, "That's when the threatened leadership calls the PVC."

"Poly volunteer Capsulators," explained Bella without me having to ask. "You've seen their truck drive through town."

"I thought that was the truck that shreds paper and old records."

"You're correct," said Cash. "That's PMS, Poly-Mingled Services. They do a little of everything in administrative services to nonprofit offices."

"A little shredding, a little encapsulating, a little board development," offered Joshua. "In times like these it's the flexible who survive." We all watched as the PMS truck stopped at a traffic light and released several balloons into the air.

"I don't understand why an agency would get rid of, or ignore, volunteers, especially those who work hard and have new ideas. It sounds as though these poly volunteers were doing things that they should." I was really confused.

Bella waved to a balloon who seemed to be a friend of hers. "Volunteers are challenged to remember their place; work silently, follow orders, and go away quietly when dismissed."

"That doesn't sound productive for volunteers or agencies."

"Of course, it doesn't." She looked at me again appalled at my stupidity. "I've designed my new class, 'Volunteers: Love 'm don't PV 'm' for that reason."

Cash stood to go. "Change can be scary, and tough times scarier," he frowned, "that's why good volunteers can keep an agency from being TP'ed, a Thing of the Past."

Social Networking

Today spring arrived in the Land of Lost Board members. How could I tell? Several locals were cleaning out their offices, briefcases and, ah, backseats? I walked by Coach Alonzo Upright as he threw fourteen latte plastic cups out of his car. "Coach," I asked, "did you drink all this during the winter?"

"No, we had an ad hoc committee meeting in the car last night," he answered as he tossed out several double cheeseburger wrappers. I looked into the back seat. Fourteen empty cups, many more empty wrappers?

"How many people on that committee?" Frankly, I couldn't see more than two people fitting back there, with or without the food.

"Six." He scrambled up from the floor and counted the change he had found. "Dollar -thirty." He smiled and shoved it into his pocket.

"Coach, I know an ad hoc committee usually has an immediate issue to solve and then is dissolved." I leaned against the open car door. "So what was this committee working on and for how long?"

"How long?" Coach scratched his head. "We've been meeting for three years."

"Have you reached any conclusions, or come up with a solution to your original problem?" I waited patiently, hoping he would invite me to help him spend his dollar-thirty.

"We were to conclude something?"

"Why did you form?" I was puzzled. "Did some chair of a board on which you serve appoint you and those five other people to look into some question, solve some issue, rewrite some policies, review the bylaws, develop an updated salary schedule?"

"I don't recall." Coach rubbed his head in deep thought.

"But you've been meeting for three years. What do you discuss at your meetings?"

"Stuff."

"Who is the committee chair, the convener, the record keeper, note taker, agenda setter?"

"Usually the person who pays for the drinks."

"But doesn't the board expect a report or recommendation for some action, or an evaluation of a project?"

"Listen here, missy," growled the angry coach, "we're just doing what we were asked to do."

"Which is?"

He rubbed his head again and stared at the sidewalk. "Maybe it was bylaws. No, no, that's the ad hoc committee that meets in the sauna. Maybe it was a new salary schedule." He shook his head. "Couldn't be, we're an all volunteer agency. By golly," he stared at me perplexed, "I forget what we were working on, but we have such a good time."

"Coach, an ad hoc committee is defined as a temporary committee to address a specific problem or issue."

"Young Cash Now told me it was Latin for 'to the beer,' you know, ad hock."

"Beer?" Now I was confused. "You said you were drinking lattes last night."

"It was chilly so we improvised with a little Bailey's." He reached under the front seat and pulled out an empty bottle.

Sadly, I found myself looking at a man who had fallen

into the trap of volunteer service, Ad Hoc Syndrome, or the 'ahs' as some professionals refer to this malady. People work together on boards, enjoy one another's company then panic when the opportunity to meet no longer exists. It's a very sad commentary on our life and our social loneliness when people dream up excuses to stay together. History is full of examples: the Hundred Years War, foreign military presence in Afghanistan, a hung jury, global warming committees, anti-global warming committees, anything sponsored by the UN. But you get the picture. There's only one solution. If you are the chair of a hardworking board of an energetic nonprofit, treat the board and staff to a little fun. Don't find out in the newspaper that they've been meeting secretly drinking lattes and eating burgers in the dark of night just to enjoy their time together.

"So, Coach, when's the next meeting?"

He winked at me, "Just as soon as I get the car cleaned out."

There you have it, dear readers, clandestine social networking masquerading as community service.

Adversity Can Be a Call to Action

Sometimes in the land of Lost Board members local citizens go over the top in their assessment of the challenges of the times. That's why, I suppose, I found my old friends singing a sad song as they warmed their hands over a sputtering fire pit. "Nobody knows the trouble we've seen," sang Bella Pelorizado, consultant to local nonprofits, as the all male, all volunteer army of singers, hit the sad notes of background doo-op.

"What do ya mean trouble?" The question came from a newcomer, the stylish, yet bubbly, Birdie Inkstain, the new community cheerleader to nonprofits. "We haven't any trouble in LOL. We only have opportunities."

"You call 'em what you want and we'll call 'em what we want," answered Bella as the chorus sang a five part, "Hmmmmmm."

"So times are tough," Birdie cajoled. "They're always tough for someone."

"Now they're tough for everyone." Bella replied. "Amen." from the chorus.

"No, it's attitude," Birdie barked. "We've got to change that attitude. We've got to take that trouble by the throat." She shook her fist in the air as though she were strangling her personal trainer.

"Gag," coughed the chorus as Bella reached for something to drink.

"Troubled, tough times are in the eyes of the beholder." Birdie danced around the fire now. It had come to life. I hadn't noticed but I suspected someone had thrown some small bits of a random executive director's report to make it flare as punctuation to her words.

"How would you like a punch in those eyes?" growled Bella. She hated having her rain paraded on. Or was it that she hated parading enthusiasm, or enthusiastic paraders? In any case, I knew Birdie was heading for trouble with a capital T.

"Look at you," Birdie turned to face Bella, "All tense and sooty. Trouble only comes to those who look for it. You have to be more positive. Know your strength. Turn your back on weakness and negativity. Wake up every morning with a song in your heart. Life will be what you make it. When you work for those in need and serve a higher good, the resources will be there. The energy will be there." She grabbed onto a utility pole and danced around like Gene Kelly in 'Singin' in the Rain.' Bella decked her, like Alex Karras punched that horse in 'Blazing Saddles.'

"Ooooooof," sang the choir as they all watched Birdie roll down the alley, under a parked car, over a manhole cover, through a pile of recycled cardboard, around a puddle of something nasty and land on her feet as the LOL trolley service stopped to let her catch a ride as she sang. (Dear Readers, I don't have to tell you what she sang, do I?)

"Maybe," offered Coach Amos Alonzo Upright, "we should consider what Birdie said."

The chorus gasped in a Dragnet tempo. Bella looked at the new challenger and flexed her fingers.

"I mean," continued the coach, "we can't just sit around in back alleys singing and feeling sorry for ourselves. It's time to pick ourselves up and....,"

"Don't say it," threatened Bella.

"Face our opportunities." Everyone waited. Nothing happened.

"I know why she didn't hit you," speculated Cash Now, CPA to nonprofits, "You didn't say dust ourselves off." Bella slugged Cash.

"I think," intoned Joshua Biggly-Huge, "there's a lesson to be learned here." The rest of the chorus waited. "We need new strategies and we should think about what Birdie said. We can be a catalyst for change, figure out ways to make a positive impact. Regroup, revitalize and reorganize." The rest of the chorus now had their eyes covered.

"There is a lesson to be learned," Bella began, as she shook off the malaise of 'same old same old' and looked to the parade and trolley passing her by. "It has to start within each agency as we shore up our strengths, jettison the marginal projects, work together to rethink need in our community then design solutions that will be long term." The chorus joined hands and hummed the theme from 'Hoosiers.'

Learn what's happening in Henderson County. Learn more about the United Way/WCCA community assessment. Find out what the talk is all about at www.liveunitedhc.org.

Praying for the Future

"Look at this newspaper." Bella Pelorizado, nonprofit consultant, waved the latest edition of the local Timely Donations at her friends. "We're praying at public meetings." They waited to hear more. "You know what that means?" asked Bella.

The gang at the coffee shop stared at her. A used napkin drifted across the street on a random breeze.

"It means that local politicians have discovered another way to demonstrate their hypocrisy?" asked Al Truistini, community benefactor.

"I can't believe you're so cynical," flounced Bella, turning her back on him. To the rest of the gang she explained, "It means if they're choosing, in spite of separation of Church and State issues and Supreme Court decisions, in spite of all that, if they're choosing to pray Christian prayers in public, they have committed to acting in a more Christ-like manner."

"What does that mean – they're going to walk on water?" The gang guffawed at Coach Upright's question.

"They already think they do that," offered Cash Now, CPA to the nonprofits.

"No." Bella stomped her foot. "They're going to make decisions that are Christian not politically motivated. They'll allocate money to feed those who are hungry."

"Right," frowned Joshua Biggly-Huge, "that means they'll take themselves out to big dinners."

"Use money to shelter the homeless," continued Bella, ignoring his comment.

"Yeah, another way to justify a posh hotel stay," snickered Coach Upright.

"Take care of the sick and infirmed." Bella was losing patience with the attitude around the table.

"I can just see them worried about universal health care," Cash Now said.

Bella looked at the scowls on her friends' faces. "Do you think they're just giving prayer lip service?" She pulled out her soapbox and climbed on. "I think this decision means that they are committed to act in a Christian manner, making all their decisions guided by tenets of faith, Christian love and concern for individuals. Why else would they stand up in the face of so many defined legal decisions to act in this manner? This is the stuff of martyrdom. This is what inspires others to make the difficult choices and perform unselfish acts – acts that are ethically and morally motivated. I believe that our political leaders were inspired by those voters who want prayer at public meetings, because they know this means that those voters want government to act in a more Christ-like manner." Just then a church choir appeared at Bella's side in their flowing white robes, trimmed in startling gold braid. They began to hum a hymn, purr a psalm, murmur a , well, you get the picture.

"How does she do that?" whispered Al Truistini as he pointed to the choir.

With music at her back and light from an invisible source on her face, Bella continued, "I believe that this will be a new day for leadership, religion wrapped around politics guiding our hearts, keeping us from going astray." She shook her fist at the crowd that had gathered. "Our elected leaders will be the guardians of all religiously directed politics, and politically motivated religion."

"I think that describes all fanatic religious fundamentalists," observed Joshua.

"Just watch." Bella was intense, now. "Our leaders will budget money in a way that shows concern for children, respect for the elderly, and protection for those facing life's challenges." Bella stood on her soapbox breathless at the thought of political Christianity. Or was it Christian politics?

"Money's money," said the CPA wisely. "When pennies count, people don't, no matter how they start a meeting."

"What will it take to make you believers?" she challenged her friends.

"Instead of closing their prayer, "in Jesus' name we pray,' they should say, "in Jesus' name we will act to do what is best for our community.' Then I'll believe they intend to be led by Christ. But for now I believe they're led by political expedience," grumbled Joshua.

"Amen." sang the choir.

Homage to Maurean

It was the usual gray day in the Land of Lost Board members. A humid breeze caressed every random piece of trash drifting down the street. The usual gang was sipping iced coffee at the local sidewalk cafe.

Bella Pelorizado joined her friends at the table, sighed, plopped into a chair, sighed, dropped her purse to the ground, sighed and sighed again. The gang waited.

"I just came from a retirement party for my friend, Maurean." She sighed again. "She was my alter ego."

"What?"

"She had no ego of her own, so I loaned her mine."

"That's crazy," challenged Joshua Biggly-Huge. "Everyone has an ego. Although I certainly can understand you sharing some of yours, you have plenty."

Bella gave him a squinty glare. "She never worried what people might think of her."

"People respect her," Cash Now, CPA to nonprofits stated the obvious.

"But she didn't care. She only cared about kids."

"She cared about more than that," Al Truistini, community philanthropist, said. "She cared about the people she worked with and she cared about the people who donated to her cause."

"I think she's respected for shifting the paradigm of community cooperation," intoned Joshua. "We donors were impressed to see various agencies come together and work for a purpose under her guidance."

"Don't you mean leadership?" asked Cash.

"Guidance is velvet leadership," stated Coach Alonzo Upright.

"Velvet leadership?"

"Bringing everyone into the tent. Sharing the responsibility and the rewards. Challenging bad behavior. Working with, working side by side, but always working." Joshua wiped his brow just thinking of all the work Maurean had done.

"She was committed to her cause, to kids, to working together." Bella was soon standing on her soapbox, bathed in light from the usual invisible source. "Maurean never let a big idea nor a small minded person stop her. She moved out in front of the issues and got behind those who could get the job done."

"SHE got the job done," argued Coach Upright.

"She got the ball rolling, the fire started, the dough rising, the......." Bella was stopped by a waving hand.

"We get the picture," said Al Truistini. "What I want to know, is what she'll do next?"

"There are all the job offers, the pleas for a good manager to rescue an agency, to fundraise until her eyes fall out, to charge into any fray without caution or worry." Bella spoke, backed up by the choir that had appeared behind her.

"I still don't know how she does that," whispered Cash as he moved over to make room for the sopranos – not to be confused with *The Sopranos.*

"But which job will she take?" demanded Coach Upright. "We're all waiting. I've got my request in."

"What do you mean your request?" asked Joshua. "I want her working on my cause, chasing my donors, marshaling my staff to higher goals."

They looked at Bella. Stepping down from her soapbox, she pulled her chair up and moved in closer to those around the table. "I heard," she began and chairs scraped as they all gathered in to hear the gossip. "I heard," she repeated, "that she wants to spend sometime enjoying her family, her friends, her garden."

"Yeah, yeah, that's what they all say," groused Coach Upright.

"Gardens," snarled Joshua. "We need her talent in my agency."

"Friends, bah," commented Cash. "She needs to teach more people about fiscal management."

"What can a family have to offer that's more compelling than working with a few distressed agencies?" asked Al.

"A hottie husband," explained Bella.

They all nodded their understanding.

This article was written when my friend, Maurean Adams, retired from her service as Executive Director of the Children and Family Resource Center of Henderson County, NC.

Organizational Culture

Bella Pelorizado was deep in thought when her friend Cash Now threw his new printout of IRS non-profit regs on the cafe table at the sidewalk coffee shop in the Land of Lost Board members.

"You scared the liver out of me," gasped Bella.

"What had you so deep in thought?" the CPA to non-profits asked.

"I'm preparing a training for new board members at the Dysfunctional Agency of Mind-numbing Narcissism."

"DAMN?" asked Joshua Biggly-Huge, local philanthropist as he pulled up a chair.

"Yes, DAMN," sighed Bella. "My goal is to help the old and new board members understand and respect the agency's culture, but give them permission to change with the times, with new philosophy or with new ideas."

"DAMN won't change," offered Coach Alonzo Upright. "I tried to convince them last year to work with my fundraising training program, Sweating for Dollars, but they were reluctant to try anything that included sweat."

"What do you want to accomplish?" Joshua asked Bella.

"I want them to look at each other."

Her friends all laughed. "Their agency vision is, 'Mirror, mirror on the wall.'" The guys sang.

She ignored them, "I want them to see what potential each new member has."

They laughed harder. "Their mission statement is, 'It's all about me.'"

Bella gave them all a scary, squinty-eyed look. "You don't have to support an agency's mission to help them be well organized," responded Bella. "After all I worked with the gum lobby."

"Don't you mean gun lobby?" asked Joshua.

"No gum, mmmmmmmmm," hummed Bella.

"There's a gum lobby?" Coach Upright was surprised.

"There must be or else all those people who stick gum under chairs and on sidewalks and in people's hair would be shot." Bella's hair stood on end at the very thought of gum.

"Now you're talking about the gunnnnnnn lobby, right?" asked Cash Now.

Rolling her eyes at her friends she returned to her original discussion. "I plan to present DAMN principles that work for any and all non-profit organizations. Many organizations elect new leadership and have a board retreat to work with old and new members to ease the transition, to review the past year and set some goals for the new year."

Bella waited for another comment, but no one spoke, she continued. "It's my experience that a change in leadership ushers in a new philosophy. Most boards have term limits to keep ideas fresh and to reorganize as the times, technology or fundraising reality demand." They all nodded in agreement.

"I remember a board in my past where we just changed the treasurer and found a whole new purpose," offered Al Truistini, community benefactor.

"That sounds inspiring," Bella praised her friend. "What new purpose?"

"Prosecuting the old treasurer."

"That's another point," offered the knowledgeable CPA. "A leadership change is another reason for an annual review of the books."

Bella was making notes for her presentation. "I want

them to understand that once they agree on goals…"

"Don't you mean strategies?"

"I thought it was objectives."

"Isn't it aims?"

"How about process, plan, method, design?" They all looked at Coach Upright who was paging through his Thesaurus.

"Whatever." Bella broke the tip of her pencil and searched through her bag for a new one.

"I want them to understand that the old ways may work, but they should evaluate new thinking."

"The goal of my strategic objective," smirked Bella, "aims to help DAMN understand that well-thought-out change is good. Old ways, methods and plans should be evaluated for relevance within their current mission and vision."

"They only have one goal, or strategy," proposed Cash, "Me first!" The gang cheered.

"Damn," barked Bella as she broke another pencil.

How To Handle the IRS

The usual gang gathered around a table at the sidewalk coffee shop in the Land of Lost Board Members. From inside the group came a voice asking, "Trouble with the IRS? Have you never filed taxes? Is the IRS coming after you?" Everyone at the table shuddered. "Don't be afraid," said the calming voice. "We'll protect you. We're retired IRS agents augmenting our retirement income by helping you when the IRS comes knocking. We'll smooth the way for you. Make the IRS treat you with respect. We'll even come visit you once a week in prison. So call us today and the IRS will be just a memory."

The gang all sat back in their chairs as Bella logged off the Internet TV programming. "This wireless street network allows us whole new ways to be frightened and confused." She was impressed with the LOL technology.

"It allows me to work and stay connected even though my agency can't afford to rent office space," sighed Coach Upright. "These IRS 990 issues have us all panicking and going underground. Access to a wireless network keeps us at-large and flexible." He looked over his shoulder.

"Your agency is in trouble with the IRS?" asked Joshua Biggly-Huge.

"I didn't think we were but I checked that non-profit website listing non-profits who haven't filed. We're one of them."

"I thought you only had to file if you raised money," said Al Truistini, community benefactor.

"Listen, I'm going to tell you one more time," growled Cash Now, CPA to non-profits. "If you are a non-profit, you have to file with the IRS. There are income requirements that determine the amount of information to be reported." Cash looked at his audience. "If you have a budget over $500,000," here everyone snorted, "you file the long form, a 990. If you're under that figure you file a 990-EZ. And if you're a non-profit who wants to remain a non-profit, but you are under $25,000, you file the 990 N (e-postcard.) And you can do that online. Please go to www.irs.gov and click on 'Charities and Non-profits' in the header."

"Big government is always in our way. How can we prosper as a country with government wanting its share?" a stranger asked as he leaned against a planter listening to the gang's conversation.

"The organizations who file a 990 may not pay taxes. Regardless of the size of the agency, they're reporting on their status, confirming that they're still reputable charities," said Bella. "The IRS website says that organizations that meet the requirements of IRS Code section 501(c)(3) are exempt from federal income tax as charitable organizations."

"What if I don't want to file?" goaded the stranger.

"Things can get expensive," answered Cash. "An agency no filing can be assessed penalties, sometimes pretty nasty penalties. It's import for all agencies to complete this filing by October. All of the information you need is at the IRS website, including a list of organizations at risk."

The gang turned to look at the stranger. He had pulled out his iPad and was furiously surfing the IRS site. He looked at their questioning faces. "Hey, I got to protect my agency. I don't want us closed down on some technicality."

"What sort of service does your agency perform?" asked Bella, always ready to expand her base of potential clients for her consulting business.

"We help people avoid," he stopped and studied his audience, "we help people hide from, that is to say, we offer interested citizens a strategy for low impact citizenship."

"Low impact citizenship?"

"Live and let live; don't tread on me; under the radar; sub rosa; subterranean" he shrugged. "We help people learn byways to circumvent government regulation. The irony is we gotta let the IRS know we're here."

"You don't have to be tax exempt," suggested Joshua.

"Then who would give us money?"

Working Together Works Out

"How sweet." Bella Pelorizado stared at the iPad screen displaying the black dog, sprawled across a carpet. She handed the screen to another Land of Lost Board member in the coffee crowd. The gang had gathered this morning to survey the first annual volunteer-where-you-put-your-money Main Street non-profit festival.

"Great looking animal," concluded Joshua Biggly-Huge. He passed the screen on.

Cash Now, CPA to nonprofits, chuckled, "I bet he eats his weigh every day."

"He's energetic that's for sure," Coach Upright stated with pride. "He can do all sorts of tricks and is a thoughtful companion."

"He talks to you?" asked Al Truistini, community benefactor.

"He understands what I say," explained the coach, "which is more important to me. I like to be listened to."

They were all sitting at their usual sidewalk cafe table on the gray and misty afternoon in the Land of the Lost. Main Street was crowded with tents and balloons as each local nonprofit worked to attract the attention of the citizens walking through town.

"At least you kept your dog home," Bella complimented the coach as she moved her briefcase before a leg lifting dog could do any damage. Returning to the table she found a large Husky sitting in her chair finishing her cranberry pecan scone.

Big and little agencies jockeyed for attention and curb space. Leashed pets jockeyed for fire hydrants and scraps of food. "Isn't this great," grinned Cash. "By bringing all these agencies together, volunteers and donors can learn what's available."

"It's also an opportunity for agencies to learn more about each other," observed Bella, kicking a dog sniffing at her shoe. The gang watched as the booth workers at the Delicate Artistry tent pushed a man leading a dog as big as a small pony into the booth promising outdoor volunteer opportunities.

"In these tough times folks might find ways to work together," nodded Cash. "Collaborations work wonders for everyone." The cafe friends had worked for months to organize the venue and bring all the nonprofit agencies to the table for one gigantic cooperative event.

"Do you think this sort of event will help agencies see opportunities for some creative partnerships?" asked Al.

"Wouldn't that be great!" Coach Upright was always optimistic. He was fond of saying, only an optimist would coach a sports team.

As the waiter carried more lattes to the table, a low-throated growl came from behind a planter. The tall cups wobbled on the tray. Another growl, this time louder, from the other side of the street, answered. The waiter barely got the tray to the table when a dog ran from the planter, leaped onto the waiter's shoulders and bounded into the street.

Potential volunteers pulled in their animals. A small dog jumped from his mistress' bag and danced in front of an unidentified mammal, forty times its size. People screamed. Dogs tangled their leashes together. People toppled over as they were woven into knots by hysteric pets.

Finally, several dogs broke loose from their owners and raced through the street. Tents tilted, tumbled and toppled.

Agency recruiters sprawled in the street. Banners of nonprofit messages and mission statements blurred.

The gang watched as people sorted themselves out, helping one another, then listening to each other. Soon someone suggested a cooperative activity, something easy, but useful to everyone.

"My, my," observed Joshua, "Things seem to be happening."

"Things that could help everyone." Bella got her briefcase. "I think I'll see if anyone needs a consultant to flesh out these ideas."

Cash stood. "Maybe some of these folks will need advice on managing funds in joint ventures."

"Maybe allowing pets on the street is a good thing," concluded the optimistic coach.

A Holiday Story

It's that time of year, again, thought Bella Pelorizado to herself. In the Land of Lost Board members Bella, the famed nonprofit board consultant, studied her calendar. "Yep," she said aloud, "It's time for the annual what good deed can I do before the year ends season." She was expected at the annual holiday meal delivery site.

She looked around her snug office then out the window into the gray day with its gray falling snow and shivered. "If I stay here long enough maybe all the volunteers will have taken the deliveries." She snapped her fingers at her plan. Be late, look concerned and get credit for showing up. The meals would be dispensed and she could return to her snug office for a holiday toddy. Yummm.

Slipping on her boots, pulling on her long winter coat and wrapping her neck against the elements, Bella slogged down Main Street in the Land of the Lost to Holiday Happy Mealtime, the agency that prepared and delivered holiday food to needy families in the community. Bella squinted through the snow and was delighted to see the long line of volunteers. She could almost feel her warm office and her hot toddy. Yummm.

The line moved quickly as volunteers grabbed the boxed dinners and followed the instructions to the homes of the very lost, the very least of the community. Bella waved to her friends; wished holiday cheer to one and all, growing colder and thinking warm, toddy thoughts. Yummm.

"Bella," greeted her old friend Al Truistini, community benefactor. "My last box for my last volunteer." He handed her the meal box and gave her directions to the last, lost home. Checking the instructions, Bella groaned.

"Al, this place is further than Gerton, on a plateau higher than Mt Pisgah and over a river older than the French Broad."

Al smiled, "And you're the person who can deliver." Al closed the door to the Holiday Happy Mealtime kitchens as he waved her off.

Bella grumbled and mumbled as she headed out of town. At the city limits of Land of the Lost, she looked back. What if she just tossed this box into a dumpster? Who would know? The snow was falling and she was cold. No one in the community can be this isolated and this hungry. No one will miss this meal and no one would ever know.

"I would know," sighed Bella. She pushed on, through the snow, over the river, up and down the mountains. After miles of driving her car slid into a ditch.

Bella climbed from the car, kicked a tire, pulled the boxed meal from her trunk. Sitting in a drift of the usual gray snow, she thought about walking back to town, or maybe just sitting there until someone found her. Then she thought about her warm office and hot toddy. They were both probably cold by now, she mused. She looked at the box and wondered who was waiting at the end of the map. Who could be this isolated and this hungry, surely not anyone in her community.

"This is ridiculous," she said to herself. "It's cold. I'm probably lost. No one is probably home. In fact, who would live out this way. I should just go home."

She thought about all the other ways she could have helped with holiday giving: send a donation to feed someone; send a donation to buy toys and clothing for someone; send a donation to keep someone warm. So why did I volunteer to deliver food, she wondered with a disgusted shiver. Leaning against a fallen tree, she thought about turning back. She put the box down. The snow would cover it in minutes. Who would know? Bella sighed.

Picking up the box she began to walk to her destination, up hills, down hills, over rivers she walked. The snow fell. The wind blew. Night settled. As it grew darker, she finally saw a small light on the horizon, just over another river and up another hill. She continued, promising herself that she would never volunteer for this assignment again.

Soon she stood before a small home, tilted against the blustery winds, roof shingles creaking, wallboards flapping, but with a flickering candle in the window. Bella knocked at the door. It slowly opened a crack as a small shadow tried to be welcoming yet keep the cold and wind at bay. A small face looked up at Bella.

"I knew you would come," said the little girl.

Domino's Isn't Just for Pizza

"Come in," Bella Pelorizado called as she wrestled with the hermetically, plastically, unassailably sealed packaged set of ink cartridges. The Land of Lost Board Members gang pushed hard on her office door and tumbled into the room. The push propelled two of them across the floor into her floor to ceiling stack of 'End of Year' giving requests. Papers and envelopes scattered across the room.

Coach Upright picked up a familiar envelope. "You haven't sent a donation to my agency?"

Bella took the envelop from his hand, not gently. "You sit on five boards, and they all want an end of year donation." She was now knifing the cartridge plastic, becoming indignant when the plastic bent her knife.

Her attitude deflated the Coach as he moaned, "That's the domino effect everyone's talking about."

"What do you mean domino effect? The Cold War is over."

"No, I'm talking about the budget crisis mindset. No one's spending, so no sales tax. No one's making money, so no income tax. Ergo, no one's making donations."

"No money for food, for heat, for clothing." chimed Cash Now, CPA to nonprofits.

"For Christmas dinner." moaned Joshua Biggly Huge, community philanthropist.

"For Christmas toys." lamented Al Truistini, community benefactor.

"Don't be silly." Bella Pelorizado, non-profit consultant, chided her friends as she threw the cartridge packet at the wall. "Sure things are a little tight. Sure everyone's rubbing their pennies before letting them go. But this is the holiday season, people will give."

"You're being uncharacteristically optimistic." Coach Upright picked up the cartridge packet.

"People will share with those who have nothing. It happens every year. We all become the person we want everyone to see us as." Bella took the packet from the coach and held the plastic over a lighted Christmas candle.

Cash Now shrugged, "That's not what my clients are saying."

"Non-profits always sing the blues." Bella dropped the package as her sleeve caught fire.

"No, I mean my other clients. The potential donors." Everyone looked at Cash. "They tell me they can't spare any money this year."

"What are they doing? Sitting on their assets?" Bella had no patience with hidden assets. Coach Upright stamped out the flames on the 'End of Year' pile of requests that had ignited.

"Are you certain you're reading your clients correctly?" Joshua Biggly Huge asked Cash.

"Yes, sir." Cash threw a glass of clear liquid on a portion of the flames that had eluded the coach. With a mighty 'whoosh,' a stack of old strategic plans erupted into a holiday fire of prancing and dancing flames. The gang looked at Bella.

"A little White Christmas toddy, you know, vodka, white wine and peppermint schnapps with a dash of fresh snow to ice it down." She blushed.

As the gang got the fire under control and looked for the remains of the toddy, Bella said, "I think we have to reframe the community's mindset. During Christmas the domino effect is in reverse." She paced her office, pouring a drink for everyone. "The Christmas domino effect doesn't represent toppling and capitulation, it represents everyone reaching out to help one another." As usual as Bella began her speech, unseen choirs sang and a light shined down from an unseen source.

"How does she do that?" Cash asked everyone. They shrugged.

"The message of the Christmas season," Bella rang out, "is share your gifts, spread your cheer, and touch a hand in need." She raised her glass saluting her friends.

"Here I got your cartridge packet open," said Coach Upright.

"That's all right I got my message out."

A Vacation DownUnder

The usual gang of the Land of Lost boards members jockeyed for a view of the airplane. Their friend, Bella Pelorizado was returning from a trip to New Zealand.

"There she is," cried Cash Now, CPA to nonprofits. They watched as Bella swayed into the lobby of the LOL airport.

"How long do you think it will be before science perfects teleportation?" she asked as her wobbly knees dragged her to the luggage carousal.

"It shouldn't be too long," replied Coach Alonzo Upright. "My new science non-profit is putting up cash prizes for innovation."

"How much money?" Bella could become really innovative for the right price.

"Enough talk about business," chided Al Truistini. "We want to hear about your trip."

"Did you meet a lot of people?" "Did you try different foods?" "Could you speak the language?"

"Yes, yes, no," replied Bella. "Put my bag in the boot."

"What do you mean no? You were in a country that speaks English."

"Wanna bet?"

"How did you present your seminar on *International Gifting Opportunities: Scams or Not?*"

"They understood me. I speak clearly." She gave her friends a flinty stare. "You all going to be a bit daggy or do you want your gifts." Bella held up her carry-on luggage.

"Daggy?"

Bella ignored the question as she handed a gift to each of her friends. Cash Now unwrapped his first and held it up.

"A letter holder?" he asked, twisting the metal in his

hand.

"It's a toast holder. You put the toast in between these wires and it looks like they're marching to the breakfast table." Bella glared at Cash.

Joshua Biggly Huge unwrapped his next. "A tea strainer?" He hoped he was correct. Bella had been disgusted with Cash.

"Right." She almost patted Joshua on the head.

"A dish?" asked Al Truistini as he held up his gift.

"I got it because it says that it was made in Levin and I visited that city," Bella said disappointed at the impact of the gifts on her friends.

Coach Upright tried to sneak out of the room. He knew he didn't stand a chance in guessing anything correctly. "Aren't you going to open your gift?" Bella asked him in a threatening voice. Coach slowly opened the package.

"Shot glasses." Coach smiled, happy that he received something he could identify.

"Yes." Bella showed her delight.

"Nothing says New Zealand," said Cash.

"What did you want? Some possum wool socks?"

"Possum?"

"Wool?"

Bella slipped off her shoes and wiggled her feet, showing off a pair of snug, warm, wool socks. "It's not the same kind of possum," she said anticipating their question.

Joshua cleared his throat. "We're grateful that you thought of us when you were so far from home." Everyone gave her an insincere smile as they held their presents.

"Of course you're grateful." Bella sometimes missed nuance. "Because I bought these things at thrift shops." The insincere smiles got insincerer.

She pointed to each item. "I got the toast rack at a Hospice store; the tea strainer came from a Red Cross store; the plate came from an interdenominational store supporting a local food bank." Finally she pointed to the Coach, "And the shot glasses came from the Sallies."

"Who's Sally?" asked Coach.

"The Sallies Thrift shop," Bella said, "you know, the Salvation Army."

"Ah," they all said as they understood.

"I learned a lot of new words while I was gone," admitted Bella. "Sallies is only one. Most of the others can't be printed in a daily paper – at least not the definitions." Bella slipped her possum wool clad feet back into her shoes. "But one thing I did learn, my new friends work as hard as we do for their nonprofits. I thought you'd all like to support their work and this was the best way. I spread a wee bit of money around at each thrift shop, just like we do at home."

Confessions

The gang settled into chairs in the conference room of Bella Pelorizado's new consultant office suite. Bella is a professional trainer, cheerleader and paid consultant for nonprofits. She recently studied international nonprofit issues. The usual gang from the Land of Lost board members assembled in her office ready to learn. They thought nonprofits needed a shot in the arm in the Land of the Lost. Fundraising was tepid, volunteer enthusiasm was vapid and leadership was insipid. At least that's what Bella had been telling them during their visits to the coffee shop on Main Street.

Today she was ramping up her pitch. Land of the Lost would learn how to move from insipid to inspired. At least that's what Bella told them.

As the gang looked around the remodeled office space, Cash Now, CPA to nonprofits asked, "What's that lettering on your door? BPINGO?"

"Nothing," she said not wanting to meet his eye.

"It means something," Cash challenged. The others, alerted, listened to the discussion.

"It means Bella Pelorizado, International NGO.

"N-G-O?" asked Coach Alonzo Upright, respected community volunteer.

"Non-government organization," replied Joshua Biggly Huge. As a community philanthropist and local small government advocate, he said, "I have mixed feelings about NGO's. They sometimes receive tax money."

Al Truistini another member of the LOL gang said, "NGO's try to provide services in lieu of a government growing bigger to provide that service. They're also useful in emergencies or in providing service when a government is small or poor, or when the service is needed in locations hard to reach from the seat of government."

"So why are you an NGO?" asked Cash.

Bella fluffed her naturally curly hair, hmmphed at the gang and walked to the head of the conference table. "As you know I've been away investigating non-profit issues. I learned that NGO's have great potential for service and in helping find solutions to many problems."

"And you have some solutions for the world, so you're becoming an NGO?" Sometimes the gang caught on quick.

"I've found a need in the NGO community. And I intend to fill it."

"What need? social, economic, environmental?"

"Acronyms."

"The world needs more acronyms?" They started to leave.

"Since all this social media appeared, I think we have more acronyms than we need," growled Joshua.

"And more than I understand," admitted the coach.

"But I'm talking about the world. International acronyms." Bella was on a roll; her hair radiated. "There are so many NGO's and so many collaborative NGO efforts that the world is running out of acronyms. I'm here to solve the problem."

"We don't understand." Al spoke for everyone.

"I'll give you some examples," she said and began to write on her white board. "WANGO is an organization called the World Association of NGOs. Then there's BINGO, Business-friendly international NGO. And TANGO, technical assistance NGO."

"What about MANGO?" called Cash.

That's management and accountability for NGOs, or Macedonia NGO, or market advocacy NGO. See what I mean? They're running out of words. I can fill the void. But I need a supply of acronyms."

"Dingo," shouted Al.

Bella scribbled on her board

"Bongo, gongo," suggested Joshua. He wasn't certain if this exercise supported NGO activism or if he supported the concept. Acronyming could get really confusing.

"GONGO is a government operated NGO," advised Bella.

Joshua hung his head. "This is going too far. First NGOs were non-government now they're government?" He was having a problem with this lingo.

"Gringo, Ringo, ingo," rhymed Coach.

"Sorry, INGO is international NGO," pouted Bella. "And we all know Ringo."

"Flamingo, fandango," called Cash as he tangoed around the floor.

Joshua studied the words on the white board and cleared his throat. "Sometimes reality is stranger than the bizarre rantings of imaginary people."

"I say Bingo!" declared Al showing his agreement with that statement

"You can't. That's already taken."

Flu Shot Roulette

"I know one of you is responsible for this," wheezed Bella Pelorizado, famed consultant to nonprofits, as her friends from the Land of Lost Board members trembled into her sick room.

They had never seen their leader so ill. Her hair lay limp and unresponsive on her pillow, her eyes watered and her nose ran. Her breath came through clumps of trapped mucus. After speaking she fell against her pillow and stared at the guilty gang with one angry eye while she daubed the other with her bed sheet.

"My dear," asked Joshua Biggly-Huge local philanthropist, "What do you mean? You think we did this," and he waved his aristocratic hand of disdain over her bedside collection of medication, "to you?"

"Who else?" she accused. "My best friends. I see you most often. Who else would give me this virus?" She fell into a coughing fit. They all backed toward the door. The angry eye stopped them.

"But we got our flu shots," said an earnest Cash Now, CPA to the nonprofit.

"Yes," seconded Al Truistini, community benefactor, "Don't you remember? You told us friends make friends get inoculated." They all nodded eager to have Bella's memory kick in.

"I thought she said intoxicated," said Coach Upright. They looked at him with panic as Bella switched her angry eye to laser and scanned the coach. He raised his arm in self-defense. "No, I mean, I got a shot, but I thought she meant I should have a drink afterward so I chased it with a few Sam Adams."

"Wait a minute." Cash was catching on. "You didn't get a shot."

"You didn't get inoculated?"

"Or intoxicated?"

"And you made us?"

Bella flopped back on her pillow, coughed until her ears turned red, then caught her breath. After sipping some water, she steadied herself and said, "It's been my plan for years, if you all get shots for flu, or whatever else is passing through the Land of the Lost, I won't need any inoculation because I'm protected." She sort of waved her hand as a weak conclusion to her congested logic.

"You didn't get a shot?"

"We aren't the only people who see you. Anyone in Land of Lost could have passed the bug to you."

"I feel really bad. These bugs came from more than one person. Maybe it was a conspiracy?" she moaned as she pulled her blankets up to her chin.

"You didn't get a shot. It's your own fault," they chorused.

"I have a plan," she whispered. They all took out their hand sanitizers. "I'm going to develop a Board Code of Health Ethics." She signaled toward a stack of papers on a nearby table. "That questionnaire must be filled out by anyone who wants to sit on a volunteer board."

Joshua leafed through the pages. "This is fifteen pages long. And it asks questions that aren't any of your business. Haven't you ever heard of invasion of privacy?"

Al Truistini tried logic. "People know when they should avoid others, when they feel ill. People stay home when they think they're contagious."

Cash had been scanning the Ethics pages as Joshua finished. "What's this question? Do you spend more money on French fries then you do on vitamins?"

"I don't want to sit around with all those high cholesterol

junkies. They probably carry grease cooties."

"Grease cooties?"

"Who's going to review these forms and verify the information?" asked Coach Upright. Bella's angry eye pinned him against the wall. "Not me," he sputtered. "I don't want to know how many times my friends have been treated for athletes foot." He stood far away from her bed, but he stood firm.

"You all have to help me," she pleaded with her friends, putting on her Bella the little waif look, the look no one believed. "Who else will look after me? You're my friends, my colleagues, we're almost family." Cough. Cough.

"Next year, get a flu shot," they shouted.

Can't Tell Allies from Alloys

"Do any of you want to help me?" Bella Pelorizado asked the gang as they lounged on Main Street in the Land of Lost Board Members. Spring was knocking at the gray mist that always hangs over the city.

"Do what?" asked Cash Now, CPA to nonprofits.

"I'm doing some consulting for a new nonprofit in town. Maybe you've heard of them – The Environmental Antiestablishment."

"What do they do?" asked Coach Amos Alonzo Upright, community activist.

"I'm not sure," replied Bella. "They seem to be against stuff."

"Such as?" wondered Joshua Biggly Huge, community philanthropist.

"Their mission statement is, "Refuse to reuse." And their vision statement says, "Say no to using anything twice.""

"Why have they called you?" asked Cash.

"They need fundraising help. So anyone interested?" They all looked into their mocha latte slushies. But Bella was clever. She nonchalantly commented, "What an interesting car." Coach looked up. The others knew better. "Ah, Coach, thanks for volunteering." Bella had him on his feet and marching off before he could run the other way.

Approaching the office of the Environmental Antiestablishment, Bella and Coach had to kick aside junk. Not just junk, but JUNK. Piles of aluminum cans, yards of tangled wire, brass fittings that looked like sculpture

Charity in Motions

mistakes, but were probably something that had once functioned something, piles of newspaper with small critters nesting on the sports pages.

Bella greeted the gentleman at the reception desk. "I'm Bella Pelorizado, the renowned nonprofit consultant. I've been asked to help your agency with some organizational issues." Coach stood in the background, ready to run.

"Our executive director is out back cleaning a spot for you to sit." He led them through some doors into a large warehouse filled with more JUNK.

"Basel, that consultant is here. She brought some guy to help." As if by magic Basel rose from the debris. Metal clattered all around him. Old brass valves rolled across the floor. Stacked newspapers slid at his feet.

"I'm Basel," the man said as the din died down. "I look forward to learning as much as I can from you. Our agency is new and we need help organizing and focusing on our mission."

"Where do you want to start?" asked Bella

"We need money," said Basel.

"No, I mean where will we sit and work?" said Bella.

"Here." He kicked aside a box of copper wire.

"What work do you want to accomplish? Why would donors want to support you?" asked Bella.

"We're riding the reactionary wave of anti environmentalism," boasted Basel. "My donors will be people who want to put a stop to clean air and clean water and, ugh, recycling. If someone says it's good for the environment, we deny it. We are out to expose the high costs of cleaning up the planet. We want to debunk myths, delouse pesky tree huggers and deploy our minions to dispel rumors and facts."

"That's quite an agenda. Do you have the money, a budget, a large membership, in-depth donor recruiting strategies? You know the basics."

"Those are basics?" moaned Basel. "We don't even have money to pay for my cell phone yet."

"What about this stuff?" asked Coach. He threw his hand out to all the metal pieces littering the warehouse floor.

"That's our battle cry," said Basel. "We won't lift one finger to recycle."

"But this is all worth money," explained Coach. "You can get big money at the scrap metal yard if you recycle this brass, this aluminum, this copper wire."

"Recycle?" gasped Basel. "But our principles?"

"Income," said Bella. With that she and Coach helped Basel cart a few tons of metal to the scrap yard. The last time they saw him he was stuffing cash into his trousers, planning his media blitz against the environment.

"Do you think he'll see the irony?" asked Coach.

"Is that another alloy?"

Follow Your Money

"Get up," Bella Pelorizado, well-known nonprofit consultant, shouted at two men who were wrestling curbside at the Main Street coffee shop in the Land of Lost board members. "What's the meaning of this outrageous display of geriatric testosterone?" She turned an angry eye toward her other two friends who were watching the slow motion smackdown.

"Coach said something about the group he met last month," said Cash Now, CPA to nonprofits. "You know, those guys you two helped with their fundraising,"

"The environmental anti-establishment?" Bella was puzzled.

"It seems," offered Al Truistini, community benefactor, "that Coach isn't sympathetic to their cause."

Cash pulled at Bella's arm to get her attention. "You know Coach is a staunch recycler. That crowd you worked with wanted nothing to do with reusing and recycling."

"And Joshua supports anti-environmental advocacy," summed up Al. They watched as Joshua Biggly Huge, local philanthropist and small government advocate, ripped off the Coach Upright's Nike and started to tickle his foot.

"We have to stop this," declared Bella. Her two friends sidled toward the next block. "Stop right there," she said in a voice so threatening that even Coach Upright and Joshua Biggly Huge came to attention.

Four frightened men stood at the curb, well, Coach sat at the curb tying his shoe as Bella walked in front of them much like Patton probably walked before his troops. "I do not find this behavior acceptable." Their heads all bowed. "I do not expect to find community leaders acting like thugs." Their heads bowed lower. "I want an explanation." She stared at them. They caved.

"He started it," said Coach. Pointing to Joshua, he continued, "I told him about those crazy people we met last month and he had the gall to say he had given them a donation to support their environmental anti-establishment efforts."

Bella looked at Joshua. "I didn't start this he did. I merely stated that I found their mission in line with my political philosophy. He started calling me names, and when I said sticks and stones he dove across the table at me." Joshua swept his arm in the direction of the overturned table and scattered coffee cups.

"You dove across the table?" Bella asked Coach.

"Maybe I just walked around to his chair and pulled it out from under him."

"Then you picked it up and threw it at me," counter Joshua.

"I was trying to knock some sense into you," snarled Coach.

"This is enough. Now shake hands," ordered Bella. The two men stared at one another, but didn't move. "OK, maybe we're not ready to shake yet, but at least we can talk about this."

"Yeah, this is a great teachable moment." They all glared at Cash, hoping he would put a lid on his exuberant youth and optimism. The two wrestlers moved stiffly, stretching to unkink muscles as they settled into chairs. Al Truistini distributed mocha slushies.

"You all know that nonprofits have a right to define their mission and to attract donors who support it. Not everyone supports every cause. If the community doesn't support a mission, that agency will probably fade away, change or restate its purpose, or merge with a similar organization."

"I can't believe people support those nuts," said Coach.

"How many crazy causes have I seen you support over the years?" asked Joshua. "Remember that group that wanted to shave cats so they wouldn't get fur balls? What about that woman who came to town with the group called Happy Trails? You gave her money."

"I thought she was cute."

"But she wanted to make the LOLDOT paint yellow lines green because it was a nicer color." Al's eyes bugged out at the very idea.

"So what? She was cute."

"You didn't believe in her cause?" asked Cash.

Coach shrugged.

"Is this another teachable moment?" asked Cash, swiping Slushie foam from his lips.

Bella rolled her eyes. "Sometimes agencies are successful because they have a charismatic leader. It doesn't mean you shouldn't investigate the mission and understand how your donation will be used." Bella gave them all her steely-eyed look. "I hope we've all learned something today."

"I learned those guys are tougher than they look," said Cash.

"And I learned he's crazy."

"Who said that?"

Politics of Poverty

"Bella, what are you doing?" The gang of the Land of Lost board members found their guiding voice sitting in a shady corner of the Main Street coffee shop.

"I'm on my Kook," replied Bella Pelorizado, nonprofit consultant.

"Kook?" questioned the chorus.

"It's my bilingual e-book reader. It reads Kindle and Nook." Bella held it out for the guys to study.

"What are you reading?" asked Cash Now, CPA to nonprofits.

"I just down loaded a book called "The New Social Safety Net."

"You mean it talks about the way all levels of government are revamping social support programs to get control of spending and their budgets?" asked Joshua Biggly Huge, community philanthropist and smallest-government-possible activist.

"There you go again," moaned Coach Amos Alonzo Upright, community activist and staunch supporter of LOL's social safety nets. "You always want to harm people, cut the knots of the safety net and let everyone tumble into the poverty abyss."

"I care about people." Joshua stomped his polished, tasseled loafer. "I just want them to take more personal responsibility. Work harder, work several jobs. Reduce unnecessary living expenses."

"The poor don't have unnecessary expenses. Food and shelter are necessary."

"What about the flat screen TV, cable, cell phones?"

"What if those were items that were acquired before job

loss or debilitating illness caused financial troubles?

Al Truistini, community benefactor, cleared his throat. "I think we need to examine the poverty you fellows are talking about. Not everyone who we might define as poor take advantage of our social safety nets. Some folks find second jobs, or become creative in finding other ways to earn money. People also learn to manage limited funds. Families make decisions regarding priorities."

"My point," Al continued, "is that not one poverty solution fits all people and all situations."

"I thought that's why we had so much variety in social safety nets," said Cash. "Some people need child care, some people need retraining, some people need transportation."

Al nodded his head. "People are resourceful. They'll knit together what they need from friends and family and safety net services. They'll do what others have done – retrench, rework and resurrect."

"I think it's time for people to realize that there are no guarantees. Everyone is responsible for his own safety net. You didn't save, too bad. You don't have any marketable skills, too bad. It's up to you to solve your own problem. The rest of us got our own lives to look after," said Joshua. "We'll go back to those days when we all took care of ourselves."

"When did you ever have to take care of yourself?" challenged Coach. "You've never wanted for anything. Today we're seeing folks who never thought they would need a social safety net coming to all the LOL crisis nonprofits looking for help. Need has visited a whole new group."

"They'll just have to learn to survive," said Joshua as he buffed his loafer.

Cash and Al restrained Coach as he lunged at Joshua.

"You fellas seem to have a lot of anger," Bella said to Joshua and Coach. The two men blushed. "Besides you're both correct. My new book says there will be challenges to people not familiar with loss of income and with cutting living expenses. It also says that the new poor are finding new avenues for entrepreneurship and new solutions

"Like what?"

"B and E."

"B-N-E?"

"Breaking and entering," explained Bella.

"Wow," marveled Cash, "personal responsibility, initiative and a touch of risk. Now that's the definition of entrepreneurship."

Settling Differences

Bella Pelorizado rounded the corner onto Main Street in the Land of Lost Board Members. In the middle of the street a crowd had gathered, cheering and yelling. Muscling her way to the center of the mob, she stopped, stunned at the sight of her two friends rolling around in the potholed throughway.

"Stop this immediately," she demanded. Joshua Biggly-Huge and Coach Amos Alonzo Upright stumbled to their feet, sweating and puffing. "What kind of behavior is this? Two community leaders carrying on as though they were teenaged hooligans."

"Look again," pointed out Cash Now, CPA to nonprofits, "there's nothing teenage about them." The two huffing and puffing geriatric wrestlers glowered at him.

Bella turned on Cash with her blazing eyes. "You encouraged this?"

"I just wanted to see them finally settle their differences. You know they keep arguing about social issues and taxes and government and taxes and poor and rich and .."

"Blah, blah, blah," said Al Truistini, community benefactor. "It's the same old fight over and over. Neither one of them listens to the other and both of them think they have all the answers."

"Maybe we need to investigate what's happening at local agencies," suggested Bella. Their first stop was the LOL homeless shelter. "We are seeing more folks every day," reported the director. "Many nights we haven't space for all who knock at our doors."

"When you give away services for free, people come for the hand out," muttered Joshua.

"No one comes here just because they want to sleep in a bed with a thread bare blanket among strangers," replied the director.

Coach challenged Joshua Biggly, "You can't admit that people are in need."

"And you won't admit people can help themselves," countered Joshua.

Bella took them by the arm and marched them to the LOL health clinic. In the waiting room there were a number of people seeking treatment. "Many people had access to health care through their employer's insurance program. Losing jobs equals losing health care," said the director. "We receive a lot of support from our medical community because helping people in this non-profit keeps the community's costs down and our hospital from providing a service more expensively." The director then turned to Joshua and said, "Thank you, Mr. Biggly Huge, we always appreciate your generous support."

"You support this organization?" asked Coach.

"Yes. And I support the homeless shelter. I didn't say I don't believe in charity, I just don't think everyone asking for a handout is in real need."

"But that's so cynical. Why would anyone ask for help unless they are in need?"

"You're so naive," chided Joshua, "it's all about what's in it for me."

Bella led them to the LOL food pantry. The director welcomed them in as she explained, "Today we're distributing fresh fruit and vegetables from some local farms as well as canned goods from our weekly donations from local churches and clubs as part of our program to get food to senior citizens."

"How do you know people need this food?" demanded Joshua. "Some folks could be taking it to sell or just to save their money."

"We only require that each person be over sixty-five or not employed. Our food distribution is monitored by volunteers who do some screening to make certain we put our resources to the most needy." The gang watched as several LOL seniors gathered at the LOL food pantry.

"Mother!" cried Joshua. "What are you doing here?"

"It's free, sonny, and I'm old." The wiry octogenarian elbowed her way up to the distribution counter. "Besides I heard they're giving out bologna today."

"You win," said Coach. "There are folks just milking the system."

"Baloney." said Joshua as he hurried his mother toward home.

One More Ask

"Not another request for money from some touchy-feely nonprofit," muttered a man sprawled on a Main St. bench going through his mail. He was enjoying the usual gray day in the Land of Lost Board Members. "How can I give money to some do-gooder who's never had to face the realities of running a small business?' He crumpled up the letter and tossed it into a trash container. Then he followed that letter with several more, all unread, all crumpled.

"Excuse me." Bella Pelorizado, consultant to nonprofits, cleared her throat. "I think you should learn more about managing nonprofits before you dismiss them as not worth your attention and support." Those listening, the usual gang who knew Bella well, were impressed with her self control.

"Don't bother me, girlie. I've got real work to do." He waved another letter in her face. "I don't have time for this make believe stuff."

At that remark, all Bella's friends reached out and restrained her. But she shrugged them off, rounding on the small businessman. "How are nonprofits different?"

"Nonprofit – that says it all."

"I don't understand. By nonprofit, it only means that these groups operate under a different structure of state and federal tax and organizational implications."

"They never have to worry about making a payroll."

"If they have employees, they do. In addition they have to worry about managing funds for their specific mission," Bella explained. The man snarled at her. She, well, she tried to attack but Coach Upright held her back.

"Maybe I can help in this discussion," offered Cash Now, CPA to nonprofits. "Many things are similar within the operations of for-profits and nonprofits. Each of you has payroll taxes, workers comp and must, on a daily basis, operate within the financial realities of your bottom-line."

"But, if my bottom-line is in the red, I don't send out letters to people asking for money."

"You're correct. You sell more or regroup, maybe layoff workers. If you think about a nonprofit appeal letter, that's like selling something. A nonprofit has to have a great product to attract donors. You know, fill a community need. If the service isn't provided economically, or the community perceives the program is inefficient, it fails just like a mismanaged or disorganized business."

"Times are tough. I have to be ready to move. These guys," he crumpled another appeal letter, "just sit around bellyaching."

"I'll tell you who's bellyaching..." Someone put a croissant in Bella's mouth.

"You're partly correct," said Al Truistini, community benefactor. "As a small business owner, you have to respond to your market quickly. That's an advantage you have. A nonprofit is usually governed by a board of directors made up of people in the community, people like you who understand budgets and making payroll. All those people must work together before a decision is reached."

"But while a nonprofit might be hampered by a longer decision making process, it has an advantage that a small business hasn't," said Coach Upright.

"Yeah, no fear of going under."

"That's not true. A nonprofit can fail financially. It may dissolve, or merge with another group or reorganize. It has the advantage of good thinkers on its board of directors working together with a defined mission and some long-term objectives. The board has usually engaged in strategic planning to some degree."

"Save me from that fluffy duffy stuff. I know my industry. I know my clients. I don't need that blah blah planning."

"You do know them and you can act quickly. But a little thought to future needs and products might make you able to act with a higher expectation of success," said Cash.

"Blah, blah, blah. You fellows need a real job."

"We have real jobs," said Joshua Biggly-Huge. "Some of us find that being a small businessman also means being a responsible community leader. Small businessmen are an asset to the nonprofit community for what they can offer in terms of financial guidance and support. That's why they are so valuable on a nonprofit board.

Coach added, "Then there are small minded small businessmen who never volunteer in the nonprofit community, but always criticize."

"Which are you?"

Post Bella Years

In late 2011 a new editor came to the Hendersonville Times-News. She called me in for a chat and told me that I could no longer write allegory. Who knew I was writing allegory! I was having fun. Well, I thought, what about the First Amendment. She replied, what about the ink?

So I canvassed my friends. Should I give up my nonprofit voice? Should I knuckle under?

The more reasoned of my friends suggested that any nonprofit voice was a plus. I should consider following the editor's demand? Suggestion? Whatever. I continued to write and continued to find information to share.

I was shocked when several of my friends commented on the new format by telling me that they could finally understand what I was saying! Who knew that the editor knew what she was talking about?

Local Funders

At a recent Community Foundation of Henderson County luncheon, my friend, Ron Partin, led the invocation and asked that we, "Lift up our neighbors through philanthropy." A charitable foundation provides a donor many opportunities to serve one's community. Philanthropy and foundations go hand in hand. But what is a foundation?

Nonprofits come in many shapes and sizes and offer many opportunities for each of us to support everything from the arts to zoo animals with tax-deductible gifts of cash, property, stock, insurance policies, donations to thrift stores and many other creative options. A charitable foundation is a legal category of a nonprofit organization that either donates funds and support to other organizations, or provides the source of funding for its own charitable purposes. Many times an institution receives land or stock or other donations instead of money. Having a foundation organized to accept such donations allows the institution the opportunity to carry out its mission and direct its foundation to manage the philanthropy.

In our community there are five hard working, successful foundations that follow the above definition. They offer donors opportunities to give funds for capital programs to support new facilities; create scholarship opportunities to encourage students; provide management for endowed funds that allow donor money to be distributed long after the donor's death. A sign of a successful, thoughtful foundation is one that matches a donor's interest with institutional or community needs.

The Community Foundation of Henderson County began in 1983 because of the vision of a small group of community leaders. The concept was to create a vehicle for citizens to give back to the community and to keep charitable gifts close to home. From the beginning this foundation has offered citizens opportunities for philanthropy in a manner consistent with a donor's personal goals for charitable giving – how to serve the community through their generosity.

In Henderson County there are two foundations, Pardee Hospital Foundation and Park Ridge Health Foundation dedicated solely to supporting their respective hospital/healthcare systems. Both organizations work with their hospitals to make certain that foundation fundraising goals are consistent with the goals of the institution they support. Many donors to these institutions have received care from the related hospital, or have a personal commitment to the long-term success of the healthcare facility and its programs.

There are also two foundations that focus specifically on education: Blue Ridge Community College Educational Foundation and the Henderson County Education Foundation. At the BRCC Educational Foundation funds are used for scholarships, equipment purchases, training and in other ways to help fill the gap created by state funding cuts, always in a manner designed to help BRCC reach its institutional goals.

The Henderson County Education Foundation distributes their funds in a manner that enriches the education of students, teachers, and the community. Foundation programs support student needs, provide creative teaching grants, support worthwhile projects that cannot be funded through school budgets, and support the Bullington Center and Historic Johnson Farm.

The above foundations in our community deserve a closer look by any donor seeking professional, meaningful advice on personal philanthropic goals. There are other foundations in Henderson County. They may have been created to support an individual non-profit. There are also private foundations, usually created by a family or corporation, to manage their charitable giving.

All these opportunities for philanthropy exist so that people may give because they feel a desire to do good in our community; because they want to make a difference; because they want to lift up their neighbors.

Small Nonprofit Business

In the world of fundraising one often hears from those solicited certain comments that suggest a nonprofit seeking funds isn't in touch with reality. The first reality challenge is to ask whether these nonprofits know how tough times are. The second reality challenge usually involves the phrase, "Never had to make a payroll." This is one of the most common criticisms of a nonprofit – they've never had to make a payroll. Wanna bet? Not only does a nonprofit have to make a payroll, they have to do it while also making certain they have enough money to provide a service that is far more realistic than any donor faces on a daily basis. Not many people, those concerned with making payroll, face down abusive husbands, go head to head in court with child molesters, or, in addition to providing jobs in the community, provide food clothing or shelter to those in need.

Of course, when a potential donor doesn't understand the impact on the community provided by a nonprofit agency, that donor is apt to make some silly assumptions. A nonprofit must follow most of the same laws and policies that a business does. Many operational policies are similar for a business and a nonprofit. Each entity pays payroll taxes, workers comp, and must on a daily basis, operate within the financial realities of their bottom-line.

When a business is at risk of operating in the red, the company takes defensive measures, laying off workers and becoming more aggressive in marketing. Many small business owners will even reduce their own salary to keep staff or to stay operational until times improve. That's similar to what a nonprofit will do.

During tough times another strategy found in the for-profit world might be merger, or streamlining services. Again that's something possible in the nonprofit environment. Two local agencies serving a similar population may join together to eliminate redundant operational and administrative costs. Or an agency may reexamine its mission and refocus on basic services, eliminating some programs that do not serve great numbers or do not serve the most at risk of their clients. In tough times, services are pared down and the clients face stiff scrutiny to demonstrate a critical need for service.

An advantage of a for-profit operation is its flexibility. A local manufacturing company, with one owner, can respond quickly to market fluctuations. A nonprofit, usually governed by a board of directors, must be more deliberative. The best part of that deliberation is that a nonprofit board is usually made up of community business leaders – people who are familiar with making payroll and responding to economic fluctuations.

One of the strengths of a nonprofit is long range planning. Although many board members joke about the falderal associated with planning, the exercise helps the board, different people with different opinions and ideas who volunteer to serve during both boom and bust economic times, work out the long-term future of the organization. A plan shouldn't be complex or restrictive, but it should protect the mission of the organization and help the community leaders who join the board in later years understand the vision, be able to use the plan as a guide in reorganizing under difficult times or help a board find its way to new thinking while holding the agency mission up as a rallying point.

Finally both a small business and a local nonprofit

should be valued for what they are – necessary pieces of any community's economic engine. And luckily for a businessperson, when a crisis strikes an employee, it's good to have the community services provided by the local nonprofits. When a nonprofit opens its doors and keeps working in the community, everyone wins. But the nonprofit gains the most when community business leaders join a nonprofit board. Community business leaders are an asset to the nonprofit community for what they can offer in terms of financial guidance and support. Making payroll in a nonprofit is a team effort – donors, staff and board members – all community members.

Pet People

There are over 200 registered nonprofits in our community that exist to support specific concerns or interests. One group of agencies providing a service and sharing a common interest includes those local organizations that work for the protection of animals.

In our community the Blue Ridge Humane Society has been operating for 68 years. Today the Humane Society has joined with Community Partnership for Pets, founded in 2005, and the Henderson County Animal Services and together they provide a model for local public-private partnerships working for a common good.

At a recent gathering, representatives of these three groups talked about the way they work together. I know many of you are skeptics about nonprofit service and about government interventions, so I went into this meeting looking for the villains.

Brad Rayfield, Director of the Henderson County Animal Services Center, opened the discussion talking about how the county commissioners encourage his department to work with groups in the community. As a result the Humane Society helps with adoptions, the Community Partnership for Pets works with the county on spay and neuter programs as well as rabies clinics. There are also some smaller nonprofits that help pet owners with fees and work on animal issues. In addition to this cooperation all those present praised the Sheriff's staff for the thoughtful and professional enforcement of the county's animal control ordinance. Hmm – no villains yet!

As a long time organization in the community the Blue Ridge Humane Society, represented by Dorsa McGuire, has worked for years to find adoptive homes for animals, and raise concerns about euthanasia. As part of the working relationship between the county and the Humane Society, and as a service for county taxpayers, the humane society accepts large rescue animals taken in or dropped off at the county shelter. Did you ever wonder what the county shelter does with a horse? The county shelter calls its friends at the Humane Society. The animal is boarded at the Humane Society property, at no taxpayer cost.

In its six-year existence in Henderson County the Community Partnership for Pets has evolved into a pet owner support organization. Its founder, Mary Cervini, talked about raising funds and creating opportunities for low cost spay and neutering for pets in our community. Helping families stop the stream of unwanted litters and working on several rabies clinics per year is part of the annual community service of this organization.

So what about the veterinarians in town, do they help out? A big YES from the animal advocates. The local vets in Henderson County work at rabies clinics, provide advisory support as members of the medical advisory committee for the Humane Society; and can be counted on to accept Community Partnership for Pets' vouchers, or vouchers from some other local groups to pay for spay and neuter services. In addition, many local vets are willing to negotiate fees with the local animal advocates to help a rescue animal become an adoptable pet.

Brad summed up their working arrangement. He says each group is still working on their role in animal issues, but with the Humane Society working on adoptability and with the Partnership staying focused on spay and neuter, the county can work on animal issues and public safety as well as community outreach. Brad concluded by saying, "How we work together and become more effective, both staff and volunteers, is still evolving, but very encouraging for all of us."

Check out the websites for more detailed information about each of these organizations:

Henderson County Animals Services, www.hendersoncountync.org/animals; Blue Ridge Humane Society, www.blueridgehumane.org; Community Partnership for Pets, www.CommunityPartnershipForPets.org.

So there you have it. A great model for government and citizens working together in a cooperative manner, leveraging each others' resources and strengths to reach common goals for the entire community. Hmm – no villains at all.

Advocacy

In this newspaper we often see the ad for United Way with the words: Give. Advocate. Volunteer. We all know what give and volunteer mean. But what does advocate have to do with a nonprofit?

In the human service nonprofit world, one doesn't stop homelessness, hunger or the many other community service needs without also advocating – speaking out. But speaking out to whom? First, speak out to friends, let them know what is important to you, what community need is your priority and gets your money and your volunteer time.

Next, speak out in public forums. Encourage your church congregation or your civic club to support your cause. Request that a representative from a specific agency visit with your group to explain the need and outline the work being done.

Finally, get the attention of policy makers – local, state and federal government representatives. Hunger or homelessness won't disappear in our community if local decision makers act in a manner contrary to those interests.

Sounds pretty simple – but it's not easy. A nonprofit must walk a fine line that is nonpartisan, never speaking for or against a candidate, but always staying focused on the issue. Point out to policy makers and to interested citizens that a policy decision may inadvertently have negative impact on many who are the least fortunate in our community, or our state. Prepare facts for elected official so that they make decisions based on all information pertinent to the issue.

There are several ways to advocate – soft advocacy – keeping an eye on the issues, informing those who make decisions and inspiring those who vote. Overt advocacy – speaking out as a designated board member, raising money for a cause. Then there's rabble advocacy – burning leaders in effigy, throwing dirt and stones – you know, asking to be pepper sprayed.

Nonprofits in our community use soft and overt advocacy. With soft advocacy, they educate and inform people in the community. They bring community members together for quiet discussions to help everyone understand the need, and help local leaders understand that we are all interconnected and that one segment of our community can't advance without bringing the other segments along.

Local agencies also use overt advocacy throughout the year with events that draw attention to a cause or issue. A good example is the Mainstay event, "Walk a Mile in Her Shoes," where men in our community put their names and faces out front – taking a stand against domestic violence. That's advocacy – adding one's name, one's voice – speaking out.

One of the biggest challenges of a nonprofit revolves around having an advocacy policy. Nothing complex, but something that designates a spokesperson and allows all advocacy to be approved by the board of directors.

Because nonprofits have boards made up of local community leaders and volunteers it is important that the advocacy voice echo the board leadership. In fact that is one of the board's biggest roles – speaking out. Put a familiar face and a familiar voice to a community need. Stand ready, as the board leaders, to educate the community, spread the word about need and speak to policy changes that will serve one segment of our community and ultimately help us all.

Speaking out takes courage. Ugliness doesn't disappear because we choose not to look it in the eye.

In this Christmas season, remember that advocacy begins and ends with giving – giving time, giving money and giving your voice for those in need.

Advocacy Part 2

Last month this column highlighted a discussion about the methods volunteers use to work for issues in our community. Volunteer. Donate. Advocate. Advocacy has many facets – speaking out to friends, being present to show support, and taking your voice to decision makers. That last option means *lobbying*, a tried and true method for moving an agenda forward.

This is not a discussion about professional lobbyists. This is a discussion about volunteers who want to affect change that will impact a specific issue. Nonprofits, though not working for particular candidates, have every right to lobby in support of issues. For example, if volunteers want more funding for certain services, they prepare their case and present it. That's community lobbying.

Lobbying for a cause will also involve interacting with local elected officials. We have just seen an example with the proposal of a soccer complex north of Flat Rock. Both sides of the issue prepared presentations that included factual assessments of the need; emotional assessment of impact on those involved; and hypothetical descriptions of outcomes depending on the future use of the piece of property. Lobbying!

Another term related to this discussion is Special Interests! Special interests define the way we slice and dice ourselves into more and more component parts and then find ourselves opposing ourselves on many issues. The best examples are those of us who demand more from education but demand that we pay less in tax money, resulting in less money to raise the level of education. There we are – sliced and diced to illiteracy!

Lobbying happens everyday, close to home and far away. Often the lobbyist is the best-prepared person in the discussion. He or she knows the facts, has plotted an outcome to serve a particular interest, and developed a solution to a problem or a new path.

The challenge for those lobbied is to make sense of the proposals, because the first rule every lobbyist knows – there's always another side. So anyone being lobbied should also be aware that the solution is going to be more complex than the lobbyist would have one believe.

In many cases, a voice speaking out on an issue by lobbying, informs officials and interested citizens about need and about solutions. The risk of a lobbying effort is that it may distract from policy development and thoughtful decision-making. Political energy may be diverted from long term solutions to sidebar conversations that take time and claim attention.

This essay seems to be getting political, but let's face it, lobbying drives many political decisions, some of which may not always be best for the common good. The solution for many committed volunteers is to develop a political agenda. Understand what you want as a volunteer and as a citizen and then determine what solutions are relevant, and then work to affect change that is important and meaningful in the long term for the community.

Remember change is scary. Also remember – don't let the opposing lobbying forces define you or your cause. Finally, remember that a lobbyist, more than any one else, is always vigilant. A committed volunteer lobbyist needs staying power to become a part of a solution.

Charity by the Drink

Recently we've all been excited about our newest industry — Sierra-Nevada Brewery. In much of the press local officials have been quoted as saying that the new business will change our local culture. In a recent item from the Chico newspaper, the reporter referring to a review of our own Times-News coverage says, "... the mention of Hendersonville's first brewery, that opened in 2011 as a private club because of state law at the time. In nine months, it had 5,000 members. You can't say North Carolinians don't like their beer." Since local government has taken steps to place "Liquor by the Drink" and related issues on the May Primary ballot, I hope that encouraging beer sales isn't the only cultural change we will see.

Looking at the Sierra-Nevada website and reading items from the Chico, California newspaper, we may get a hint of other cultural changes. Local officials have recruited an industry that takes pride in its presence and in its relationship to its local community.

To some degree, that sort of presence and community commitment is part of the business culture of most of our successful employers, large and small. From the perspective of the nonprofit community, success and continued services are available because local businesses respond to critical need. They are the backbone of the United Way campaign. They are the sponsors of local newsletters, local capital campaigns, and local special event fundraisers.

Sierra Nevada will be coming to a community where the business culture is one of commitment and local support. However, with the infusion of a new community partner, and as a sign that the local economy is on the upturn, our local business community may be encouraged to invest even more in the nonprofit sector.

Many of our local businesses try to share their donations with as many worthy groups as their budget allows. The new guys in town seem to be interested in environmental issues. Time and again in news reporting the new investors spoke about our natural beauty, clean water, and many other comments that spoke to a respect for and interest in preserving the essence of western North Carolina, our quality of life. Sometimes it takes an outsider to draw attention to what we may take for granted – sort of like helping us see the forest and the trees.

It will be exciting to watch our community culture and business interests expand to more intensely draw attention to environmental issues. Local government will now have a visible community partner to support them and local nonprofits in steep slope ordinances, strengthening local soil erosion and flood plain ordinances, managing water quality issues along French Broad tributaries above the Mills River drinking water intake and, finally, preserving viewscapes. After all, a local business partner who invests in land because the water is great, the views are knockouts and the quality of life is the best will certainly find local environmental nonprofits, and local governments ready to work together to preserve what is our best foot forward – our natural environmental quality.

It will take two years to build the brewery. That's our environmental window of opportunity to shore up and refine our local commitment to environmental issues, from run-off to billboards. After all, we've seen what unrestricted development and clear cutting can do to the land around us. When we owe a portion of our prosperity to our trees, mountains and water we should be working to protect what has value to us.

Local governments and the nonprofit environmental community should have a beer and discuss how we preserve our assets.

You've Got Mail

I love technology! Working through my computer, answering e-mail, verifying information online, these are all things that make life less complicated for me. You want to ask me a question, or set a date, e-mail me. I hate using the phone for this sort of non-conversation. On the other hand, I offer you Renee's rule for electronic media: nothing is secret and nothing is real.

Electronic exchange among nonprofit board members as a tool in efficient management is a swift, clear, timesaving option. It is of some importance to understand since the state legislature action of 2007. Session Law 2008-37 states, since 2008, that nonprofit corporations are allowed certain votes by electronic transmission. This legislation expanded the way nonprofit boards may take action. Many local boards that use e-voting reserve the actions for a quick response to noncontroversial items, such as the acceptance of a new board member to fill out an unexpired term. Or they use it as my friend, Elisha Freeman, executive director of the Children and Family Resources Center says, "Our board has used e-mail for quickly needed decisions...when a quick turn-around decision had to be made." In all cases, before taking action electronically, especially e-voting, the agency bylaws must be amended to allow for such activity. In addition, the bylaws should outline a method for reporting the action in the official board minutes. For example, if a board votes electronically to accept a new member, the agenda of the next official meeting should reflect as an item of information, the outcome of the vote and be recorded in the minutes of that meeting.

When I asked if it were useful, Elisha replied,

"Convenient." Her board chairman, Jaime Laughter states, "With board members all over the county in professions that do not readily allow us to convene at a moment's notice it (e-voting) allows us to support Elisha with informed and expedited direction."

There are many other ways local nonprofit boards take advantage of electronic communication options. Most local boards send out electronic information for each regular meeting. Often called the board packet, this information usually includes agenda, minutes, financial reports and any other reports related to agenda action items.

It is possible for board members to review items, submit questions prior to a meeting and have members and staff prepared for meaningful discussion. Again Jaime says, "We live in a world where things can change at a moment's notice and being able to work collectively on e-mail to obtain information, process it and make a decision makes us more efficient as a organization and allows us to leverage opportunities or react to challenges as they present themselves instead of days or weeks later."

One of the most interesting options I have seen recently was a board that receives a flash drive instead of a three ring binder as a board manual. This drive includes bylaws, policies, and other information usually handed to new board members but with the option that as changes occur in any of the documents, a board member need only delete the old document and accept the new via e-mail or other method, including taking the drive into the agency office for an upgrade!

The biggest advantage to all of these methods is saving paper, ink and postage while sharing information in a timely manner. On the other hand, I recently heard a marketing professional comment, "People are receiving so much e-mail, that to get someone's attention folks are going back to sending a letter." To which I say, electronic board communications only works if, 1) all boards members have access to the Internet and have an e-mail address, and 2) all board members read their e-mail at least once a day!

Technology and Nonprofits

Almost daily, technology changes the way we do our work and even speak – twitter isn't just for the birds and a cloud is a place, sort of like heaven and hell, without dimensions, but where we meet our friends. So it's only good business for our local nonprofits to adapt to the technologies that help them serve their mission and goals.

Most of our local nonprofit agencies take advantage of the Internet and sharing information through e-mail. Agencies are also moving into other social networking. Although, how can it be social when there's nobody in the room but you and your computer? Sorry, that's probably my age piping up.

Recently I asked my friends at some local agencies to explain their social networking philosophy. My friend, Elisha Freeman, at the Children and Family Resource Center says, "We use Facebook, Twitter and electronic e-mail blasts to communicate with the public at-large....We announce special events, share program/staff news, etc. We use these media to keep the Center on the public's mind and to keep the community informed."

I asked the same question at Pisgah Legal. Katie Russell Miller, Development and Communications Manager, said, "We created our Facebook page several years ago, but recently started posting more regularly. We post information about events, success stories, volunteers, etc."

Years ago I attended a fundraising training at which we were all advised to take advantage of the internet as a mechanism to reach donors. We were warned that old donors might die before they catch on to technology, but finding one's place in cyberspace should be the goal of every agency – to wait there for the young tech savvy to grow into donors. I left the workshop feeling the grim cyber reaper breathing down my neck.

So I had to ask – does e-money work for agencies? Elisha said, "Donors have the ability to make a donation via PayPal from our website. We are exploring more ways to allow donors to give, including: onsite credit card machine, multiple laptop sites for online donations, cellphone, text donations, monthly automatic deductions."

Katie replied, "We accept donations on our website through Network for Good. This is a well-used feature, particularly during our end-of-year campaign. We also use this feature for online ticket purchases to events."

And purchasing tickets is really easy! Last week I attended "Are you Smarter than a Fifth Grader," sponsored by the Blue Ridge Community Health Center. I was able to purchase my tickets at their website; print my receipt and take that to the event as my admission ticket. Hmm. Maybe I'm not as old as I thought.

The name of the game these days is getting a donor's attention as well as getting financial support. If donors are more and more available online through various social networking locations and feel comfortable using options such as PayPal (the same method many use to shop online), successful fundraisers have to maintain a presence there.

However, there is one very big challenge – feeding the beast. It takes time and attention from someone in an agency to stay tuned in and networked – someone who's job is to develop and post items on Facebook, to Twitter clients, volunteers and donors about up to the minute breaking news. If agency volunteers prefer e-mail to a phone call, or if an electronic newsletter reaches more supporters for much less money than the cost of printing and postage, it may be time to adapt to social media. Keeping track of the results – funds raised, friends made, supporters informed – will help a board determine if the investment in staff time is worth the return.

Local Hunger

A few Sunday mornings ago I heard Fareed Zakaria mention that over fifty years ago President Truman used television to broadcast from the White House to talk about hunger in war torn Europe. He pledged American surpluses to feed the hungry during those recovery years. As it happens my friends at church that same Sunday were raising money for Feed the Children Coalition, a program that provides a Friday evening meal to youngsters in our community. Hmmm. Fifty years later and we're still feeding the hungry, but this time on our own doorstep.

So who's hungry now? Locally schools feed children free breakfast and lunch depending on a demonstration of financial need. The American Red Cross gives funds to disaster victims to among other things, provide food as they try to sort out the impact of a calamity on their family. Council on Aging provides Meals on Wheels to people who are home bound but in need of adequate nourishment. Some of those clients may have the ability to pay for food, but are unable to leave their home to shop. We feed people in our community for several different reasons and under a variety of programs.

What's heartening about hunger in Henderson County is the cooperation among agencies and churches to address the need. I sat down with Pat Fisher and Dick Ranges, members of the Hunger Coalition Board to learn about hunger in our county. Members of twelve different congregations sit on the executive board of the Hunger Coalition while many congregations, large and small, will participate in the major Hunger Walk fundraiser in September.

Pat Fisher swears that the Hunger Coalition executive

Charity in Motions

board is the best group of hard working committed people anywhere in town. Without paid staff they will, as they have done since 1983 or so, manage an event in September that touches many people – volunteers who walk, local merchants who provide food and drink for walk participants and especially touch the lives of those who are hungry.

But we're back to my question. Who's hungry? Dick and Pat offered me information about the agencies who feed those in need. IAM served over 9,458 clients last year, Fishes and Loaves Pantry at Etowah United Methodist had 8,803 client contacts last year, while year to date the Calvary Episcopal Food Pantry in Fletcher has had 7,289 client contacts. The Council on Aging reports that they serve about 210 meals daily and the Hendersonville Rescue mission serves an average of over 4200 meals per month. Manna, the regional distributor of bulk food, sent 786,540 pounds of food to Henderson County, distributed through various agencies and church ministries.

In addition to the above providers, many local nonprofit agencies such as Red Cross, The Salvation Army, Mainstay, WCCA, The Storehouse, and the Blue Ridge Community Health Center have food components as part of client services. That doesn't even highlight all of the local churches operating food pantries and other services through efforts of dedicated congregations.

In recent years, there has also been a focus on children's food needs after school. A group of local residents as Feed the Kids Coalition work through several churches in Henderson County as teams to prepare meals for children at the Boys and Girls Club on Friday evening. Manna also packs backpacks of weekend food and snacks for over 700 youngsters at sixteen Henderson County schools.

A large part of non-profit support and success comes from volunteer workers. I marvel at the ways we enhance our lives in this community by giving our time and talent for programs that are worthwhile and from which we as volunteers gain such inspiration and fulfillment.

One group of volunteers who represent commitment to program and clients are the people who work for the hungry. Whether its collecting food, working in food pantries, cooking for and serving meals to those in need, or as many do, raise money to help.

But donors want assurance that money is well spent and that the needs are real. Are we helping make a difference? Pat Fisher reassured me when she said, "You won't believe how all the agencies cooperate and work together in Henderson County." The need is not just hunger. It's clothing, shelter, health – crisis needs. Next month, come back and read about crisis management in our community. How a Walk for Hunger can lead to a bag of groceries or a hot meal which leads to help for a family. And it all begins when great volunteers take the first step.

Hunger Part II

Looking into the issue of hunger in our community has led me to some interesting people. After visiting with Pat Fisher and Dick Ranges of the Hunger Coalition, I dropped in to visit David Cook at IAM. This agency receives support from the Hunger Coalition through funds collected on the annual Hunger Walk.

At the beginning of our conversation David confirmed what Pat Fisher had said, "This community works together." David explained the Emergency/Caring Coalition that brings together service providers in our community to help agencies share resources and help clients through difficult times.

Local agencies meet monthly to share information and collaborate on services. In recent years this partnership has been chaired by Caron McKay, Director of Services for the Council on Aging. David Cook says all participants are grateful to Karen Smith, executive director of the Council on Aging for encouraging her staff's leadership.

The coalition works to leverage community resources, help those in crisis and deal with clients who seem to be in chronic need of service in our local support system. David explained that a client with chronic needs goes beyond the services of one agency. With the client's permission, the agencies share data and help a family move beyond their crisis. The Emergency/Caring group can discuss a client's situation and work with the clients to encourage them to work toward solutions for themselves. Once the agencies receive consent and begin discussing a client, coalition members are never surprised to learn that most clients are already dealing with multiple agencies.

Caron McKay says, "I'm very proud of this coalition. I'm surprised this isn't being done in more communities."

When I met with Caron, she invited Donna Lovelace from the Department of Social Services, Adult Protective Services, to join in the discussion. This clearly made the point everyone had already made – we all work together. Donna said, "I learn so much about what services are available from all the agencies. I learn where to send clients with certain needs. In addition, I bring to the meeting current information on programs and funding availability from the Department of Social Services. Everyone at the table learns what DSS has to offer."

Caron described a meeting agenda for the once a month meeting. The first item for discussion is to review the cases of clients who have signed a waiver so that information can be shared. Then each agency member present is given an opportunity to speak about new programs and share other information.

Donna and Caron have been active participants in the coalition for many years, with Caron chairing it for seven years. Caron says, "The meetings allow agency members, both government and nonprofits, to look beyond our own services and help us see what other agencies do and help us find more ways to serve our own clients."

"To start with, our coalition," said Donna, "helps each agency with the cost of staffing by reducing demand for duplicate services. By working together through the case management program, we can determine which agency is best suited to take the lead in serving a client."

Finally, Caron points out that the coalition is not a private club. Any service group dealing in human service issues is welcome to join the group. The current membership includes local nonprofits, local churches and local government and public schools. It's a great place to learn about services that will help each client and it's a great place to share ideas and effectively manage the resources available in our community.

But this isn't all. In July come back to learn about the way technology helps community services work together.

Hunger Part III

Learning that IAM served over 9,458 clients last year, Fishes and Loaves Pantry at Etowah United Methodist had 8,803 client contacts last year, while year to date the Calvary Episcopal Food Pantry in Fletcher has had 7,289 client contacts, that the Council on Aging serves about 210 meals daily and the Hendersonville Rescue Mission serves an average of over 4200 meals per month and that Manna, the regional distributor of bulk food, sent 786,540 pounds of food to Henderson County, distributed through various agencies and church ministries has had me investigating local hunger services for several months.

How can so many of us need food? What are we doing about it? To make our community work better, work together and spread resources further, many local groups have come together in a service coalition. This cooperation and collaboration has been going on a long time. Members of the Emergency/Caring Coalition work together, stretch their resources in day-to-day combat with community needs. All of the groups – nonprofits, local government, public schools and churches – represent local citizens working on a solution. And these days technology adds a new level of resource management and client support.

After meeting with representatives of the Hunger Coalition, Patricia Fisher and Dick Ranges, and with folks who work together in the Emergency/Caring Coalition, especially Caron McKay, the chair, David Cook from IAM and Donna Lovelace from DSS, I moved on to talk with Ruth Birge and David Jacklin of United Way.

Our topic was agency cooperation and information management. Last year the Community Foundation underwrote participation for interested agencies in software called Charity Tracker (www.charitytracker.com). This added another dimension to community agency cooperation, allowing information to be shared instantly – no more phone calls, or waiting until the next meeting. Everyone knows when everyone else knows, what everyone else knows, and how everyone proposes to deal with the knowledge.

This year United Way is underwriting Charity Tracker licenses for some additional community members, such as churches. As the agencies learn to use the software and as more community information is entered, the folks at United Way see participation in this web-based software as a tool to help pinpoint need. Ruth highlights the system, "Clients get what they need through electronic referrals to the team. It eliminates redundant paperwork for the client and adds efficiencies to the service."

David pointed out that this type of connectivity will also be helpful in a local natural disaster because the information is web-based. He gave an example, "In the event of some emergency this evening, such as a fire or flood, an agency worker can enter client information on the network at the site so that first thing in the morning other agencies are alerted and ready to support the victims."

Ruth says, "I think this will be helpful for our faith-based community. They have worked hard to make their congregations aware of hunger as a community need. Being a part of Charity Tracker will make them aware of other needs and help them, as well as other groups, manage their charity dollars, stretching them further."

But who's still hungry? "Hunger in our community continues to make news. Henderson County's rate stands at 15.1%. That's more than 16,000 of our residents who struggle with hunger," said Ruth.

That doesn't sound like progress to me. "Yes it is," argues

Ruth. "Donors are aware and being generous. The letter carriers collected 36,000 pounds of food last month (May) in Henderson County. And look at the folks cooking meals for kids. Our community is working hard."

Is it enough? What happens if federal and state tax dollars are reduced even further for these programs? What happens when donors think the problem is solved? Or trumped up? Or never existed because it's all a UN conspiracy? Or what happens when another need demands community wide attention?

That's where we are. Collaborative efforts to feed the hungry, and serve other needs, exist in our community because citizens on agency boards, elected officials and staff along with citizen donor/taxpayers, want it to work right, to work efficiently and to work for all of us and make us ready for the next collaborative solution, which is – effectively serving the homeless.

It's possible, as we've learned, to feed the hungry – it will be more challenging to the community, to each one of us, to shelter the homeless. But the agencies working together have a good blueprint for crafting solutions – solutions that need support from all of us.

Organizational Review Time

For many non-profits, July begins a new fiscal year and often a new organization year for board members. As the board gathers for its July meeting there may be new officers and some new board members. It's time to reassign committee responsibilities and review the board's role in the organization.

Some of the items to consider: make certain each board member understands the role he/she fills on the board; make certain each standing committee understands its purpose; make certain each board member understands that part of board service is to be an active donor to the agency.

I'm probably two or three months late in suggesting how the new board leadership should have prepared for this transition, but life happens and this is where we are. In fact, that's the first rule for all boards – life happens. A strong board can adjust to a personal emergency of one of its members. Although challenging, a strong board can reorganize if a member of the leadership, or an active committee member has to resign or take a leave of absence. Planning for life happening means that a board has some plan of succession, formal or informal – who steps in if the treasurer needs a hip replaced; what happens if the chair of the fundraising committee has to help with triplet grandchildren? In this town we've all been there!

If it didn't happen in May or June, all new board members need an orientation, or if it did happen in May or June, they need Part II of the orientation, an understanding

Charity in Motions

of the board organization structure and a discussion about assignments for each new member. If a new member was recruited for a specific role, such as the finance committee or to help with personnel policy, get the assignments in place and get the new members acquainted with the committee chairs.

Another consideration in Part II of the orientation is to help new board members understand their role in relating to the staff. A thoughtful personnel committee made up of board members and sometimes, other volunteers, should understand the current personnel policies and should bring recommendations to the board regarding any needed adjustments. On every board the personnel committee should function as a welcome and willing advisor to the executive director – in part to protect the board. Any actions, hiring and firing done by the executive director, may haunt the board unless all actions are done with knowledge of the personnel committee at least. Getting into HR issues is very tricky: understand the ED's role; understand the board's role, and understand the agency policies and labor laws that govern all actions.

A third area for review and support revolves around board training and governance. This is a standing committee that should also have the responsibilities for keeping a board informed on the services provided by the agency; current issues of board concern, such as legal responsibilities; fundraising issues; staying on task with or developing a strategic plan, short or long term; nominating strategies, that is keeping new member recruitment a year round function, not manic action in March and April.

Finally, a finance committee with the responsibility of working with auditors or reviewers should be in place to understand the monthly ebb and flow of funds through the organization. This is NOT a fundraising committee, but a committee who keeps the fiscal operation of the agency in its sights, and advises the board on any concerns; recommends changes in response to audit recommendations; keeps the agency financial policies up to date.

Over the next months we'll look at these and other board responsibilities in more detail so that the board functions at its best to keep the agency strong and to keep the mission as the driving force, not board malfunctions.

Board Responsibilities

Volunteering on a nonprofit board requires that members keep up with changes and challenges from outside and inside the organization. For example, a crisis through natural disaster, loss of funding, or a staffing crisis can be handled by a well organized and prepared board – that is a board where all members take responsibility for the work to be done, bring experience and energy to each meeting, and understand the expanse and limits of their role.

On the other hand, a board that is forced to stick ten fingers in a dike because of lack of experience or training prevents that board from moving toward any solution. In my opinion, there are three internal priorities for a good board: well-established culture for interaction with the executive director; well-defined board operations as formalized in the by-laws and policies; and, healthy finances – an engaged finance committee and fundraising committee.

Let's look at interactions with ED and staff as a topic today. Is it clear to board members and staff: Who's in charge? Who talks with whom? Who should the staff listen to? Who should speak to staff? Where do board members take concerns?

The ED rules in day to day operations. He or she sets the work schedule and takes responsibility for implementation of the personnel policy. The Board's role is to hire the ED, conduct an annual review of the ED job performance and adopt the personnel policies that guide the agency. Board members should be available to consult with the ED on issues. A board member should never have a quiet chat with a staffer then approach the ED about responding to those concerns.

The basic role of the board is to hire and evaluate the ED. All other staff members are supervised and hired by the ED. In a small community, friendships may grow between board members, staff and volunteers. It is always important to respect the management boundaries, no matter the existence of long-term friendships. Serving on a well-organized board, keeping the board culture businesslike and professional, helps everyone involved understand the boundaries of administration and management.

The board is responsible for the ED evaluation. Often an ED has had the job longer than some of the board members have been serving on the board. However, the board still has responsibilities and ED performance evaluation is an important one. In most cases, the executive committee, or another group designated by the chair, develops an evaluation instrument based on the ED's job description and agency goals. This instrument allows the board to look over the ED's current performance, compare work done with goals set at performance evaluation of the previous year, and allows comment from board members.

I have served on a board that contracted with an outside professional to interview board members and staff members on ED performance. It was an interesting exercise – everyone offered insight and observations to the third party. The ED's evaluation was developed from a variety of points of view. After the interviews with board and staff and an interview with the ED, the third party presented a confidential report shared with the executive committee and ED.

In the performance review I always think it's important to help the ED set personal goals for the coming year. In a small agency, as often happens, an ED works many hours with a tireless commitment to clients and mission. Make certain the performance interview includes encouragement to take time off. It is also important, as well as useful, for the agency to encourage the ED to participate in training classes that will help in areas such as finance, human resources, overall management training, or professional development. Each training helps enhance an ED's skills and helps an agency and board gain from a well-trained executive.

One last tool I have seen used in agencies is an exit interview. Even an employee leaving on friendly terms has something to say. If board members have a concern with employee turn over, think about using an outsider to interview departing employees. A board needs to know if turnover is related to dissatisfaction with agency management, job demands or low salary and/or lack of benefits.

And I can't stress confidentiality enough – what is discussed with an ED, what is said about the ED and what may be learned from exit interviews all should help the board grow a stronger agency – but none of the information learned and discussed should find its way out into the community. Nothing is as deadly to fundraising as a whiff of floundering or incompetence on the part of the board or ED.

Boring By-Laws

By the end of October a nonprofit board should be reviewing and examining a few procedures to insure good operation for the coming year. We're not talking about fundraising. That's a constant. But there are strength-building exercises that should be in place.

Review the By-laws. (I hope I didn't hear anyone groan or snicker!) Two or three board members can do this over coffee or wine some afternoon. Things to look for: when was the last time they were reviewed; do the by-laws reflect the way the board operates; are they written clearly; how long are they; are all the tasks defined in the by-laws being carried out; do they allow flexibility so any operational change does not mean a by-laws amendment?

If the by-laws have not been amended since 1970, there's a big problem. Laws and improved management philosophies effecting non-profits have changed considerably over the years and the by-laws should reflect external as well as internal changes.

When the committee reviews the by-laws, if they feel as though they're reading a fairy tale, it's time to, either organize the board along the lines defined in the by-laws, or redo the by-laws to pattern current operations. For example, do the by-laws say, "Meet every fourth Tuesday" and for the last three years the board has been meeting on the second Monday? Consider rewriting the meetings section to say, something like, "Meet monthly at least eight times per year."

Is there an attendance section which states something like, "Members who miss three consecutive meetings will be beheaded?" If no one is enforcing the attendance requirements, take a deep breath, talk to the executive committee, encourage them to get heads rolling. Then offer an amendment that allows members to take a leave of absence. Finally, accept a resignation. Don't encourage someone to stay on the board in name only so that the roster is filled. That only means that the faithful members get more work, and resign also.

It's clear that by-laws should be understandable so that you know when someone has missed a meeting quota, or how you can plan a coup. Renee's rule: if the agency budget is under $100,000, more than five pages is too many for by-laws. And if your thirteen-year-old grandchild can't read it through aloud and understand what is written, rewrite it!

When reviewing the by-laws, look for process – how is the board elected; term of service; term of office; what are the responsibilities for officers; what committees are named, and do they function? What the by-laws committee may find is that the by-laws are fine, but no one is working the outline!

For standing committees I think you need a finance committee and a nominating committee, someone following the money, and someone trolling the community for new blood and new leadership. After that standing committees should reflect the work that must be done year in and year out. There is the executive committee, with a large board of over five members this is the committee that can work quickly to steer through an emergency or crisis between meetings. The roles and term of the members of the executive committee, usually the officers, sometimes including a past president or other member, should be defined in the by-laws.

Board governance, board development, board education, are all, in my opinion, the nominating committee dressed up. That's because the nominating committee should be working year round, trolling for talent, training the new members, creating opportunities for board members to learn by encouraging members to attend conferences and trainings, or by providing such training at board meetings. Every board needs a quick review of parliamentary procedure, or training on fundraising, you know, making "The Ask."

The other committee that should be defined is fundraising or as it is sometimes called, development. Following the money is one task, getting it into the agency coffers is another very big and very unique task. After defining those standing committees, allow a section giving the president the authority to create ad hoc committees. These committees last for the time of the task, designing a volunteer appreciation dinner, 2 to 3 months. Building a new facility, 2 to 3 years.

Other things that may be in the by-laws are: purpose of the agency, maybe mission; removal of a director – for various reasons like absences or stealing or some other unacceptable activity; process to amend by-laws; board compensation – as in no one receives compensation for service. Each agency may have certain processes that should be etched in the semi-concrete of by-laws. For example, if the agency is part of a national organization, it may be necessary to reflect the relationship and define the level of autonomy for the local board. Finally, make certain that the by-laws have a notation at the end stating the date that the board accepted the amendments.

Remember keep the by-laws simple and relevant. Use board policy to direct day-to-day operations.

Following the Money
Part 1

The biggest challenge to any nonprofit board is money. I'm sorry to be telling you something you already know, but truth is truth. Managing the way the money flows into (donations, grants) and out of (salaries, services, rent, etc.,) an agency is a big part of the board's job. The degree of direct responsibility that falls to the board depends on the size of the agency.

A small agency with no paid staff operates with financial realities different than a large budget operation with professional staff managing funds moving through the agency. However, both need good financial policies.

If you currently serve on a nonprofit board that is a 501(c)(3), you should be familiar with the agency's financial policies. What? You don't know what I'm talking about? No one offered you a copy when you joined the board? Sounds like we have an agenda item for the next board meeting.

Financial policies should segregate responsibilities around finances. Someone should be designated to open mail, someone to prepare deposit slips. Every agency needs to designate at least two check signers with dollar limits for checks needing one or two signatures. The finance policies should reflect how money flows through an organization, who is involved at each point and outline the safety nets to protect funds and ensure best financial management practices.

In addition to basic fund management an agency must

have policies that deal with 21st century issues. Does the agency use online banking? Who knows the passwords? Who can enter into contracts? What about an agency credit card? Who can use it? What are the limits? Are there prohibitions for credit card use? For example, no mojitos on the agency card.

There should also be some guidance on dealing with petty cash and reimbursement to staff or board members, as well as a conflict of interest policy. Should a board member do business with the agency, if so under what conditions?

There should be a method outlined for reporting on financial status. A good rule is to have a treasurer's report and financial statement at every board meeting. The information is then entered into the minutes and the reports are filed as part of the official record.

The above questions are the basis to begin developing finance policies. They, as your bylaws, need not be complex. They do need to reflect the reality of the funds received and managed and reflect the number of people available to do the work.

Locally, most nonprofits have finance policies, and it may be time to review those policies. Times change, new things happen that should be included in a policy. For example, does your policy include reference to online banking? Is there a gift policy? Some gifts should never be accepted. Every agency has a story about a gift that turned out to be more challenging than it was worth. Set some guidelines in your policy.

And a stock policy. The gift of stock may be a great tax benefit to the donor, but if not managed in a timely fashion by the board, the gift may lose much of its value to the agency. So the policy should reflect who can authorize a sell of stock and how soon after receipt it should be executed.

Before we even discuss the need for an audit, take a little

time to Google "nonprofit finance policy" or visit www.ncnonprofits.org. This is a member organization to which many local nonprofits subscribe. As a member you have access to a variety of reports and studies on many nonprofit issues. While Googling I found more sites than there was time remaining in my life to visit, but I did visit www.nonprofitassistancefund.org. They had a lot of downloadable information, including sample policies. I also visited www.blueavocado.org, a site that also provides information to nonprofits. They had a good story about how some board members dealt with the arrest of the agency's ED and an embezzlement crisis (someone needed better financial policies!)

As you can see, managing the money means that a plan should exist to follow it. Once that is in place, it is time to establish methods to measure and report on an agency's financial health.

Audit. Is that an agency's only option? Come back next month.

Getting at the ITCH

With financial policies in place for tracking money through an agency, it's necessary for a nonprofit board to consider the pros and cons of an annual financial review and to determine just what type will work.

First of all, there is no discussion – yes, there must be an annual review of financial status. After all, the work needs to be done to file the 990 with the IRS. I hope I didn't hear anyone out there ask, "What 990?" Because everyone knows that no matter the size, a nonprofit must be submitting a 990, paper or paperless with the IRS. That's how an agency stays a legitimate tax deduction for donors. I'm certain the IRS has many complex, distrustful and paranoid reasons for demanding the filing, but, trust me, the only reason important to anyone is that an agency maintains its legitimacy. So don't get bogged down in nonprofit conspiracy theories, humor the IRS. Just get it done.

The big question is HOW; a second question is WHO; and the final question is HOW MUCH DOES IT COST?

Start with the third question. If an agency is considering an audit, evaluate the cost. Working with an audit firm costs several thousands of dollars. If the agency annual budget is less than the cost of an audit, consider some other option. If, however, the agency has a robust budget, wants to attract bigger donors and apply for grants, and/or, is a United Way agency, an audit is a required and necessary investment.

What does an audit do? This professional assessment of an agency finances validates the Integrity, Transparency, Credibility and Honesty of the agency for donors, clients and community partners. I call that the ITCH factor – **I**ntegrity, **T**ransparency, **C**redibility, **H**onesty.

The agency audit process brings in outside reviewers who will go into detail on the financial processes as well as check the math. The auditor will look for: segregation of duties around finances; track transfers and how money flows including who is involved; credit card receipts and management; online transactions; reporting, who sees reports, how they are filed; gift policy; conflict of interest and confidentiality policies; reimbursing staff; petty cash; stock as gift policy. Note: This is why last month we talked about an agency's finance policy. The audit begins there.

The final audit report will include recommendations for process improvements. The auditor works with the finance (or audit) committee of the board and throughout the coming year that committee works with the ED and board to address and correct, or modify process to the auditor's recommendations. Then it's time for the next audit. Following the money, maintaining that ITCH factor, goes on year round.

An audit is expensive, but choosing to do an audit only every other year or every five will cost more in the long run. Taking that first step is tough, but an agency may have no choice if dynamic and successful service is part of the Strategic Plan.

However, if the audit would represent a third of an agency budget, consider something less. Maybe the agency is only interested in minimal growth, its existence is only to support a small annual effort and the books are kept by a volunteer who has QUICKEN on her computer. Do they need an audit? They need something much less.

They can have a friend of the agency with financial background do an internal review. It's usually free but, if the friend is knowledgeable, it's a helpful exercise for the group. The friend would look for many of the same things as the auditor, but on a more basic level, including; did the 990EZ get filed; deposit slips, purchases; comb through the checkbook; make certain that the treasurer balances the books each month and reports to the board (this is in the minutes of the board meetings); pay attention to segregated funds, such as a donation received for a specific purpose. It's obvious that even a small internal review by a friend takes time and effort. But it should be done for the very same reason that an audit is performed – ITCH!

And because the world is the way it is with more areas that are gray than black or white, there are review options available for agency books that aren't quite an audit and will not give an in-depth look at financial status with analysis and recommendations, but, with a contracted professional, may result in a review and report on some specific phase of an agency's financial system. This type of review may overlook unsavory cash or credit habits (or as we say in the business – OUCH).

Any type of professional review comes with a fee and weighing that cost against information received, an agency can determine which is a better investment.

I can't close the December piece without acknowledging another ITCH factor – It's time for us to support the **I**mage of our **T**own as a **C**ommunity of **H**ope. During this Christmas season give time, treasure and talent to those agencies who fill our community with hope.

Asking for Another Year to Operate

Another year begins and it's time for the great nexus of annual cash flow in the American home – several dozen requests from local and national nonprofits that we ignored over the Christmas Holidays meet the 1040. The great accounting – how did we measure up in 2012 – too generous? too stingy? too strapped for cash to be helpful?

This is the time of the year to be proactive, plan for your 2013 donations. Look at the requests from 2012 that were unanswered. Look at the donation receipts in your files. What money went to charities last year? Are there services in the pile you ignored that you wish you had supported? Maybe others in your donation receipts that no longer excite you or no longer, in your opinion, fill a need you think is necessary at this time. Those are some hard decisions. Every well-organized and managed agency is doing its job. Being a responsible donor is your job.

Five years ago my husband and I developed a donations calendar. We started with those organizations that receive automatic donations monthly and quarterly and certain annual donations that we are committed to for the next year. We marked those donations on our calendar then budgeted an amount of money for each month to be given in response to requests. Of course this means we had to talk.

Although talking to Stan is like the fiscal cliff – he's not hearing anything until the last quarterback gets flattened, or is it the last bowl tips over? That means I have until after Super Bowl Monday morning wrap-up to look at 2013 donations. It doesn't matter. When this discussion occurs, we'll learn so much about one another we'll wonder how we've ever stayed married.

He likes to support a charity or two that his parents supported during their lives, sort of legacy gifts. I'm not that sentimental. Of course my parents were a little more heavy handed. Dad just sent me raffle tickets or event tickets and told me I owed him money. The time I won a cash prize he called to tell me he gave it back to the group as a donation because I probably didn't need it anyway.

We both support children's issues and environmental concerns. But every now and then Stan likes to buy a cow or a pig for someone in some foreign country. He speed dials donations for any natural disaster – tsunami, floods, hurricane – at home or abroad. You get the picture. He's a nicer person than me

All I'm saying is that the meanie and the person with a heart in your family need to have the nexus discussion this year. Learn what is important to each of you. Many of our local nonprofits have sized down, reduced services and still manage to keep the lights on and provide support services in our community. They need us. When giving in 2013, make certain that a good portion of your charity dollars stay local. You'll see the impact of your dollars every day.

It starts with research. As you collect information for your 1040, analyze your giving. Where did you put your money last year? There is always the debate as to whether one small donation to several agencies is better than a few large dollar gifts to a small number of nonprofits. Whatever. Every penny counts. An agency appreciates your gift at any level; appreciates your volunteer time; and is thrilled if you make an appointment to learn more about its work.

Not sure about who or where, or how much? Check out an agency's website. The annual report, quarterly newsletter or calendar of activities may be posted on the site, giving you a good idea of the work done and the openness of the agency. In addition, most agencies are also found at social media sites.

Once you've done a cyber study, ask to visit. Maybe you have a friend who is a supporter. Talk. Or a friend who has received service. Talk. Or a friend who volunteers. Talk. You worked hard for your money – put some effort into donating it thoughtfully. It's up to us to keep necessary nonprofit services functioning.

Human Relations

Recently I heard an executive director of a local nonprofit remark about the challenge to help young staffers understand the relationship between staff and board members. He said that staff members work to design new programs and bring new methods into an agency. They are always frustrated when implementation has to wait until the board approves any new programs. In his view, inexperienced staff always wants to by-pass the board and move forward quickly.

In board training it's always necessary to remind members about the formal and professional relationship between staff and board. It is also necessary, in new staff orientation to help new employees understand that same relationship. New staff members must understand that there is a respectful and professional relationship with the board. They should understand the role and responsibilities of the board, especially the part about raising money to fund programs and salaries.

Both board members and staff must understand that formal discussions are channeled through and facilitated by the executive director. That means the ED has the responsibility to make certain that all involved understand their roles and understand the work each has to do. For example, most staff members provide the services for an agency. They provide counseling, do intake work, provide meals or manage shelters. But they don't run fundraising programs. Sometimes they may be asked to give a presentation to potential donors on the work done at the agency, but the final ask comes from the board or the ED.

On the other hand, the board is not expected to meddle

Charity in Motions

in service delivery or office management. There's always a fine line. In a small community like ours that line may be sometimes hard to define. For example, staff and board members may attend the same church or belong to a club that brings each of them routinely into informal contact. It is important to understand that these informal times are not appropriate for agency discussions.

The staff, the service professionals, determines best approaches to a problem. This is probably the area in which the staff takes a leadership role. The board members are bystanders in the development, but become participants when the assessment is made as to costs, staffing levels and outcome measures. Once the program is defined, the board must determine its path. No wonder an inexperienced staffer wonders why the board has any say in program.

Staff orientation should include a basic understanding of the role of the board in agency mission, financial management and strategic planning. Strategic planning is a joint staff/board operation. Usually the staff sets the course with regard to program goals, mapping out future services and developing steps to attain those program goals. The board usually outlines board and administrative objectives. In fact, the agency strategic plan is a good illustration as to the way board and staff work together. Each has assigned tasks, all wrapped up in one document, the map for a successful agency.

Finally, it is the board who develops and adopts the personnel policy. But the board has no responsibility to hire any staffer except the ED. The ED through appropriate methods hires the rest of the staff. The board usually works with the ED in establishing salary levels and employee benefits such as retirement or health care packages.

One exercise to help board and staff get acquainted is to invite staffers to board meetings. Often, the board chair allots a short period of time before a meeting and invites a staff member to present a program and take questions. In my experience, this is a time for a staff member to shine and to develop support for a program, as well as gain the board's respect for the quality of work being accomplished. Board members impressed with the staff and with the service being provided are able to solicit support from donors with real enthusiasm.

Board and staff; it's not us and them; it's a partnership.

Giving Over Fifty

The most recent *AARP Magazine* features an article "Give Yourself a Happiness Makeover." There are ten suggestions in the piece about ways to make us happy and lengthen our lives. Of course, those of you who read AARP magazine regularly know that one of the happiness hints is related to sex. In fact, just as an aside, I've never seen so much sex talked about in a magazine since I gave up *Cosmopolitan*. Can you believe the articles: sex over fifty, dating over fifty, and conquering ED with, or without, a pill, and I don't mean **E**xecutive **D**irector?

Now I'm blushing, because you're all going to suspect that I read the magazine from cover to cover for you-know-what kind of information. Well, sometimes I just go online to review an interesting article, you know, to make sure I read it right the first and second time.

Anyway you can imagine my delight to learn that in addition to suggestions that happiness is related to finding a soul mate and getting a dog, the author suggests that to be happier one should ignite one's passion for compassion because giving feels good.

The article states that several studies exist to show that givers are happier people. Happier than what? Happier than all the tightwads around them? Happier than if they just won the lottery? AARP needs to explain that study a little more. On the happiness scale, are they measuring against the curve or against some inner thermometer? Personally, I'm all for outward happiness. Those inner glow sorts of things leave me feeling, well, feeling, but without the outer happy dance of showing it off. Maybe I've missed the point of that study.

However, another study is cited that shows that altruism

stimulates the same pleasure centers in the brain as sugar and cocaine. I guess sex doesn't have anything to do with that part of the brain.

Anyway the study doesn't talk about amounts – the size of the donation that will make you happier. AARP always seems to leave us with more questions when they quote studies. What we need is a tool for price setting on donation thrills. To be helpful, I'm proposing a donation measure. The old saying, "give till it hurts," should be replaced by "give until you feel the rush."

Of course, the AARP article concludes by suggesting that making a donation isn't the only altruistic way to feel good. No money – then feel the rush by volunteering. It does the same for your happiness and brain stimulation as sugar and cocaine, but without a tax deduction.

Of course, this isn't just for people over fifty, the rest of you want to be happy, too, I'm sure. So donate and volunteer. It's the way to keep the lines from your face and the stiffness out of your joints. I'm certain I read something in AARP magazine about all that stuff, but maybe it was related to sex.

Another topic often covered in AARP magazines is the good old days. The *good old memories* discussion frequently revolves around what we learned as children and what we should pass on to our grandchildren. Most of us learned early on, from the activities of our youth, organized clubs, our churches and our families, that giving and volunteering should be a part of our lives. Now that we're older, do we remember those lessons? Are we passing them on?

The number of nonprofits in our community and the time and dollars we invest in altruism locally is a testament to those lessons. We all remember and we all give – until we feel the rush!

Calling for Help

Recently the Times-News reported that Sheriff McDonald's department worked with a consultant on an "internal audit which led to an action plan ..." This is an important step for any organization. It can be important and revitalizing for government offices, businesses, and nonprofits.

One of my first experiences in the early years of volunteering and board service with a nonprofit was dealing with consultants. Consultants are everywhere. They called themselves various names – facilitators, coaches – but it all boils down to one thing, they come from out of town, show their clients the yellow brick road to the Emerald City, then leave with a car full of Munchkins, while the client tries to subdue a witch, or raise money in a capital campaign, or draw up a strategic plan, or reorganize services, or rebrand ... hmmm ... subduing that witch sounds a whole lot easier, doesn't it?

Consultants have a service to offer. They are skilled in helping their clients focus. They know how to rein in the silly and bring reality to a plan. But, they don't do the work. That was the first consultant lesson I learned. It didn't matter that the consultant sold himself as someone who helped with a capital campaign, I soon learned that he didn't make donor calls. The board did that. He didn't know who the potential donors were. The staff and board knew that. Besides, we all know that donors don't want to give money to a guy from out of town. A donor wants to give locally to someone local. They like to watch their money work. But a consultant *does* help frame the campaign message, train those who will do the 'ask,' and help prioritize donors.

Consultants who help with strategic planning are another breed. They come prepared to squeeze out of any board a mission statement and goals, long and short-term strategies or outcomes – I get confused with all the words. They throw around input and outcome and all sorts of other jargon. Because most boards have gone through retreats and planning processes, the consultants are clever and change the game, the format and the team building exercises on a regular basis. Most consultants can get a board and staff to put an organized document down on paper, then it's up to the board and staff to get it done. In the article the sheriff let us know he understands follow through, because he put a high priority on "identify the problem, then fix it."

That's the other consultant lesson I've learned. No matter how well written a plan may be, it's the execution that counts. The consultant doesn't stay around for that. The contract may include follow-up sessions, or coaching for the ED and board chair, but the work has to be done by the board and staff.

Are consultants worth the investment of time and money? I think so. As long as each board understands the limits of the consultant's role, it will be a successful partnership. A well-defined strategic plan can be very helpful to a board. Each quarterly review (Oh yes, look it over at least every ninety days – don't put it on a shelf) helps everyone measure what has been completed, holds board members or staff accountable, shows the board that a project may be unrealistic and should be dropped or moved out to a longer completion date, or, in a surprise to everyone, that a project has been completed ahead of schedule.

As long as a board understands the limits of a consultant's role, contracting with a skilled professional will help the board and staff work through challenging times or critical events in the agency's history, shake out the ennui, or set the agency up for it's next success. Just remember, the consultant's advice is only as good as the board's response in delivering on the vision.

As the sheriff's consultant is quoted, " ...do you plan on following through? Because if you're not going to follow through, I don't need the money badly enough to come."

That says it all, a good consultant wants to help his client grow and succeed.

Wait a Minute

Keeping records for a nonprofit organization is very important. And there is no end to the records that should be kept. Most boards should have a Retention Policy that outlines what information to keep forever, and what to discard after a prescribed amount of time.

One of the forever items is minutes. This is the eyewitness history of any organization. Each filed minutes of a meeting includes the date of the meeting, attendees at the gathering and records of all actions taken. Minutes should include excused absences, "my husband broke his leg," and also unexcused absences, as in she just didn't show for the meeting. Should attendance of a member come into question, the minutes are the corporation's word on who was there on that day.

The minutes should report a motion, explicit wording of the motion, that it was moved and seconded. Should the names of those moving the action be recorded? In my opinion, routine actions, approving the minutes of the previous meeting, the treasurer's report, don't need a name attached. When a motion comes from a committee chair, the chair's name will be part of the report, as in Igor, chair of the ad hoc committee on dungeons moved as a recommendation of the committee that ... The stuff that makes history, the actions that move the agency in a new direction should be in the official minutes. Not every argument needs to be reported – that the discussion occurred, that the motion carried or failed is important. In addition to action, include reference to all reports given or submitted in writing.

However, when a board gets into a discussion that will have long term effect on the future of the agency, take names.

Sometimes, after a profound discussion, members may choose to bring the item back for discussion at the next meeting. It is important that those who discussed and voted on the issue at the last meeting be present. In some very important discussions, the board may want a roll call vote. If that is done, include the members' names with their vote.

The agenda is a great outline for the secretary to use when preparing the minutes. It's a great tool for the chair to use to keep the discussion on track. It organizes the meeting to make certain all items of importance are considered. The minutes of the previous meeting help organize the next agenda. For example, the minutes may state that the committee will visit the ex-treasurer in jail and report back at the June meeting. The June meeting agenda should have a place for that report – and I bet everyone attends the meeting to get the update.

Speaking of the treasurer, it is also important to have the minutes reflect that the treasurer's report was accepted. This is proof to everyone reviewing the minutes that the board has seen the status of the finances and that board members are receiving the information. If said board member isn't reviewing the report – that's not the treasurer's fault.

What should not be in the minutes? Anything that is personal, like the president asked the treasurer to help plan a baby shower for her niece, or the finance committee chair complained about his allergies, should be ignored.

Also it is not necessary to include verbatim any report that has been submitted in writing. Reference the report and file it with the official copy of the minutes. The minutes should just reflect that the report was submitted.

And what if the minutes are incorrect? Every member has the opportunity to read the minutes, usually at the next meeting, and offer corrections. When the minutes are corrected, the secretary corrects the original set, marks them approved and files them. Do not clutter up the succeeding minutes listing the corrections – just say they were approved as corrected.

These days, most agencies deal electronically with a board packet – the minutes to be approved, a treasurer's report, other reports and an agenda all may arrive days before the meeting. Of course that means that all boards members read the information before hand. Meetings move very quickly when the information is in everyone's hands in advance.

One final piece of advice to all secretaries – get the minutes done as soon as possible after the meeting. No matter how clear your notes, or that you are a techie typing the notes into your laptop, as time passes, the sense of the notes lose out as memory fades. Minutes are too important.

Being a Responsible Donor

A recent letter writer to the Times News cautioned donors about the potential of scams or out right mismanagement in the nonprofit sector. His recommendation was to investigate a charity before sending in a donation, even referring donors to a website.

This is a wise rule when dealing with any charity. After reading the informative letter, I thought it was time for me to remind readers that the NC Secretary of State's website, www.sosnc.com has a lot of practical information pertaining to nonprofits operating in North Carolina.

One interesting download available from this site is a form to use when dealing with a phone solicitation. The form called "The Donor's Telephone Checklist" cautions a donor to "Check before you write One." We all get those meal interrupting phone call solicitations when a paid solicitor places a dinnertime call to see if we'll support any number of causes from politics to the arts. Do what the Secretary of State advises: be cautious, use the checklist to ask important questions to help you decide whether or not to make a donation. Or do what I do – hang up. Or do what people much smarter than me do, use caller ID!

Is it a crime to hire a professional fundraiser/solicitor? The answer is no. Contracting with a fundraiser is one option many charities use for various reasons. One reason is that a phone canvas is short term. Yes, the fundraiser gets a fee. Could the fundraising be done internally, by staff or agency volunteers? Certainly. But it would involve hiring additional staff or finding more volunteers. So the challenge a nonprofit board faces is whether to contract with a fundraiser/solicitor or take on additional staff, which may be a full-time position, because raising money is full-time.

Other features on the Secretary of State's website include tabs to review charities in North Carolina, helpful donor tips and notices of current scams. An article worth reviewing is from "2001 Independent Sector, Give Five" brochure. It's called *Ten Tips on Giving Wisely*. One of the tips: Be an informed giver – emphasizes the point made by the recent letter writer. There are a number of other tips, including the suggestion that a donor should be aware of how much is really tax deductible in a donation for an event. For example, attending a fundraising dinner for any nonprofit, means that the cost of the meal is not a tax-deductible part of the donation. When buying a ticket for a fundraising dinner, donors should be advised as to the meal's value, thus reducing the tax deductible amount by the cost of the meal.

Another feature on this website includes notices of current charity scams. The most recent one as of this writing is a warning about scams following the Oklahoma tornadoes. The first suggestion is – if a donor wants to support recovery in Oklahoma, give to established charities such as the American Red Cross and the Salvation Army who are equipped for an immediate response to tragedies. On the other hand, be wary of "pop-up" charities or emails or Facebook requests for donations. Secretary Marshall invites all those interested in making donations to these tragedies to check www.sosnc.com.

A donor should do a lot of research, study services, look at administrative costs, but, my recommendation – do it locally. The best way to follow your charitable dollar is to give it in Henderson County – from the arts to human services there are enough organizations doing great work – work that you as a donor can see every day. You can even volunteer and work along side your money. A hundred dollar donation, given to a local nonprofit goes a long way. Each agency in this community can outline for each donor the impact of every dollar and how close to home the money makes a difference.

Being a responsible donor takes time and effort. You should work as hard to give your money away as you worked to earn it.

Fundraising Forever

For most non-profits July 1 is the beginning of the new budget year. In everyone of those nonprofit budgets, the income side of the outline has a large number that represents the amount of money to be raised for the year. The headings probably include: store income, if the agency has a viable thrift store, another line or two reflecting other income streams, such as Mainstay's new Dandelion restaurant, or it's a line item that might just be called *Fundraising* or *Donations*.

Whatever it's called it means *Work!*

How does a nonprofit get from a line item to actual cash in the bank? They do it with a fundraising plan! An established nonprofit already has a fundraising calendar in place. Even though July 1 initiates a new budget year, a long established agency already has the Fundraising plan in place, maybe even beginning the new fiscal year with funds already pledged. How does that happen? If the agency has an annual fundraising event, chances are the planning efforts never stop. Once the event occurs and is wrapped up, planning begins for the next year's effort. A small committee of staff and volunteers, including a board member or two, already have the date of the new event lined up, are outlining plans to meet with current donors, have initiated steps to invite new donors to become financial backers for the event, and are doing a dozen other tasks behind the scenes in preparation for the upcoming event, probably eleven months away. Whew!

A "Gala" dinner, entertainment or something new and different like Hands On! Mud Run will be an agency's signature BIG effort in the plan to raise a large portion of the annual funds necessary to sustain the agency's programs and services. Another part of the action plan probably includes some sort of direct mail effort – sending out a letter to a well-defined list of annual supporters to ask them to renew their support, think about increasing their support and tell their friends.

All fundraising efforts by an agency must be coordinated – the big fundraising event invitation cannot arrive in the mail to a donor on the same day as the annual appeal letter. The newsletter, or online prompt for support, must be scheduled between any big donor appeals.

And through it all the back office operation of the agency revolves around donor support tasks – getting information correctly into donor software, that magic computer database that keeps a record of donor giving history and correct addresses, as well as specific confidential information, such as donor requests only to be visited in June, or donor indicates interest in an estate gift discussion.

And thank you very much! Every fundraising plan includes several opportunities each year to thank donors – a hand written note from a volunteer or board member or a recipient of services. Donor contacts also include invitations to take a tour of the facility, to learn more about a new program, to lunch with other volunteers, to stop by the agency for after work drop-ins. Engaging each donor in opportunities to hear from or meet face to face with the agency and its representatives, helps that agency line up support for the fundraising effort for the coming year. The budget may be an annual exercise. Fundraising is long term, well-planned, everlasting and eternal work.

Planning Past Our Noses

There's a lot to be learned from reading the Times-News. Just last Friday (August 2) there was a front-page story about United Way of Henderson County. The leadership of this community organization spent several years of study to examine ways to ensure its work in our community would be effective and its funds invested wisely.

Of course, this is only ink on the Times-News front page if you're not a regular donor to United Way. For those of you who are sitting on your checkbooks, let me explain. United Way supports, with annual donations, many services in our community. In fact, through its member agencies, it's a large part of a public-private partnership with local government and local business providing a social safety net. Not only that, but United Way is always ready to listen to new ideas and accept your help through, advocacy, volunteering and donations. There it is, the opportunity to follow your money and watch it work. But this is not a want ad for United Way volunteers and donors. This is a conundrum.

In life there are advantages to looking long term and there are advantages to looking short term. Nature is great for showing us examples. In the long-term category there are animals that prepare for winter and live to the next spring to raise a new generation. Or there are examples of the short term view, bugs that hatch to live for three weeks having sex and laying eggs. In that case the next generation takes care of itself. Is it better to look ahead and plan for the next generation or to just have sex and die off, letting the next

Charity in Motions

generation take care of itself?

United Way of Henderson County had just presented their assessment of county need and their proposal – Henderson County 2025. The leadership plans to focus on: kindergarten readiness, school success, financial stability, affordable housing, healthy youth behaviors, and curbing obesity. Ho hum, you worldly wise, free marketeers respond. Or maybe you laugh. Solve these problems by 2025? Ha!

United Way leadership has spent time interviewing community service providers and other community leaders as well as collecting and evaluating data from many sources. United Way has set goals for the next decade to improve conditions in our community in the focus areas. They have been in the human service support business for decades, they state that their plan has it's focus on children – long term – a next generation commitment!

In the Sunday paper (August 4), Mike Tower's column "Corporate Thinking is Short Term." Hmmm. Mike points out that through the years, based on the need for corporations to serve investors, corporations have developed short-term games to increase stock value. Mr. Tower says, "Such short term thinking by corporate leaders has led to the elimination of millions of American jobs, and even entire industries, over the past few decades." He goes on to say, "Our federally elected officials are supposed to protect our citizens ... but they have all been too busy trying to remain in power by doing the bidding of special interest ..." No one here is thinking about the next generation. What kind of data do you think these guys are studying? And what problems are they trying to solve? And what kind of problems have they created?

Has the free market been replaced by the closed market with big players taking the cash and running in place, not running to secure the future? Is this the example of short term choices – buggy sex and death?

In the world where public-private partnerships are viewed as a good way to work together, it seems to be that two sides of that triangle, government and private corporations, are doing the short-term dash. While the third side of the partnership, non-profits dealing in social issues, are the only people looking long term.

So I wonder how can United Way and similar organizations see needs to be addressed and propose solutions as we look toward 2025? But not anyone else?

It Stays in Vegas

Last week a friend commented to me about a board disagreement in an organization in which we both participate. He was part of the leadership team and I humbly work in the trenches as a volunteer. When I said I wasn't aware of any disagreement, he was shocked. He thought that other members of the board might have contacted me because I write a column and profess to know all. Yeah, right!

He described the discussion that had occurred over several board meetings and then outlined the resolution. I was grateful that I hadn't been asked to help form a solution – and I was pleased to hear how an organization I value solved its problems.

This experience got me thinking about all that had been done correctly. First, the board discussed the issue, AND kept the discussion in the boardroom. No other members of the organization were sucked into a popularity contest or leadership struggle or made to feel as though they had to take sides. It's called leadership for a reason – lead! No board member should be out in the membership or among the volunteers lobbying for an outcome to a board discussion. This isn't congress where every comment is interpreted as a challenge – a non-profit is made up of people working for organizational progress and success.

Second, in the midst of diverse opinions, the board chair, as reported by my friend, listened to all sides. The chair didn't play favorites, didn't act as an outraged despot, but listened. In fact, he seemed to have listened for several weeks. Time is always a luxury. When making a strategic or, at least, a precedent setting decision – take time. It will pay off in the future as the decision is implemented. There will be a history of discussion (the minutes and an action plan) that helped form the response and will help others, especially future board members, understand what happened and continue to follow the plan.

Open discussion at board meetings is necessary to make certain all board members understand the choices. It's also necessary that the pros and cons of the issue are understood in a manner that tells everyone that this is not a popularity contest, but a meaningful discussion that should lead to a well-informed decision.

The third reason that board discussion and debate should stay in the board room is that anything that devolves to talk on the street hurts the organization. This is a reason many boards ask its staff and members to sign an annual confidentiality statement. It's a reminder to everyone that talk, from discussions of property purchases to gossip of out and out brawls, stays in the meeting – not in the minutes and not at a local coffee shop.

One of the reasons for a board retreat or some sort of team building exercise is that it helps a board work through challenging issues without a "take no prisoners" attitude. Although many board members scoff at the touchy-feely interchange of a team building exercise, it's a way for board members, who probably meet once a month as a body and other times in small committees, to get a true sense of the other members of the board. Of course, one of my solutions is to always recruit your friends to serve with you. That has its own challenges. A small tight knit group can overwhelm and undermine the chair. But that's another column.

Board retreats help members learn about one another and develop plans for the organization to move forward and develop ways to talk to one another that are tempered by those common goals. When the chair and the board review their decision, they should be proud that it worked, that it never disintegrated to a food fight and that the integrity of the organization is intact.

So don't kiss and tell, zip your lip and leave it all behind in the boardroom.

Happy Returns

Some of the best, well-run and energetic nonprofits are here in Henderson County. I know that because many of my friends serve on those boards and many of my friends staff the agencies and many of my friends volunteer. And sometimes my friends are helped and enriched by the services provided. I'm such a Pollyanna – it's disgusting.

But we have the best, and sometimes, the best just are hard to forget. In the last several years we have seen three respected executive directors leave our community for various reasons and then return to their former jobs. I say former, not old, because each returnee I spoke with felt they and the job had evolved. No one found the same old place nor slipped into the same old rut.

In 2006 Chris Comeaux, left Four Seasons Compassion for Life to return to Florida, to take a challenging position and to be closer to family. Kevin Lauritsen retired from the Boys and Girls Club in Henderson County in 2011, thinking he needed a respite from all his years of nonprofit work. Jennifer Henderson resigned from Blue Ridge Community Health Center in 2012 to explore a job with more administrative responsibility in a larger agency and was back 2013.

Chris left for a job that kept him on the road and away from his family, but it was a job that, in his opinion, helped prepare him for the executive director position when it became available again at Four Seasons, in 2008. He says, "I was not handed the job, but was reinterviewed by the board." He says he came back, "because there is no better place to raise a family and because the job in Florida grounded me in healthcare, ready for the challenges" he would find in Hendersonville.

Kevin talked about the serendipity of being rested and ready when his old job became available. He says, "I came back and looked at everything with fresh eyes, and had the fire to do it again."

Jennifer says, "Moving away helped me see what was important for me in a job. It is core beliefs about people and focusing on primary care policy and service delivery." She missed that when she joined a bigger organization.

All three of these directors spoke highly of their boards. Kevin remarked, "I returned to find a stronger board." Both Jennifer and Chris give their boards credit for managing the agency until the issue of a new executive director was resolved.

Kevin and Jennifer also noted that they found the staffs within their agencies stronger. And as returning executive directors, they felt they moved into a more relaxed method of managing, allowing staff to continue to learn and grow. Jennifer said, "Staffers got a better understanding of the entire operation. They had to move beyond their specific areas."

Chris had a slightly different conclusion. He had spent his early years at Four Seasons helping the agency grow and develop a strategy for the future. Upon his return, he said he was able to see what worked and what didn't and correct his mistakes.

Chris also speculated, "This must be the only county where people return to leadership positions." Then he added, in case I hadn't gotten it the first time, "It's a great place to raise a family."

Nonprofits are part of the economic engine of a community. They provide jobs, services and in many cases manage budgets competitive with local small and medium businesses. We all gain when those nonprofits are led by professionals like, Kevin, Chris and Jennifer.

Passing the Baton, the Minutes, the Coffee Pot ...

Recently I worked on a committee to deal with bylaws and policy in an organization. It is one of those civic, member driven clubs that exist for a certain purpose. But just like a big nonprofit, the club generates records, accumulates assets and stuff, while following all the same rules.

What do you do with all the stuff??? A large community nonprofit like the Children and Family Resource Center and Mainstay have their own space. Just imagine what they could squirrel away if they didn't pay attention to organizational jetsam such as old minutes, old donor lists, old board lists. Because space is finite and precious, they probably have in place good policies to manage old records and inventory control systems to keep track of computers as well as coffee pots and desks.

Then there are the rest of us – civic clubs, garden clubs, quasi-political groups, disbanded groups of all sorts. You can bet each group, still thriving, or disbanded, leaves (or left) behind monthly reports, minutes, old banking information, maybe a banner or two from marching in the Apple Festival Parade. So I ask again – what do you do with all that stuff?

Two suggestions: a records retention policy and an inventory control policy.

I heard some of you shudder. You're a small club, under a hundred members, you meet monthly, pay dues, have all the basic organization needs, officers, bylaws, checking account. You don't need policies, *shudder*, or an inventory management system. Wanna bet? Who gets the coffee pot when the current hospitality chair resigns, dies or quits in a snit? In fact, does anyone know where she keeps it?

Do new members realize that all those Styrofoam cups are bought by the club, kept someplace and must be replaced by someone? Who keeps the booty between meetings – the fake creamer, the fake sugar, the coffee can? *AND* has anyone checked the expiration dates?

So let's start with an inventory management system. Many clubs probably own some basic items. Where are they kept? Who has the responsibility for keeping them safe? An inventory, reviewed annually allows the officers to consider the list, confirm that Joe still has the club banner, and Faye has the coffee pot. One officer should quickly contact those members and verify the information, and give the person an opportunity to decline further involvement with the banner or the pot. Or it might be reasonable to designate certain committee chairs as responsible for each item. The items may move every year or so – but things will always be assigned to active members.

A records retention policy is a little more tricky. You're a small club, under a hundred members – what kind of records could you have? Minutes, banking records, items compiled by a club historian (news articles, special events, fundraising activities, photos.) I know this sounds complex and more work than is done all year by the entire membership, but review those storage boxes and determine what to keep. With a records retention policy a club sets a date when something can be tossed. Online research will help you set those standards. Should everything be tossed past its useful date? Some information needs to be kept for the clubs history and to demonstrate its service to our community.

My friend Chuck Elston, an archivist in his former life, drew up suggestions of things a club should archive: board minutes and records, including annual budgets, financial statements and tax returns; newsletters, brochures and other publications; membership directories; Articles of Incorporation; bylaws and policies and procedures; scrapbooks of clippings and photographs; annual reports of officers and committee chairs.

Is every scrap of paper archive worthy? Chuck offered some evaluation criteria. Does the information represent a policy, function or activity or have legal value? Does the old notebook have informational content, uniqueness, and understandability? Does that file have a relationship to other records? Chuck says the challenge is to archive documents with an eye toward cost of storage, available space and volume of records.

He closed his notes with this quote: "The archivist seeks those records with the greatest research significance, covering the broadest range of activities for the longest time, with the smallest volume of the most easily understandable records."

The hard part for a small group – those organized around a hobby or specific community service – is that the group has no "home." If your group relies on someone's attic for storage, you're in trouble. A death, divorce, or fire can send all records and assets into oblivion. Let's face it, Mom takes a tumble, the kids swoop in, clean out the attic (look at all the junk she hoarded!) send the records to the recycle center, and get rid of the club coffee pot at the garage sell.

So let's get organized. The records review committee or someone will reduce the club's archives to three small boxes. It's great information – but no one wants to keep it in their attics. Come back next month for a solution.

We Are the Attic

Last month we had a discussion about sorting and storing records. You've had a month to get through all the stuff stored at various members' homes. I don't want to hear any whining about Christmas distractions. You should already have your greeting cards in the mail and have sent off your year-end donations to the great nonprofits in town. What's left? Just as I thought you have plenty of time.

Using last month's article you've surely taken time to look through records and track down the things the club owns. You have a good inventory policy in place. How many half used containers of fake creamer did you find? And how many different types of throw away coffee cups? You followed the guidelines included last month and now the archived information, the club's history, is ready to find a home and everyone in the club has said, "Not me!"

Then the only place to go is the Henderson County Genealogical and Historic Society. One volunteer told me, "We are the attic!"

Virginia Thompson the society president for many years met with me to talk about old stuff. In fact she's very respectful of historic records. She says visitors often ask about old membership lists and really like to review old photographs. As she says, "You never know who's looking for what." She and the other volunteers work to preserve our past.

But is just any club that important? The answer is yes. Many clubs already have given archived information to the society for safe-keeping, those still in existence as well as those that have disbanded. Virginia outlined many of the items that we referenced last month as items valued by those preserving local history and by those researching local citizens. She also pointed out that many church records preserve a big part of local history and the society is grateful to hold them for research.

In addition, the history of local non-profits is another area that is worthy to preserve. Researchers like to review board lists when looking for a relative. That kind of information helps understand and define that special family member. What was important to her, or where did he put his volunteer time? That kind of information rounds out the memories of a special relative.

When deciding to store archives of an organization, it is important to prepare a brief statement about the club's purpose, activities, leadership and include news clippings. Some of the bits of information Virginia said researchers value include meeting location and photographs. She says that a photograph gives a lot of information about the past – clothing, architecture, cars.

Another source of information that can be found at the society office at the corner of Fourth and Main includes family files. Don't throw anything away before the volunteers at the Genealogical and Historic Society have a chance to look things over. There are no funds to purchase documents, but they are happy to preserve and protect what you hold as valuable to local family and club history. And they are happy to help determine what should be kept and what should not. Finally, if your club archives are on hand in their office, all records are accessible for research Monday through Friday from ten am to four pm.

Are you still wondering if going through those old boxes is worthwhile? Was your organization a value to our county? Did you have a place in local history, participate in special events? The answer is all community groups and clubs were and are important. They help people in the future understand who made us such a great place.

Check out www.hcghs.com or stop in for a visit.

Business Partners

When we bought a new car recently, we were advised that the national corporation would donate money to five designated national charities. We were told that because we bought a Subaru the manufacturer would donate $250 to five selected charities and we could allow $50 to go to each or distribute the funds more specifically and our choices would be honored.

This event re-enforced several of my life axioms.

First, I was reminded that I should never believe my husband when he says he thinks he'll just "stop in" at a car dealership to "look around." When Stan's new car itch begins, the scratch inevitably follows. So here we are with a new car and an opportunity to let Subaru donate money to five worthy causes.

The second axiom to be reaffirmed – Can Stan and I be more different? Whatever made us get married when we have nothing in common, and never see the world in the same light? That's right. Over forty-five years of marriage and we couldn't agree on what to do with Subaru's offered donations. Stan is kind of a Weather Channel spontaneous donor – flood, tsunami, hurricane, volcanic eruption – where's the checkbook. I look at long term, steady support for basic human progress. Both are valid – but we had limited choices and limited funds.

I thought making a donation of all the money to one recipient made fundraiser sense. A larger sum is always more helpful. Stan thought that made sense, too. So he offered his pick – which was not my pick – which led to a discussion of human priorities, environmental priorities and dogs and cats – and probably education, music, art and space exploration.

We sort of got beyond the original offerings.

Which kind of finally resolved into the Solomon-like solution – you designate half and I'll designate half. Whew!

After all was said and done and said and done, etc. I reflected on a third truth of life – how much the nonprofit world benefits from the business world. We see it everyday in our own community. Without regard to economic ups and downs our community has a faithful contingent of local businesses, whether with national, international ties or local family connections, which can always be counted on for support.

We see that support when a business adds their logo to the participants' T-shirt of a 5K. We see it when a business donates to a local capital campaign and is honored with a naming opportunity. We see it in gifts for silent auctions and we see it in sponsorships at many fundraising events.

Most visibly we see it in United Way where our business leaders work side by side with nonprofit leaders to run successful campaigns and promote community priorities. Mark Morse, President of Selee Corporation and the past Board Chair of United Way, said in a recent Times-News article, "I have met many nonprofit executive directors and staff, and I know they are working hard to improve Henderson County. The work they do is more valuable than most people realize .... They are amazing stewards of the funding and trust we invest in them."

He called on people in the community to join him and work with those nonprofit leaders when he said, "What difference can you make? Probably more than you think. It's not a one-way street; what you give to our community, you will get back through the satisfaction of knowing you made a difference."

I think that reflects the intentions of our local business community and is put succinctly in another quote from

Mark: "Follow your passions when you choose a volunteer activity. Encourage others to volunteer with you. Lend your muscle. Find an outlet for your creativity, talents and business acumen."

That's not just a call to the business community – but to all of us. So in this New Year, remember, take a lesson from Subaru and from Mark – be generous with your time and money. Be excited about the potential of our community and, above all, be there.

Fundraising Is Like Gardening

The snow is gone. Maybe. The temperatures are climbing back up. Maybe. I just checked my camellia bushes to see if wrapping them saved the buds. Maybe. And then, there in Parade magazine was an offer for a free hosta! Of course, it was free if I paid shipping and handling. So while I was on this website, getting my FREE hosta, I thought I might as well shop around. There were those photos of happy geraniums, sophisticated iris, and feathery ferns. But the final temptation – $20 dollars off my purchases this month only! I wonder how long until my plants arrive?

Then it struck me! The perfect metaphor for successful fundraising. The plant catalogue got me to give money with a promise of blooms in the spring, summer and fall. Just like any local nonprofit with a good fundraising plan, the plant catalogue presented a case for my money.

But is it simple and easy?

Fundraising. The two words that are like fingernails sketching across a blackboard for many board members, but the two words that make an agency succeed or fail. Take a page from the plant catalogues – make your case, show photos and tell client stories. And yes, everyone must be engaged in the effort. But the process works best when the board and executive director hire the right staff person to work with them.

Wouldn't it be great if during the interview process, the skies opened and angels descended on the best candidate to hire? Well, that doesn't happen. So I went to one of our

Charity in Motions

regional fundraising consultants, Alex Comfort (www.mn-ps.com), and asked how to get that angel feeling.

The first question – when is it time, in a small or new agency, to hire a fundraiser? The answer – when you're ready to deliver on your mission. In addition to volunteers and advocates, an agency must work with staff and board to set a fundraising plan in place. Alex had one caution. Don't hire a fundraiser as a last ditch effort to survive. No donor wants to receive a call to be asked "Your money or our life." No donor wants to throw money at a sinking ship. A fundraiser should come into the organization with enough time to cultivate the agency's donors, maintain a dialogue with them, work on various types of fundraising – annual campaign, major gifts, endowment, capital campaign.

Then we talked about the qualities a fundraiser needs. Alex suggested that when you're in the market for a person to staff that role in your office, look internally. Look at your volunteers or one of the agency's staunchest advocates. Fundraising is mission centered so look for someone who is committed to the mission.

What about other qualities? Alex offered some other traits for a successful fundraiser. Likability. Someone donors and volunteers trust. An extrovert. And his final trait was "act like a celebrity." Really? After some discussion, I think I can explain it as someone who walks into a room with confidence. A fundraiser is someone who believes in the mission, isn't afraid to ask, and definitely isn't afraid to hear "No."

So you've found that special person for your organization. What next?

Training!

That's not as hard as you think for those of us in the mountains. Recently in conjunction with Lenior Rhyne University Center for Graduate Studies in Asheville, Alex ran a bootcamp for fundraising. Regionally the Association of Fundraising Professionals has a very active chapter (www.afpwnc.org). The Association of Fundraising Professionals in WNC works to train and mentor fundraisers in the region. They organize and run workshops and trainings for just the reason Alex mentioned – find a person inspired by the mission, the training is close by.

Making Friends

For many of us the news is always more interesting when it concerns someone we know. For example, when we have a loved one in military service serving abroad, the international news has a certain pull, riveting our attention to places we have never seen. Knowing someone in a danger zone puts a face on the survivors, the injured and the dead.

These days, my husband and I find ourselves riveted to the international news because of our interest in Friendship Force International. Our local group in WNC has entertained people from all corners of the world. We have shown them DuPont State Forest and Biltmore Estate. We have introduced them to local elected officials, toured them through our medical facilities and provided time for them to talk with teachers, public safety professionals and managers of local non-profits.

In return we have been welcomed to visit their homes. And that's why we are riveted to the news. The two weeks we spent in Kiev and Lvov were a delight. Imagine our dismay when we see the many places, still vivid through our digital photos, now scenes of rioting and police action. While in Ukraine we stayed in the homes of teachers, business people, physicians and other professionals. We had an opportunity to dine with survivors of political imprisonment. We learned of national history and visited sites of painful historic memories. What has happened to our friends?

On a recent visit to Thailand, we spent several days in Bangkok, another friendly and energetic city. On that occasion we were invited to the US Embassy for a briefing arranged through a friendship between one of our group members and an embassy staffer. The briefing was

Charity in Motions

interesting, but the security was eye-opening. However, even though embassy security was strict, our new friends toured us through the lovely city and even took us on a delightful stroll through local neighborhoods. What has happened to those neighborhoods as citizens riot?

And Jakarta – between volcanoes and unrest – we are concerned about the friends we met in that city. During our two week stay in Indonesia we were hosted by both a Christian family and a Muslim family. Both generous, kind and warm people. We were such a novelty that both of our host families arranged for many of their relatives to come by to visit us. We met grandparents, in-laws and children, each as friendly and gracious as the next. We toured the biggest Mosque in Jakarta, and toured the Roman Catholic Cathedral – just across the street! We hope our friends are doing well.

This is only to tell you that working with a non-profit can expand your world, can fill your heart and can cause you to worry about someone half a world away, just as though they are a friend across town.

Note: My husband and I travel internationally through Friendship Force International and participate in home stays. Some days the news gets close to some of our friends.

Keeping in Touch With Donors

Earlier I wrote about hiring a fundraiser for your agency. The hiring is just the beginning of the process. Your new hire needs the right tools, or nothing positive will happen – no bags of money, no flood of grants. But what sort of tools? Remember, if you have hired a person with background in your mission and commitment to the agency's success, you've won round one.

Round Two – training – get that hire off the starting block.

Arriving at Round Three means that you have provided the basics – training support, phone, computer, and some software to help manage information on the donor base. The work strategy for Round Three requires that you have a plan to personally take the new fundraiser around to your long time supporters. You know, over coffee help your new hire meet the lady who gave the biggest gift for your Annual appeal or the gentleman who gave a donation to add the new heating system to your offices.

What? You don't have donors like that? Are you sure? How long have you been with the agency? It's my experience that every local nonprofit has an Angel List, those people who supported the mission from the very beginning, gave time and money to open the doors. Those angels were there when the first clients overwhelmed the office. They ponied up the cash to keep programs functioning while the agency got on its feet. They stepped in with time and money when

Charity in Motions

disaster struck – flood, hurricane, fire. Those angels . .

What do you mean you don't know who they are? Who's keeping up agency history? Where's the scrapbook of news clippings showing the ribbon cutting when the agency doors opened? Who are those people smiling? What scrapbook, what history?

How long have you been involved with this agency? Certainly you can put your hands on a list of board members from the agency's beginnings. You can't?

Some how Round Three is turning into a KO. Before your new hire puts a photo of her kids on her credenza, she's behind. Donor records, board minutes, newspaper stories. All that history needs to be at her fingertips.

I've heard more than one story from donors telling me they were asked to support an appeal or capital campaign by a fresh hire and that the new person had no idea about the donor's history with the agency. Embarrassing? I think so.

So here are some suggestions. In the first weeks, as you establish your new fundraising hire, begin with a history lesson. The fundraiser has to be able to tell the agency's story as though he or she lived through it all. Then, the donor lists have to be reviewed to make certain that your records are up to date. Spend time getting all the information organized. No use talking to a potential donor who may be insulted that no one remembers that they are a part of the agency's history.

Even if you don't think your agency is big enough to hire that fundraising person. Organizing history and donor records is necessary. Someone should take time to review the past, maybe reconnect to people with whom a connection has been lost. Re-thank those early donors, invite them to the office so that they see the changes, experience the impact of their early donations on program and clients. Those early donors need to witness their success – see that they backed a winner.

Then the new hire, as well as the executive director, needs to remember those donors – not just when asking for money – but at the grocery store, at a high school football game, in church. When someone has given you money they expect to be acknowledged, waved at, smiled at, hugged, because the act of giving support to an agency after a well organized 'ask' has created an intimacy – We're on the same side; we're in this together; we will succeed.

When a fundraiser only has time for a donor on the day of the 'ask,' the donor may not have time for a future 'ask.' Showing respect for your donors is a year-round job. It begins and ends with your donors understanding that they are a part of the agency's success.

Social Media and Nonprofits

Have you ever wondered how I can keep going on about nonprofit operations? I must have covered everything by now – probably twice! Not so. Things keep coming up. Five years ago who would have thought we all needed to consider adopting a Social Media Policy? One can only imagine the kind of policies that will be needed in another ten years!

My friends at the Mediation Center did a survey and reported that in 2013 of 25 local western North Carolina non-profit agencies, 96% reported using social media websites. So why does it need a policy? If the agency has an active website, who should control and approve content? Who may enter information? Can employees create a site that uses the agency name without direction or approval of the agency? For example, if an agency, Goody-Two-Shoes (GTS) wants a presence on the Internet – Does a staff member throw up a website, create a Facebook page or should the activity be coherent, be directed by agency policy, follow agency rules for confidentiality, privacy of staff and board members and non-discrimination? No wonder NSA can have an electronic field day across cyberspace – nothing is secret!

You can see where this is going. An agency should be represented by a social media presence that reflects mission, professionalism and respect for clients, staff and volunteers. To begin with, an agency like our friend, GTS should begin by developing some protocols and standards for the agency social media uses. The protocols will determine who writes copy, who approves and, interestingly, who controls the passwords. Think about it. The most tech savvy staffer in the office establishes social media sites for the agency and one day leaves in a snit. The passwords walk out with the snit. So, maybe two people should know the passwords. For approving content, maybe the executive director is the best person, or the marketing person, someone who is responsible for image and consistency.

And that only begins to deal with the agency presence. What about staff as it relates to their personal use of social media? First, that's sort of First Amendment. Staff can maintain a personal site. However, they should be aware that using agency logo, documents, and photos, etc., are prohibited. And staffers, please use good taste. We've heard enough of how prominent people get a lot of news time for posting indiscreetly. That's not something a local non-profit wants to deal with just as the annual fundraising program kicks off. It's worthwhile to direct employees to not use their work email addresses to register for personal social media accounts that will truly be personal.

And that's another thing. It should be real clear to all involved that there are personal email addresses, to be used for personal exchanges, and business email addresses to be used for work. For example, when I email my son, I use his personal email. I don't want to use his business account and have his employer ask, "What did you do to make your mother so angry?" That goes for all employees. No executive director needs to know which employee missed Mom's birthday.

Give some thought to working in the social media arena. Make certain the agency image gains in the process. Make certain that staff members understand what is personal and what is professional. And manage those passwords

Doomsday Is Around the Corner

Above we considered that as times change there are always new ideas to evaluate adding policies and plans as we serve on nonprofit boards. Well, sometimes things never change, they just go from bad to worse – and everyone needs a plan for those times. How bad can things get? Fire, flood, Martian invasion – things can get pretty bad and sometimes it's not even my fault.

Every agency is prepared for the basics, fire escape plan, snow days policy, maybe even lock down procedures if someone is threatening staff or clients. But sometimes an agency needs something with a little more depth. The plan may be called a disaster policy, or something that uses risk management or continuity in the title. In any case it's the road map for action when things go to hell in a hand basket.

Defining hell has challenged theologians for centuries, but here in Henderson County for purposes of talking with nonprofits, hell can be as simple as the executive director falling into a coma, a roof falling in or the office building falling into a chasm. This sort of plan is geared to make certain that the agency survives the crisis to serve another day.

But a disaster can also be hell to a greater degree – a plague strikes the community, a fire destroys downtown, tornado, flood – things we see happen every day on any TV channel. This level of hell would require a plan that includes working with others to survive. Are you seeing some direction in this discussion?

To help me think through this doomsday concept I sat down with McCray Benson of the Community Foundation of Henderson County. I know what you're thinking. Of course the Community Foundation has plans just in case – they've got assets, they've got money, furniture, computers. But when I challenged McCray on that fact, he was quick to point out that not every agency needs a plan as detailed as the one his board and staff developed.

To prove it he asked some basic questions. If an agency lost organizational documents in a fire, how would they prove they had ever received a letter of determination from the IRS – you know that wrinkled, yellowing piece of paper in that old file drawer. Requesting another letter from the IRS is its own level of hell (McCray didn't say that, I did.)

So start with the basics no matter how small of an organization you are – scan a few documents that are important, your IRS letter, incorporation documents, make a list of account numbers and passwords, how about a list of physical assets, bylaws and basic documents outlining mission and purpose, special certifications. There are a variety of documents and maybe not all the same for every agency, but things that should be on hand to start over after picking up the pieces. Scan the papers. McCray suggests saving them as pdf because that's a format readable by most computers.

Then put them some places safe. Yes, places. McCray calls that redundancy. In a bank box, with the ED and an assistant, with someone the agency and board determine as a reasonable protector of information – someone who would be accessible when the need arises.

Thinking about being prepared is probably the first step for any agency. Board and staff should consider what is important to save. Even if the original documents are stored in a safe place, consider creating electronic backups to be stored on a thumb drive. Then consider what else should be saved on a thumb drive and how often the information should be reviewed and/or updated.

McCray credits his board with working as hard as the staff to organize their records in what they call a Business Continuity Plan. It takes time, it takes thought and it takes keeping at it even with the daily distraction of agency activity.

As we talked about the Community Foundation's plan, I asked "When do you stop with storing information, with redundancy plans?"

McCray said, "It's different for every agency depending on their size. Plans can be less complex for small organizations." But he pointed out everyone should weigh the consequences of not having a plan when all hell breaks loose.

Succession Planning

Queen Elizabeth isn't the only person who thinks about succession. Any nonprofit board worth its weight in donations does the same thing. When I first heard the term succession planning I really did think about the Queen. Why did my board and our agency need to consider crowning someone – sort of a royal executive director? Can you just see it? Going to the United Way office and having the new ED walk down that long corridor to the training area. Board members, with the agency strategic plan over their hearts, lining the wall. Faithful volunteers taking their places in the room as a quiet slide show of agency history and annual report plays across the walls.

Do you feel tears in your eyes? Well you will if you haven't given consideration to succession planning. This sort of planning is designed to help an agency and board deal with leadership change. It happens. Key staffers leave; better jobs, death, pregnancy – all the normal life stuff. Are you prepared to weather those changes?

Let's begin by considering some of the issues that should be outlined in a plan: Who's in charge in the interim? Who begins to look for new leadership? And does that committee know what to look for?

The first step is to make certain that the agency keeps functioning without a blip. Who should be in charge? Taking time to develop a plan should help the board answer that question. Who is the staff person or board member who can easily step into the management role? Hmm. Maybe it's not that easy. There also has to be a list of job functions that the departing ED did. Does that exist? If it does, have you, as a board, worked with the ED prior to this eleventh hour and identified and trained an interim manager?

There we are. The first question has set up the board for some thoughtful planning – understanding the job of the ED – not philosophically, but physically. Of course, it's different for a large and for a small agency, but the basics are the same. Identify the basic functions on the job that must be done regularly and begin to train one or two staff members or board members to be able to step in to keep the office running smoothly. I say one or two people because it's reasonable to ask a staffer to step into the interim ED role, but having a back up is always helpful. Besides of all the tasks to be addressed, one person may not possess all the talents to get the job done. Succession planning thy name is redundancy.

You've got step one of your plan in place – an understanding of the functions of the ED's job and a plan to train someone(s) to know the basics and some sort of compensation plan for those who step in to save the interim day.

That done the board meets at a local brewery calling itself something like 'transition committee' to start talking about replacement options. The easy answer is to let the interim move up and everybody shift to a new spot. Really? The board may decide to hire the interim, and as we know in our community calling someone from the bench has often worked well – raising expectations of an employee has often raised a good employee to become even better.

But there are things to consider – this might be a good time to assess the skills needed to continue the agency's mission. Maybe the search committee should look for an employee with some skills that are different that the former ED. All the talents to consider include: grant writing, human resource management, budgetary skills, technical know how, donor support, volunteer recruiting. Maybe the balance of the skill set should alter a bit for the agency's current needs. You know, more time working with donors, less time grant writing. A shift in staff is a great time to refocus or redesign the job and make certain it is directed by the mission.

Once the transition committee has determined the type of skills needed then reviewed and reworked the job description, the next issue – do you just advertise – or ask an agency to come in and lead the board through the process, taking responsibility for the first review and vetting of applicants. Again, this all depends on the size of the agency. For example, the City of Hendersonville hired a consultant to help them search for a new city manager. Many small operations in our community rely on the professional talents of board members to serve in the role of reviewing applications. Your call.

A succession plan is like a royal ascendency. Your board is selecting someone to represent your agency throughout the community, woo donors, sweet talk volunteers, manage clients and maintain the positive image and community presence that the board and staff have worked to create and maintain. Just as challenging as the Queen thinking about Charles or William.

More Meetings Than Days

Must a board have to meet monthly? No. But a board does have to meet. To be successful those meetings should be regularly scheduled. They should also be well-organized and have some purpose. The regular meetings allow board members to build trust and cohesiveness. They learn about one another so at those times when big, tough decisions have to be made, the discussion can move forward in a thoughtful manner.

A good meeting is an opportunity to educate the board about programs; a good opportunity to present ideas that need in depth discussion in the coming months. A board meeting is the place for committees to offer reports, keeping other members up to date on work being done.

A board meeting doesn't just happen. If the board meets on a monthly basis, there should probably be an executive committee meeting to help the chair and the ED sift through issues that need full board discussion. It's easy to talk, or write about what should be "reality." But how hard is it to deliver? Really hard in the summertime.

That's when some board members become suspicious that the executive committee is making decisions and keeping the full board in the dark. Then of course, the ED wonders why the executive committee always agrees on everything. Are they meeting secretly and keeping the ED in the dark?

Suddenly once thoughtful board members want to see all

Charity in Motions

the minutes from committee meetings and other members think emailing a committee report is sufficient because full board meetings should take 60 minutes or less once we're on daylight savings time.

While the ED is feeling paranoid and various board members are checking for hidden cameras, the policy committee forgot to meet, the treasurer can't explain the cash discrepancy and no one knows who's in charge when the ED goes on vacation or falls into a coma.

Don't you just love summer?

If you are the board chair, about June you're beginning to wonder what happened to that great group of folks you worked with in September? They hit the ground running, got the fundraiser off the ground, worked with an ED who wrote 150 grants and was awarded 90% of them. Yeah, those people.

Some board chairs use various methods to keep members engaged at a meeting. That big bowl of chocolate candy? It can be helpful until members start fighting over who took all the peanut M&Ms. Maybe some toy distractions, something to keep members' hands busy. After all, as you look around the room you can see that at least two members interrupted some gardening tasks to attend the June meeting. They smell of bug spray and fertilizer. And another member was up really early cooking breakfast for six grandchildren who are all now sitting in the agency lobby waiting to go zip lining as soon as the boring meeting is over.

You hear from other members that they plan on being out of town and the next meeting won't make quorum. Won't make quorum? Then you learn that two members are announcing their engagement – who knew working on a by-laws rewrite could be so thrilling? And another member says he's taking time to hike in Tibet for a few weeks.

A board is a living breathing entity, sort of the sum of its member parts. And those parts sometimes need to rest and regroup. For example, you saw Brazil crumble in World Cup action. That's what happens to a board in summer. And a good coach, like a good chair, knows when to call time out.

When the summer silliness hits, it's time to take a break. The best thing to do is take July or August off. There's the beach, maybe a cruise, or a family reunion. So what's a governing body to do? Cancel the July meeting. Then come back ready to work when everyone can focus again.

A Walk in the Clouds

As many of you are learning as you look into risk management and disaster recovery issues, nothing is ever simple. As you begin to look at where you are now, you realize that you are in the past. That's correct, all that technology that you invested in a decade ago is old, at risk and passé. In this day and age, being "now" only lasts about a nanosecond.

New technology exists today that allows an agency to work smarter using phones, tablets and laptops. Many years ago an agency invested in desktop computers and a server housed somewhere in the office. Today that has all changed. And getting the best answer for your agency requires a review of your current operations, what might be available to you now and what may be smart for the future. Then it's time to find how the game has changed with regard to technology methods. Many agencies now operate in cyberspace through various systems that allow staff to share documents, pass along information and work together developing action plans.

The game has also changed in that there are many options today to store and protect your information. As I explored the concept of data and storage I learned that the only thing stored in the clouds is heaven, everything else has a physical location. So all that "cloud" dependent work that an agency staff produces, plus all the past work saved, is living someplace.

I recently did an informal survey of four local nonprofits regarding their technology choices. Everyone is in a "cloud." So I asked about where their information is housed. One agency said they were already housing their data with a company that offered them security and information backup.

The second agency said they were still using a server housed in their building, wondering what they should do next, because they questioned the security of the aging hardware. The third agency said they were in "the cloud" and when I asked where their data was stored, I was told, "I don't know."

A fourth agency who seemed to be further along in the storage issue told me that security of critical data was important to them and they were looking into off-site storage with security and easy access to their data as criteria.

I find this concept of data storage very Star Trek-y, all that we create through our computers is grounded someplace. And deciding where to store it becomes an important decision in an agency's technology planning.

Trying to make some sense of all this, because I'm old and still remember typewriters, I visited Brad Tompkins and Amy Crossman at a company called Immedion (www.immedion.com). They have offices in Biltmore Park and provide sophisticated services for data storage, security and data backup. I learned that selecting a technology method requires that staff and board review their operation by considering: What type of services do you need? Where will your data be stored? How accessible will your data be? Does your agency have access to the bandwidth necessary for the services you think you want?

Meeting with Brad and Amy I learned that their clients may choose from several methods and levels of secure storage. Brad offered me some reasons why he thought Immedion should be a choice for data storage. Those reasons include security, redundancy and access to your data at all times.

He also acknowledged that there are other similar providers and encouraged any agency looking to this kind of service to do due diligence review of the many providers available. He stated that Immedion is SSAE 16 compliant which is a third party certification to ensure the security of processing and storing sensitive data. He also pointed out that many agencies deal in Personally Identifiable Information (PII) because they maintain information about staff and donors. Protecting this information is important and may be more securely done in a data storage facility.

The challenge for an agency is to find a method of technology that fits your budget, gets the job done while keeping the staff connected and the work available to all who are getting the job done. All services cost money – either in monthly fees with a data storage contract or through investment in onsite hardware and in a back up server stored elsewhere for security.

Reviewing an agency's technology and determining how to upgrade hardware and software and services will take time for an agency staff and board to process. Remember everyone should understand why the upgrade is important and how it will work.

Brad suggested that the agency committee understand the work being done in house; determine how this upgrade will make the agency more efficient; do a due diligence review of possible vendors and the levels of service offered; be aware of where your data will be stored; investigate the costs involved. Brad pointed out that finding solutions to your current technology requires that you first understand the problems that you are trying to address.

Any organization with a rich history has boxes of files – those old minutes, yellowing and typed with charming typo's and erasure marks. What a simple time – paper, erasing. Not any more.

Aging and Volunteering

A little stiff these days – I have the cure – You don't need Aleve or Ben-Gay, you need to volunteer. Finding that you don't think as fast as you used to – volunteer. Feeling down in the dumps – volunteer. Not ready to pack it in and meet St. Peter – volunteer.

Isn't it obvious? The other day a lively, charming community participant told me he was 89. I was shocked. He has a sparkle and a bounce to his step and he proved to me that being active in the community keeps a body that claims to be 89 looking and acting much younger.

My friend and healthy aging advocate, Marcia Caserio, sent me an article that outlined research into the value to one's health when a life includes volunteering. The paper says, "Whether older Americans can delay or prevent disability associated with aging will depend in part on how they spend their time after retirement." And researchers conclude that older adults have found one way to maintain mental and physical health longer is by engaging in community activities such as volunteering. Hear that? I don't mean to say that if you're stiff and achy you're not busy enough, but studies have shown that there are health benefits associated with volunteer activity.

Volunteers tend to have higher self-esteem and volunteering may distract from personal aches and problems. In fact, the study says that most people who volunteer report that they see their health improving. Volunteering, according to another study, increases psychological well-being. And volunteers have a lower rate of depression than non-volunteers. My healthy recommendation: Help out at The Free Clinics, you're pains will dim and you'll help those with challenging health issues and personal emotional problems.

Volunteering improves physical functioning, or as I see it, volunteering keeps you moving. Older adults develop arthritis (no kidding!) and other health problems that limit mobility. But volunteering helps increase your level of physical activity. You know, driving your car when you deliver meals for the Council on Aging gets you out of the house; helping your church group cook meals for kids keeps you hopping; gardening at Bullington Center makes you bend and stretch. All this motion improves flexibility and strength.

Volunteering improves your mind. One research paper calls it "better cognitive functioning." This occurs because volunteering often involves interacting and coordinating with others. So, call Big Brothers Big Sisters – mentor a youngster. Because other studies show that working with kids increases cognitive stimulation, or as I see it, it improves your "heart."

In other conclusions, volunteering lowers risk of hypertension, a risk factor for cardiovascular disease. Volunteering at least a 100 hours a year can lead to better health and an extended, active life.

But there is one more consideration – accountability. As donors we demand that nonprofits receiving our donations be transparent in the service they provide and demonstrate good use of our money. As parents we have demanded accountability in our children. As employers and supervisors we were steadfast in our expectations that those we hire demonstrate that they have earned the money they are paid.

But are we accountable to ourselves? Do we take responsibility to do what's best for our health – what keeps us available to enjoy our families? Are we giving at a rate that we are able? Are we giving in ways that make a difference to ourselves and to others? Are we holding ourselves accountable for improving life around us – supporting a meaningful life? The outcome will be better health, and a longer, fuller life for us and for those we touch.

Stand Up and Be Counted

Recently I had a conversation with a friend of mine, Bill Ramsey, on the turn his life has taken since publishing his book, *Me Now – Who Next?*. This book recounts the odyssey of a young woman, Angels Leigh Tucker, who, as a result of a violent traffic accident, suffered through traumatic brain injury (TBI). By late 2008 she was a patient in traumatic brain injury (TBI) rehabilitation trying to find her way back to life.

Here it is 2014 Angela has returned through heroic struggle to a state of physical and mental independence and Bill is meeting with medical researchers and speaking, either alone or with Angels, to various interested groups personally or on radio and other social media discussions explaining TBI, sharing information and educating all who will listen.

You know what that makes Bill – an advocate! A person who feels so strongly about an issue that he or she devotes countless hours and personal time to educating others to understand the issue and working with victims to help them through a trying time by sharing experience or life changing information.

That discussion with Bill got me thinking about advocacy and it's role in our lives – sort of a philosophical search as to what makes us speak up for or speak out to or stand up against – anything. Who touches us that deeply? What does it take to move us?

This community is filled with people like Bill who have found an issue or cause or person that has given them a voice – a voice that rings out for justice, for caring, for support, for understanding. Look at our community, or any community, in which non-profits exist because someone felt about someone or something the way Bill feels about Angela and other TBI patients.

In our community someone cared enough about victims of domestic violence, sexual assault, the homeless and the hungry to stand before their congregation or our community to fire up interest and support for other members of our community with crying need.

Sometimes that advocacy has worked in a manner that brought together various groups to join into a larger, more forceful entity to pursue advocacy. IAM is a fine example of the churches in our community coming together decades ago to serve and advocate for the neediest of our community. It continues today as church groups work together to feed children and seek solutions to meet the needs of homeless children.

But what is advocacy? After a lot of Internet research I can answer – no one knows for sure. Sometimes advocacy is defined as grassroots action on behalf of others and sometimes as civic or political action. Advocacy includes public education to influence public opinion or public policy. It can be large, mobilizing throngs of supporters or it can be small, making friends and neighbors aware of the needs of another community member. It can be working for environmental ideals or for humane treatment of our pets. One thing is certain advocacy is action, moving beyond what is comfortable to what is necessary.

The hard part about advocacy is doing it. I had a t-shirt when I was in grade school that said, "Stand up and be counted." It's taken me a lifetime to understand what it meant. But, now I know I was looking at the definition of advocacy all those years ago. That personal journey we all make when we find commitment in ourselves and lose ourselves in what matters most to us. Have you found that issue, have you made that journey?

The Kiss of Advocacy

Last month's article talked about the role of advocacy and commitment to a cause. Many groups have formed in our community because they felt strongly about an issue. Advocacy within a nonprofit to support its mission can take many forms. For example, within the last weeks many groups in our community used fundraising opportunities to get the word out about their mission and service. These groups included: Pardee Foundation's Women Helping Women annual event to raise awareness for women's health issues; the Children and Family Resource Center's annual Harvest dinner to celebrate client successes; the Chamber of Commerce annual golf tournament to support its small business programs. Then the supporters of Only Hope WNC brought advocacy up a notch by sponsoring a Sleepout at the Historic Courthouse. This was an effort to draw attention to the needs of homeless youth in our county – a lot more dramatic than a dinner or a tournament, but clearly an action that got our attention, sparked our interest and, possibly, made us willing to take a part in the success of the agency mission.

The range of speaking out, advocating for issues, can be as benign as the public education and information many nonprofits share with their donors in a newsletter or through an event as dramatic as Only Hope WNC's Sleepingout and Mainstay's, "Walk a Mile in her Shoes," and as loud as the physical act of protest to draw attention to an issue. Advocacy is that and everything in between.

There are dozens of different types of nonprofits as defined in the tax code. Here we're talking about the traditional 501(c)3 non-profit, the agencies that deal with any number of human interest issues on the local level and often lobby for their client interests before the community and before local government. And yes, you saw that four letter word, lobby. Every nonprofit may lobby, they may present their case to elected officials and public policy makers, help others understand need, and work to address solutions.

The challenge to many nonprofits is first, defining advocacy for themselves. Will it be loud or soft, discrete or overt, advocate or lobby? Second, deciding how much money should be dedicated to advocacy/lobbying? You know, the quiet way – all the board members sign a letter, or a more dramatic way – the board and staff rent a bus to Raleigh to speak out in front of the legislature. Some donors and staff members may want their money to serve clients directly while others want to affect change in the future. This is a big policy discussion for the board.

Which means that an agency has to make certain that any advocacy meets the guidelines set by its board. What? Your staff hasn't a clue how the board wants advocacy to be carried out? In the normal course of activity most local nonprofit agencies have a relationship with local government. That relationship is soft, not asking for funds, but making certain local elected officials know about the work of the agency and know about the impact their service has on the community. That's advocacy/lobbying. Many local agencies also have a relationship with local elected officials to help those officials understand the impact a decision may have on local citizens. That's advocacy/lobbying.

Remember whether the advocacy is benign or vociferous, it's the agency's way of promoting better outcomes for clients and better investment of funds from their donors. It's a tough decision. But advocacy and lobbying are tools to help agencies find solutions to the challenges their clients face. Advocacy, lobbying, any difference? – I think you just wear more makeup when you want to lobby instead of advocate.

The Giving Season

Things have a way of raising my hackles even as they turn grayer, my hackles that is. We all survived Thanksgiving Day to roll into Black Friday, which I might point out started advertising and selling before Thanksgiving. Then there was Cyber Monday when we were all supposed to purchase, I presume online, all the techno gadgets we need for the next six months because by then they'll be obsolete. Cyber Monday was quickly followed by Giving Tuesday, another co-opted day, just like speak like a pirate day that occurs sometime in September. (I wonder how those pirates got so powerful?) Anyway, Giving Tuesday is to be followed by Thanks for the donation Wednesday.

And then there it was, wading through all that email about the designated post Thanksgiving days, the defining message – posted on Facebook – "All I want for Christmas is someone to remember my December birthday."

That said it all, Giving Tuesday, Thanking Wednesday, probably followed by Return your Cyber Monday on Thursday gifts day, followed by Follow-up Email Ask Donors Friday and finally, Closing out Last Black Friday Sales Day Saturday.

There you have it – another birthday missed in December. I really feel sorry for friends and family who celebrate birthdays even closer to Christmas. I won't even mention those relatives who celebrate a birthday on January first, another lost in space day. It's a wonder to me that the calendar can still function from Thanksgiving through January first without it's pages spontaneously combusting.

Take a breath, I reminded myself, it is the holiday season.

But it was a miserable opening week – sales and rain and fog and mist. Some first week in December. Until the combined program of high school and middle school bands, the public schools' All County Band, struck a chord for the season at their program at BRCC on Thursday evening followed by a Friday morning program presented by the Immaculata School choir. All those kids have a way of putting things in perspective. It is the giving and sharing season.

So did you?

You know, give?

Right, you want to review your other gift giving commitments first. Do you think your aunt really cares if you send her another fruit cake? Unless you're sending a gift card for the grandkids to buy what they want, you're wasting too much time thinking about what to give them. Think about what you could give someone really in need.

Even if you missed Giving Tuesday, there's always time and money to give to a good cause, a focused mission. And if your snail mail is anything like mine, most nonprofits are staying with the old game plan as they adopt the new. End of year solicitations are upon us.

Do your holiday spirit some good, give it a jump start, you've missed my birthday, but a donation to a worthwhile organization, especially here in our community will put you in the right frame of mind to ring out the old and ring in the new. When you finally realize it's January second, a donation now will make your spirit prepared to face anything the New Year brings.

Remember what every Christmas card and holiday program will remind us – the wish the youngsters in our community have shared – Peace on earth, good will toward one another.

Is Anyone Listening?

On New Year's Eve I sat in a pew at Immaculate Conception celebrating the vigil of one of our Catholic holy days. (No, this is not a theology lesson ...or maybe it is?) At the closing of the Mass the congregation sang *Let there be Peace on Earth (by Jill Jackson Miller and Sy Miller, 1955)*. As we sang the words I looked up at the crucifix above the altar.

Are You listening? I asked.

This is an especially poignant song to me and many of those who are members of the Friendship Force. It's our anthem. It's the song we sing, we have sung, around the world, holding hands with our hosts in many countries or with our guests who are visiting here in the United States. My friends from our local club have sung it in recent years in Russia, South Africa, Indonesia, New Zealand, Peru, Japan. We have hosted people who have visited western North Carolina from Belgium, Russia, Australia, Moldova, Canada, and Netherlands. Every exchange is concluded as we sing ...

Let there be peace on earth ...

Hearing those words makes me recall the places and people with whom I've shared this song. Two stand out in my mind. In Yogyakarta, standing beside my Muslim host we sang. He was a man who shattered all my assumptions about Muslim men. He loved his wife, hugged his children for all the world to see, and sang all of John Denver's songs with me. The other strong memory is the evening we sang in my

Charity in Motions

kitchen with several Moldovans and toasted our similarities and our differences.

... the peace that was meant to be ...

Friendship Force is not the only organization in our community reaching around the globe. Civic clubs such as Rotary continuously sponsor exchanges to other Rotary International clubs. Their teams bring medical support and help raise funds to provide services to remote villages from Asia to South America. They teach the lesson that businessmen and women have a responsibility to help build community. And then there is the group supporting the Sister Cities project, sharing ideas and experiences at a local leadership level. Watch the paper to see what other civic clubs do for international friendship.

... with God as our Father, brothers all are we ...

And the local Churches! Weekly we read stories of local congregations sending their members to small foreign communities to reach out, supported by their beliefs and by local funds, to bring medicine and education, fostered by the Gospels, to people in need around the world.

... let us walk with each other in perfect harmony ...

I was told by one of our Russian visitors years ago that he had been cautioned that he would find that Americans were nothing like the people represented in propaganda. We were a warm and welcoming people. We live in small towns, raise our children, and value friends and family. Which leads me to the ask, will our example to the rest of the world serve Peace in 2015?

... let there be peace on earth and let it begin with me.

Note: This piece was circulated among members of Friendship Force International. My work traveled far and wide.

Going Your Way

It takes time to gear up for Christmas and it takes time to decompress from the holidays. So at the front end of the holiday drama I found myself paging through *Consumer Reports*. Those Christmas gift lists almost demand it – the best 55 inch HDTV – who knew the current 48 inch in the man cave at our house was now inadequate! And maybe a new camera? Or some exotic techie device? My fingers fairly vibrated at the thought. So there I sat wanting to be a responsible consumer, paging through the Holy Grail of responsible, committed spending. And there it was – a consumer's report on "Going Your Way" – sort of a thoughtful spender's guide to, well, to dying.

The article offered a survey on "How We Want to Die." It reported that 86% of us want to spend our final days at home; 50% of us prefer pain management and comfort care over other medical treatments; 47% of us over 65 have completed an advance directive (living will); 42% have provided end of life care for a friend or relative; and 61% of us have never heard of palliative care!

What? Those of us in Henderson County know better. We're probably the 39% of the respondents who know about palliative care because we have the national award winning Four Seasons Hospice and Palliative Care in our community, in fact they serve all of western North Carolina.

As I read the article, I found a lot of useful information about end of life issues. In addition to the survey, the Consumer Reports article offered a list of characteristics developed by the National Hospice and Palliative Care Organization (nhpco.org) that should be consider when evaluating care for end of life patients – relatives, friends, yourself. As a responsible columnist I thought I should check out how Four Seasons stands up against this criteria. Here's what the NHPCO says to look for in a hospice:

Not for profit status and 20 or more years experience

Hospice-certified nurses and doctors on staff and available 24 hours per day

Palliative care consultants who can begin care if you're not yet ready for hospice

An inpatient unit, where patients can go if symptoms can't be managed at home

Ability to provide care in nursing homes and assisted living facilities

Social workers and chaplains

Medicare approval. That way, Medicare will cover services, including equipment and home health aides as needed, plus counseling and grief support for the patient and the family

I sent an email to my friend, Chris Comeaux, the director of Four Seasons Hospice and Palliative Care. I emailed the above list and asked, "Does our local Hospice meet these criteria?"

If you know Chris, you know that when he talks about his job and his organization he has a lot to say. Sometimes he says it all without taking a break, so I was surprised when he responded to my query with this very brief reply. "Per the below (list) yes Four Seasons meets all these."

Wow! I set a date to talk with him in more detail about his organization.

When I met with Chris and his VP of Sustainable Resources, Derek Groves, we talked about how the services of their programs meet and exceed national standards. We talked about the professional level of staff (200), the concept of serving their patients as a team through an interdisciplinary focus and collaboration, and the value and role of their volunteers (450). Using the professional criteria as a measure, Four Seasons offers us exceptional services and support close to home.

Sometimes life takes challenging turns and sometimes we find that we and our families are not prepared. Take some time to review the article, in Consumer Reports -- an online guide to comprehensive information about end of life issues and concerns can be found at ConsumerReports.org/endoflife. It offers resources and advice to help with the difficult medical and personal decisions patients and caregivers often face.

And take some time to consider how fortunate we all are that at Four Seasons when going your way gets tough, staff and volunteers are there to work with you and your family to help you find your way.

The Perfect Medium

Recently I attended a workshop designed to convince me and my friends that our organization should be on Twitter and Facebook. I left the training a cynic. I don't want to be that in touch. A few days later I happened to be out to dinner with my husband and we had no reservation so we were part of the pending diners lounging around the entry. Everyone, except me, spent that waiting time on their phone presumably complaining about the wait and staying in touch with friends who were probably waiting someplace else.

That's when it hit me! This was the point the trainer made in the social media workshop – people are staying in touch and sharing information. If my organization wasn't there we were missing opportunities to engage donors, volunteers and even clients. Hmmm.

Not always willing to believe someone from out of town I went to visit Chris Burns with Summit Marketing Group and Erica Allison with Allison Development Group, both here in Hendersonville.

I started with the first question, Should my nonprofit be on social media? And got an unqualified "Maybe." Well, I guess it was more qualified. Chris explained that it helps an agency communicate with it's audience, if it's done right. Erica cautioned that social media must be part of an integrated marketing plan.

Chris also said that if Facebook were a country it would rank third in population worldwide. He also went on to explain that the social media methods out in cyberspace seem to keep multiplying and that each new generation of media seemed to appeal to a newer generation of users (or as nonprofits see them – donors.)

At this time Facebook seems to be a world leader, but who knows what's next. Erica pointed out the same concept when she said that you don't own your Facebook page. All of Facebook could disappear and with it your contacts. That's why she and Chris both saw any social media contact as a way to bring people to you and engage them through other methods, you know old-fashioned email or electronic newsletters.

To illustrate how fast things move, both of them mentioned that photo ops through Instagram created more overlap opportunities. To my amazement all these social media can be linked to one another, making the concept of 'web' even scarier.

Both of my marketing friends saw a role for social media in nonprofits, but they saw it as part of a bigger strategy. They also were realistic to point out that managing the media is a commitment of time and staffing talent. Someone at the agency has to be checking social media outlets for replies, comments, attacks, etc. Chris said it is like a for-profit customer service approach.

If your agency is still wondering what to do, here are some of the pros and cons. On the up side it doesn't cost much money – you sign up for Facebook or Twitter or any other social media outlet. That's it. But, the cost is in time and talent. Somebody has to be responsible for content and contacts and connections in a manner that serves the agency, daily or weekly – as defined by your social media plan. It means engaging people in a manner that brings them into your fold as donors, volunteers and clients or users.

In the beginning many agencies jumped on the Facebook train because it was something everyone in the staff was doing personally and it seemed as though there would be good outcomes. But I recently learned (from the time I began writing this piece to the final draft – I told you technology moves fast!!) Anyway, I learned that grantors and sponsorship donors (those who look at "branding" and joining in an agency's social media train) ask about social media policy and social media measures. How do you measure what you only cyber? Easy: Facebook followers; Twitter followers; e-newsletter subscribers; website traffic. Who knew?

Many agencies have found that it takes time and thought to maintain a coherent and cohesive social media presence. It takes time to make that presence work for you in conjunction with the agency mission and goals without becoming a distraction.

I'm old and a cynic about social media – but it can be an essential tool for your nonprofit. But listen to my friends, Chris and Erica – Do it right!

Learning from Each Other

People who research other people – archeologists, anthropologists, criminologists, telemarketers – like to talk about, or write about, what they interpret as the culture of long gone civilizations – how we operated and how we treated one another. When you think about it, we're just a civilization in waiting for someone to dig us up, or dig up our meeting notes, or uncover newspapers or carryout menus, you know the things that will explain who we were and how we functioned.

Sorry, but I can't wait until someone digs us up to talk about our civilization. I want to talk now! Like what we should learn from life around us – for example, what makes local nonprofits dissolve or merge or disappear and the way it reflects on our culture. Most agencies reorganize or merge to expand service area or to work more efficiently with less money.

Recently we have seen several nonprofits in the region come together is various amalgamations to continue their missions. From experience and observation I can tell you coming together with like groups in neighboring counties brings you in close contact with some very nice people. It also takes the consolidated staff time to rinse out and coalesce.

The obvious challenges are centered around office functions – phones, technology, communications, volunteers. Do you want one phone number for each county, or one number for all the counties, but no number that costs clients a toll charge? You get that cultural thing? Should the agency keep all office locations open or operate a phone system that makes it appear that way. When you call a phone number looking for help – are you happy when the support is obviously off shore? Not! So why would a client be happy when he can only reach help by calling Macon county? Are you starting to see phone culture? A refigured agency tries to find a phone system that allows everyone to communicate with everyone seamlessly.

The techno challenges are easy in this day and age, but there are some cultural challenges. For example, one office and board may operate more informally than the others, that's its culture. One board may meet in the evening over wine and cheese, another board may meet in the morning over coffee and leftover Easter/Halloween/Christmas/Valentine candy. Blend those two cultures and what do you get? afternoon wine and chocolate – but a productive board! Helping staff learn to work together, or figuring out how to keep the donors and volunteers grounded in their county, but accepting the operational and administrative changes of a multi-county organization, require work and solidarity on the board.

Here are some cautions and no solutions.

First, the new reconfigured agency board has the responsibility to refine the mission statement and vision. That doesn't mean that all the good work in each county will be abandoned. It does mean that some programs may function well in one county but not translate to the rest of the organization sites. The future challenge to the amalgamated board is to decide what stays, what grows and what may be reasonable to remain as a signature program in only one or two counties but not all.

The second caution – plan ways to keep local donors and volunteers engaged, locally. Maybe a reduced staff size or operating hours, while still maintaining a local office or presence, or regular gatherings of a county group to help volunteers stay in touch are practical options.

Third caution, working in a new reconfigured agency serving a larger area means road trips. Board meetings and committee meetings will not always be a ten minute drive, but something longer in distance and time. But prepared. Also be on the lookout for those willing to make the road trips for board service or committee work.

My fourth caution is to donors and volunteers. Help make it work. If the agency is holding to the goals you support and working in a manner you respect, stay with them. Reserve judgment and help when you can.

As I said at the beginning, when we are dug up will our notes and strategic plans reflect people who were territorial or people who could figure out ways to work together?

Hatching Ideas

There are two comments I frequently receive from those of you kind enough to read this column regularly. The first is a generous statement along the lines of saying the column contains useful information. Thanks. I try. The second usually starts, "You should, or have you thought about …?" So there you have it. I'm busted. If you think I offer good information, it's because someone else had the idea, suggestion, hint, or outright command that an idea be pursued.

Today's piece began as a suggestion – encourage participation. It started out with a simple conversation about recruiting board members for nonprofits. Most nonprofit boards face the same issues – finding board members, finding board leadership. But the conversation moved to a darker place – others who need board or committee members – like local government! What? How can local governments need anything? They tax us, don't they? What else do they want – blood? No, but they could certainly use a few good citizens willing to give time on the many boards and committees that elected officials turn to for guidance and advice.

Guidance and advice? Yes. Henderson County commissioners appoint citizens to thirty four boards or committees. The information about those appointments is available on the county website (www.hendersoncountync.org) at Citizen Participation under the Commissioners pull down menu. The municipalities have similar citizen participation needs.

I attended the commissioners' May 4 meeting and learned that there are vacancies available and not enough citizens willing to be appointed. Here's how it works. A citizen already serving on a board will be asked, when the term is about to expire, whether that citizen wishes to continue to serve. At that time on the agenda of a commissioners' meeting is an item – Notification of Vacancies. Boards and committees with upcoming openings are listed. Those vacancies are usually acted on at the next commission meeting. That explains the next item on the agenda – Nominations. At this point the commissioners nominate citizens to the various vacancies, taking into consideration those citizens who indicated an interest in reappointment and those citizens who have sent in an application to be considered for service.

At the May 4 meeting there were Notification of Vacancies for nine boards that included 33 vacant positions. Under Nominations there were thirteen boards with 37 vacancies. At this meeting thirteen vacancies were filled and twenty-four positions left unfilled.

To be fair, some of the boards and committees require people with certain professional credentials. For example, the Board of Health requires several appointees with medical training; several boards have residential requirements; some boards, mandated by the state, require that certain members hold specific government positions, such as an educator or someone from law enforcement.

What types of appointments were available last week? There were opportunities to serve on boards dealing with children, senior citizens, planning decisions, and environmental issues.

The Clerk to the Board of Commissioners, Terry Wilson, who manages notifications and vacancies said that there are several boards that are hard to fill: Juvenile Crime Prevention Council – there are many designated positions and at large positions available; Nursing/Adult Care Home and Community Advisory Committee – it's not an easy job. Terry receives applications of interested citizens and sees that the commissioners have all that information as they consider appointments.

SO – if you're interested in becoming an active citizen – go to the website and download an application. Review the opportunities for service, also available at that site, and send Terry your application.

Several years ago, the League of Women Voters of Henderson County (celebrating fifty years of community service this year!) conducted a survey of county boards and committees. The goal of the study was to verify transparency and openness of meetings. But the League learned some other things. They learned that most participants in appointed positions enjoyed the challenge, felt they were respected for their work by the commissioners and were proud of their work as citizens.

It's fun to sit back and know all the answers. It takes more brains and courage to put opinions into play, to take time to serve. Think you know it all? Got some special skills? This is your opportunity to stand up and be part of the solution.

Public and Nonprofit Partners

To give or not to give – the taxpayers want to know. We have witnessed the Board of County Commissioners wrestle with the issue of giving funds to local non-profits. It's a challenging issue.

What, you don't think so? Maybe you think that all those local non-profits are just giving money to people who should handle their own problems or giving money to people who don't see eye to eye with you, promoting a mission that contradicts your beliefs. You should consider the number and depth of nonprofit service in our community and reevaluate your bias.

Historically, and practically, governments large and small have supported nonprofits, because they can extend the responsiveness of government and operate more swiftly in emergencies or in a crisis, or can devote more time and effort to a specific issue when a government can be easily distracted by day to day operations.

Our local nonprofits work in concert with local governments to provide swift, secure service for citizens. Our local governments deal with many nonprofits daily from economic development to public safety. For example, our volunteer fire departments were organized as nonprofits. They have boards of directors and by-laws and all the administrative trappings as any other nonprofit in the county.

Recently the newspaper reported the reluctance of the commissioners to invest tax money in local nonprofits. At the same time, our own economic development arm, Partners in

Economic Development (a non-profit) explained to the commissioners a need to create a nonprofit (not another one in town! you gasp) to help with property acquisition issues that would be helpful when recruiting industry. This new entity would extend community efforts to foster job recruitment and industrial growth.

Since I believe that local nonprofits serve everyone of us every day just as local government does, I think that our friends in economic development, under a nonprofit umbrella, will work through recruitment issues and work for us with their current and proposed 501(c)(3). New businesses will benefit from property solutions through a new nonprofit, but they will also be happy to find a network of childcare facilities for employees developed in partnership with Smart Start, Children and Family Resource Center, Boys and Girls Clubs and DSS. Old and new businesses know that certain employee problems will be addressed by local non profits – Housing Assistance Corporation, Habitat, Council on Aging, IAM, Mainstay, Healing Place, Mediation Center – to help employees with personal issues which left unresolved can cause problems at home and in the work place.

Then there is health care. Pardee Hospital Foundation, Park Ridge Hospital Foundation, Blue Ridge Community Health Services, and The Free Clinics (all 501(c)(3)) work together with local government departments to see that community health and wellness activity receives support and encouragement. Many local nonprofits often team up with and gain support from our local hospital foundations for community wellness and health education projects.

The commissioners showed support for human service nonprofits, those agencies providing direct services to citizens that are not provided by, but appreciated by, county government. However, they had concerns about other types of nonprofits.

I don't know what to say about nonprofits requesting county funds that are deemed "arts and culture." I classify arts and culture as I do parks and recreation – things we do for ourselves to make our community a better place to live. And sometimes I wonder why we're so stingy. Our community is an extension of our home. Don't we repair when necessary and decorate to lift our spirits or to show our pride of place?

I think the commissioners gave a lot of thought to the current budget, and it wasn't easy. They personally support various nonprofits in our community. They may have even enjoyed some services such as an art class for a grandchild or a meal delivery to an ailing relative, but they are spending our money and they were cautious. We have to understand the value of nonprofits in our community. They are employers, safety net providers, protectors and enhancers of our quality of life. And maybe we have to understand that the biggest value of a nonprofit is the ability it has to provide a needed community service for less money and more efficiently than local government.

And maybe we should let the commissioners know we appreciate them and nonprofits and especially appreciate the way it all works together.

Recommended Summer Reads

In the last few weeks this newspaper carried two very informative pieces on nonprofits. David Cook the executive director of IAM offered a review of the economic impact of local nonprofits with regard to service, jobs provided and money spent within our community to local vendors. The second article was a summary by many local nonprofit employees regarding the importance of making donations to reputable agencies – *We should Be Generous but Cautious,* published June 30, 2015. They offered a list of steps to follow to gain more facts behind a solicitation call or letter. I hope you taped that article by your phone! In fact, if you missed it, look in the Times-News archives and reprint a copy.

But no matter how practical a nonprofit is, as David pointed out for those who like to count, and no matter how thorough a donor is in validating a funding request, no matter how many volunteers work long and hard for a cause, there's always more to learn, more ways to improve and new management ideals to explore.

Which gets me to a summer reading list. Do you know how many people write books and maintain websites to help nonprofits manage themselves better? Probably more people than write for Harlequin Romances! Hang on, I'm getting to my reading list.

Just returned from my family reunion – the grandchildren of Luigi and Elvira. There were twenty-one of us – all first cousins. There are now nineteen of us. With spouses and children and grandchildren we add up to a manageable number and travel around each year to someone's home, unlike some of my friends who all meet in Disney World, or plan reunions that include hundreds and happen every five years and even have T-shirts. Needless to say, our small gathering allows for deeper discussions, and great belly laughs – but my point is – oh, right, summer reading.

One of the cousins at my reunion wanted to talk about his company's support of nonprofits and the guiding corporate philosophy. He recommended a book – *The Go Giver* by Bob Burg and John David Mann. It's a fast read – if you get an "e" version you can have it read before Amazon bills your credit card. It is sort of a parable threaded with a homily, but Cousin John insisted that his company encourages employees to be guided by the Five Laws of Stratospheric Success:

- Your true worth is determined by how much you give in value than you take in payment
- Your income is determined by how many people you serve and how well you serve them
- Your influence is determined by how abundantly you place other people's interests first
- The most valuable gift you have to offer is yourself
- The key to effective giving is to stay open to receiving

Hmmmm – sounds like what our local nonprofits do naturally every day.

Another quick read is *Good to Great and the Social Sectors*. This is by Jim Collins and is billed as a monograph to accompany his book, *Good to Great*. Mr. Collins' thesis is that business thinking isn't always the answer to nonprofits looking for greatness.

Reading both of these makes me think businesses and nonprofits can learn a lot from one another – maybe that's why we work well together in our community! Now you can spend the rest of the summer thinking about how both of these books blended together could be a helpful jump start for the new board that in many nonprofits took over the governance of many agencies on July 1. Think about your mission and evaluate it through Mr. Collins' good to great framework for the social sector; think about who you are and measure your agency against the five laws.

And when you need a break from all that reading and thinking and discussing, pick up my favorite summer read! It's published by the Blue Ridge Literacy Council. Do you want to meet clients, hear from the volunteers, learn of their challenges and their success? Each one of the tutor and student writers is working to follow the Five Laws of Stratospheric Success and they move from good to great. Pick up their book, *Voices*. It's five bucks. Read it and weep with joy.

Family Memories Are Gifts Forever

A friend stopped me and asked for the rest of the story. Last month I mentioned my family reunion. There is a lot more to the story. The food, the memories and the joy of sharing with one another. Each year I'm always amazed at the stories that we recall about our grandparents. Some poignant and some riotous. And, though sometimes we hear the same stories, those stories aren't just for us, but for our children and grandchildren, you know, all those next generations who need to know what family is all about.

I remember many things about my grandparents, like the day I was delighted to meet a small lamb tethered in their backyard. And my dad said, darkly, "Don't get attached." You got it, Sunday dinner! And I remember those days when we sat with grandpa and pulled grapes from stems – eat your heart out Burnt Shirt and St. Paul's – we helped make our own wine. In fact, my high school Chemistry project was to make wine – I had several canning jars that I used and each week started a new batch of grapes so that I demonstrated stages of the fermentation process for all to see. I took my jars to school with a bottle of grandpa's best as a sample of the final product. The instructor got the final product and I got an A!

A few years ago, we cousins decided that we should hold the reunion at the old family digs in Bugnara, Italy. Off we went. It's a small town hanging off a mountainside. We walked throughout the town, finding cousins and enjoying a tour of the old farm where our grandparents lived before settling in America. Walking through the village church we were delighted to see a pew with the brass plate – a memorial to our family for the donation sent by Luigi and Elvira to help renovate the building.

And that's what it's all about – memories – passing the family stories and the family spirit to the next generations. It's a thread that tethers my children and grandchildren back to Italy and it demonstrates the power of investing in the future of something important to the family.

Luigi and Elvira made a statement when they made a donation in the family's name. The church and the village were important to them.

In our community we see that every day as we read reports from various nonprofits thanking donors and volunteers for a successful fundraiser, sharing photos of donors and gifts received. We see it everyday in the obituaries. Families ask that if we choose to remember their loved one, please donate to something that was important to them. A gift in memory of – is a gift that helps carry on a dream after a committed donor or volunteer passes on.

If you do have a favorite, or several favorites, please look into the options that are available to make a lasting gift. Check with your attorney or accountant. They have mysterious ways of helping you – well not so mysterious – just more than I understand. But there are many opportunities to make lasting gifts that make memories.

Make the memory for yourself. Leave a bequest, make a last and lasting gift, something that will help your work for an agency last longer – last into the next generation. Something to show your family a thing or two about charity and commitment.

Friends Don't Ask Friends

Recently I read an article on the Blue Avocado website that was very interesting. (As a side note, any person working in nonprofits should be getting the Blue Avocado newsletter. Always something there to think about.) Anyway, this article had to do with making the big ASK! You know, knocking on doors and setting up coffee dates to solicit funds for your special nonprofit. Or as most board members like to name it – Kill me now!

All you board members will be happy to know that the article validates your/our attitude. The author postulates that people don't mind asking people for money, they just don't want to ask their friends. What a cool thought! The author, Jon Snow, says:

Resistance to asking friends is not just "a learned fear of asking." It's more likely legitimate resistance to:
Uncertainty about whether one would be overstepping the invisible bounds and hierarchies of the social network and
Reluctance to incur social (and perhaps financial) indebtedness.

Sadly, I'm not certain I have friends who get philosophically caught up in this *invisible hierarchy* thing, but all my friends and I understand this you scratch my donation, I'll scratch yours, or something like that. Although

Charity in Motions

I don't think we name is *social indebtedness*, a term which makes me think everyone I know is having a party and doesn't want me there.

Jon Snow goes on to say, "These are real concerns that will not be swept away by practice sessions at board retreats. If we don't confront the real obstacles to asking friends and relatives for donations, we'll continue to have fun but ineffective trainings."

He's right. I never seem to get much money from my friends, and the biggest single donation I ever personally reeled in was from someone I didn't know, who didn't know me, but who believed in the work the agency was doing. I could have been a toad and the money would have rolled in – the donor believed in the work that much.

There is also another side to this asking chore. Asking my friends for donations to the various agencies I've supported over the years may have confused them. What did I really believe in? Anything? What did I really support? Last year's cause or this year's capital campaign? Or did I just get a high from holding out my hand and begging? Well, not begging, but still asking, and confusing to us all.

Recently I spoke to a few great folks on an agency board retreat. We all believed in the agency and the work being done. Someone asked me on what boards did I currently serve. That's when the subtext of asking friends for money sunk in. I was uncomfortable acknowledging my current interest because I didn't want those present to think I had moved my support away from the agency we were all discussing at the time. A real conundrum.

Yes, I believe in those agencies I've worked for in the past, and yes, I believe in the agency for whom I currently volunteer. Does that make one better and one worse or does it mean I'm trying to confuse you?

And I have friends who also have special, and competing,

interests in various social, environmental and cultural causes. We all, at times, seemed to be asking each other. That always ramped up the confusion

The author's solution is to "think more deeply ... about how volunteers can integrate their work with their conversations to talk about a particular nonprofit ... We need to acknowledge and value the invisible, nuanced aspects of relationships rather than act as if they don't influence asking."

You want nuanced and invisible?? Think *Strangers on the Train*. That's right, swear an oath with a friend to flip asks of friends – I'll ask your friends and you ask mine. Of course, make certain you're five degrees of friendship away from the askees so you don't run into friends of friends who are your friends. Or you'll be right back where you started – overstepping the nuanced invisible hierarchy of social indebtedness on a train to nowhere.

Lobbying for Sex

Once I interviewed a novelist for Blue Ridge Bookfest and asked her where she got her ideas. Her name is Kerry Reich and she had been in a successful law practice before following in her mother's footsteps to become a writer. Kerry's stories revolved around some interesting legal-social issues such as who owns the fertilized eggs in divorce or death and how does one reconcile surviving an illness when others have died under similar suffering. She told me that she got her ideas from stories buried in the pages of a newspaper, those stories that were signaling the beginning of legal-social discussions.

That was a very kind and thoughtful way of expressing another author's acknowledgement of why he was inspired by stories of the day. To quote him: "You just can't make this s*** up!"

And that's where I find myself, sometimes the news is just too real to be true! For example in the September 17 edition of the Times-News, buried on page B3, was an article with the headline, *Sex Scandals carry public costs, consequences*. There was so much information that the report covered half of page B3 – the top half! Who knew that state legislators could get into so much trouble? Within the story highlighting misdeeds of state legislators is a statement: "Some states have no particular prohibition against (sexual relationships between legislators and lobbyists)... North Carolina Ethics Commission ruled earlier this year that sexual acts between a lobbyist and a state official are not considered "gifts" that must be reported on lobbyist disclosure forms."

Really?! I mean seriously? Really?!

Charity in Motions

My first comment is no wonder the session lasted so long – all those non-gifts were taking up too much time. My second thought is that I need "gift" defined as in a gift to or a gift from. The giver might have found it to be part of the job, sacrificing for a piece of legislation. On the other hand the giftee might have thought of it as part of the job of servicing constituents.

Sorry – my mind is drifting.

(Deep breath)

I'm back on track. I've tried to be useful over the years to help nonprofits understand that advocacy for your cause is like lobbying, but on a higher plain. And that educating legislators and the public about the work you do is a respectful activity.

Did I mislead you? Should I have been talking to you about safe sex? The world seems filled with people who want to force their conservative homophobic view on the country. Maybe those folks should step up and patrol the state legislatures. There seems to be plenty of stuff going on that has to be anti-biblical – harassing interns, hetero-legislative couplings, bragging of the types of favors available from lobbyists. (You've just got to search the blueridgenow.com archives for this titillating bipartisan report.)

Last year when I wrote about advocacy, I tried to explain the difference between lobbying and advocacy. I wanted you to know that "advocacy and lobbying are tools to help agencies find solutions to the challenges their clients face. Advocacy, lobbying, any difference? – I think you just wear more makeup when you want to lobby instead of advocate."

That's what I said last year. I've amended my opinion – when you want to lobby instead of advocate, I guess you don't wear underwear. Safe lobbying is called advocacy.

All I'm saying is, don't be discouraged, legislators probably like to hear about community need and good work and they probably want to help when possible. Always be prepared with information and data to provide a full picture of your agency's work. Always act professionally. And always remember that a legislator responds with respect if that's the way you present yourself.

Calling Attention to a Cause

In his ads my friend, Joseph Laughter, showcases folks in the community who shop at his clothing store and find items that are stylish and up to date and that enhance their image. We're talking about people who are well put together and who know just what they need to keep themselves on the stylish edge. But why do those customers allow themselves to be in an ad? I think it's because they want us to know that they liked the service, they liked the way they were treated and they liked the product.

You all know that when we're talking about the cutting edge of fashion, I definitely don't pop into anyone's mind. I'm just happy that I manage to find the clean pair of jeans without the hole in the knee when I get dressed in the morning. I think Joseph likes me anyway – he always smiles at me when we meet – at least I think it's a smile, he's too kind to smirk, and too well-mannered to roll his eyes.

But why am I talking fashion and style, when I'm so fashion challenged? This isn't about fashion and style, but the other message in Joseph's ads. Those ads celebrate his customers, his service and his success – a lesson many nonprofits could take away from this discussion – except substitute volunteers for customers.

Although many agencies do take the time to recognize volunteers and award them and celebrate them, there are always those who forget or who do it unevenly. Unevenly, you ask? Sort of like one year there's something called the annual volunteer recognition and it happens in March, then maybe the next year in November and before you know it, a year or two have gone by and someone wonders why you don't have that great luncheon, or fun brunch like the old ED or volunteer coordinator used to have.

Everyone has to be appreciated. And appreciation brings dividends – volunteers with enthusiasm, volunteers that go the extra mile and volunteers who keep coming back to give more time, effort and, often, money.

Volunteers are a great investment and volunteers are also great investors. One of the things volunteers do best for their agency is to talk. They talk about the time they invest; they talk about the people they work with; they talk about the lives they see change; they talk about the great professional staff they work with. Even though confidentiality is a must with many agencies, volunteers find a way to let their friends know how much they respect the staff and admire the service provided and enjoy the fulfilling work of a volunteer. Talk. That's what it's all about.

You want social media? There's nothing more social then a good volunteer telling several friends at a social gathering about the latest good news from the world of volunteering. And the lucky agency who has this volunteer all ginned up (and I mean that in a good way) gains a few more folks who have it on good (read happy volunteer) authority about the great work being done; a few more folks who have a reason to open your Annual appeal or your Christmas appeal, or your monthly newsletter and know that your plea for funds or the report of your successful work is true, sincere and, hopefully, should be supported with a check – a check to quietly honor a friend.

When someone sends a check in response to a nonprofit appeal, inspired by a friend who is a volunteer – it's like going to Joseph Laughter's store because you saw his ad or heard one of his customers talk about his service, his product and his success.

That kind of loyalty in volunteers – and customers – you can take to the bank.

Support Fantastic Nonprofits At Christmas Time

The world is a really crazy place – and there are many serious and concerned folks who worry about our safety and security. But sometimes they worry in a strange direction. There are far ranging discussions on TV, radio and other media, talking about overall philosophy on national safety and protection. However, some folks kind of get into the weeds and get distracted as they work to protect us from ourselves. Just when the forty-three Republican candidates for president have us believing that less government is best, some New York Democrats are up to no good, trying to stretch more government into places that should be 'don't ask and don't tell' – and I mean fantasy football. Just tell me why I should care that some big gut loser who thinks that scratching his bare belly as a precursor to foreplay, loses money because he couldn't figure which Manning was which. As it stands now, he doesn't put a wrinkle in the tax code and only his wife is angry, and maybe disappointed, but this isn't a marriage counseling column.

Back to the fantasy of it all. I happen to be married to a retiree and anyone who knows he-who-shall-not-be-named knows that he is an ESPN oracle, as in the Browns should have listened to him about Johnny Manziel. So when he speaks on sports I sort of listen. And when he said "I don't think fantasy football is any different than day trading," I thought he had a point.

Should I care if someone wants to call this gambling and initiate another sin tax? In fact, the more folks find sin to tax, the more sin we seem to find, or tax, or something. My take on this whole fantasy thing is that where money is involved taxes can't be far behind. They tax pot in Colorado and brag about it. It was only a matter of time before the next target came into view. We all seem willing to give up principle for money – look how we all fell all over ourselves to vote in liquor here in Henderson County. But I'm not trying to be your conscience, I'm just wondering why something called fantasy football but looks so much like day trading is being called illegal, and/or taxable. Sin and taxing are certainly flexible. But I'm getting morally sidetracked.

With all the similarities of dreaming up teams and dreaming up investments – quick action, educated guesses, hunches, fast pay outs, big wins, bigger losses, who can tell the difference? Of course, I have several solutions, the simplest is to call it fantasy day trading and every team and player is assigned a code that looks similar to NYSE stock identification. That way you'll be taxed on making money, a respectable pursuit, not on gambling, one of those sin thingies.

Don't like that idea? Then try putting your money to more concrete uses. Take the fantasy and risk out of day trading and football. Put your money into a local nonprofit. There will be no fantasy about the results. Trade your computer screen for some real time visiting agencies that are doing great work. Watch your money grow something good – food for someone who is hungry, art and music programs that celebrate the Christmas season and warm the heart.

And through it all, you'll win – big.

❄ ❄ ❄

Thank you for reading.
Please review this book. Reviews help others find Absolutely Amazing eBooks and inspire us to keep providing these marvelous tales.

If you would like to be put on our email list to receive updates on new releases, contests, and promotions, please go to AbsolutelyAmazingEbooks.com and sign up.

About the Author

Renee Kumor has lived in North Carolina for over forty years. She was a stay-at-home mom for several years developing a personal ethic of community service. Through the years as her children aged, she became active in the political and non-profit life of the community. She began writing a political opinion column for the local newspaper, but retired from writing when she announced her candidacy for local political office. After eight years as a county commissioner, she returned to non-profit service and began writing a monthly column for her local newspaper on non-profit management and service issues. Renee has been married to her husband for forty-eight years. They have four children and four grandchildren

AbsolutelyAmazingEbooks.com
or AA-eBooks.com

www.ingramcontent.com/pod-product-compliance
Lightning Source LLC
Chambersburg PA
CBHW050247170426
43202CB00011B/1585